Jazz and Christian Freedom

Jazz and Christian Freedom

Improvising against the Grain of the West

by BRADLEY K. BROADHEAD

PICKWICK *Publications* · Eugene, Oregon

JAZZ AND CHRISTIAN FREEDOM
Improvising against the Grain of the West

Pickwick Publications
An Imprint of Wipf and Stock Publishers
199 W. 8th Ave., Suite 3
Eugene, OR 97401

www.wipfandstock.com

PAPERBACK ISBN: 978-1-5326-4959-2
HARDCOVER ISBN: 978-1-5326-4960-8
EBOOK ISBN: 978-1-5326-4961-5

Cataloging-in-Publication data:

Names: Broadhead, Bradley K., author
Title: Jazz and Christian freedom : improvising against the grain of the West / by Bradley K. Broadhead.
Description: Eugene, OR : Pickwick Publications, 2018 | Includes bibliographical references and index.
Identifiers: ISBN 978-1-5326-4959-2 (paperback) | ISBN 978-1-5326-4960-8 (hardcover) | ISBN 978-1-5326-4961-5 (ebook)
Subjects: LCSH: Jazz—Religious aspects—Christianity. | Liberty—Religious aspects—Christianity. | Free will and determinism—Religious aspects—Christianity.
Classification: LCC BT810.2 B66 2018 (print) | LCC BT810.2 (ebook)

Manufactured in the U.S.A.   12/13/18

Contents

Acknowledgments

I OWE A DEBT of gratitude to the faculty at McMaster Divinity College for providing listening ears, resources, and good advice over the course of this project. My supervisor Dr. Steven Studebaker and second reader Dr. Wendy Porter provided assistance and advice not only over the course of writing the dissertation the present work is based on, but throughout my doctoral education. Dr. Mabiala Kenzo and Dr. Rick Love provided me with encouragement and support when the idea of connecting jazz and theology first occurred to me while working on my master's degree at Ambrose University College. My church families at Northside Bible Fellowship and Mission Baptist Church gave me valued friendships and opportunities to put my faith into practice. I would like to thank my family for their help and patience over the course of this project. My parents provided me with a great deal of support and encouragement over the course of my education. My children, Rowenna, Elowen, and Nigel, brightened my busy days and helped me to keep things in perspective. And my wife, Lealla, has been a patient, faithful, and loving companion on the ups and downs of this journey. There is no one I would rather have taken it with.

Introduction

CONTEMPORARY WESTERN SOCIETY IS becoming increasingly polarized. Political divisions on the left and right are widening. Unbridled subjective liberty and narrow fundamentalism pull away from each other in mutual loathing. What does freedom mean in such times? Does it entail celebrating and affirming every conceivable mode of self-expression, or do these modes of self-expression merely reflect more subtle forms of enslavement? More specifically, what does, or what can, Christian freedom look like in this context?

Freedom is central, not peripheral, to the Christian faith.[1] Paul boldly declares, "It is for freedom that Christ has set us free" (Gal 5:1a NIV), encapsulating the biblical narrative of oppression and liberation, of bondage and deliverance. Yet the Church has often been complicit in stifling freedom rather than promoting it.[2] My objective is to recover and reconstruct a theology of freedom for the Church that plots a way through the confusion about freedom and its enactment in the Western world. Just as the biblical authors often used parables and metaphors to get their point across, I use jazz improvisation as an analogy for Christian freedom and how this freedom might function in our contemporary world. I will demonstrate that *jazz is an effective analogy for a Christian theology of freedom in a postmodern context.*

---

1. See chapter 3, "Constructing a Biblical Theology of Freedom."

2. A survey of Christian history reveals harsh treatment of dissenters (see Moore, *War on Heresy*, for an account of how heretics were persecuted in medieval Europe), support of slavery (see Ker, *Slavery Consistent with Christianity*, for an attempt to theologically justify slavery in nineteenth century America), demeaning views of women (see Clack, *Misogyny*, 49–94, for a selection of writings from the Church Fathers on women), and colonialism (see Njoh, *Tradition, Culture and Development*, esp. 31–50. Njoh is prejudiced against Christianity and must be read with a critical eye, but this does not disqualify his observations concerning the relationship between missions and colonialism in Africa).

So, what exactly, does jazz have to do with Christian freedom? Just as jazz improvisation relies on successfully navigating constraints such as the history and traditions of jazz, jazz theory, and musical instruments, so Christian freedom also relies on constraints such as the biblical canon, Church history, theology, and the Church itself. By understanding the freedom jazz musicians enjoy in making music together, we can better understand how Christian freedom might be enacted in daily life. But before jumping into this undertaking, I clarify what I mean (and do not mean) by Christian freedom by offering a couple of caveats. I also situate my project in relation to other works combining jazz and theology and explain how analogy works.

CHRISTIAN FREEDOM AND PROVIDENCE: A CAVEAT

By the phrase "Christian freedom," I do not mean speculation on whether or to what extent human beings are free in relation to God's sovereignty. I do not propose a solution to the question of how (or whether) human free will relates to divine providence. In fact, I am sympathetic to Jacques Ellul's view that "Holy Scripture absolutely does not help us to resolve the problem of metaphysical freedom or determinism."[3] Instead, I presuppose human agency, appealing to the way human beings perceive the world and the way human agency is presupposed by passages in Scripture such as Josh 24:15, where Joshua calls upon the Israelites to choose whom they will serve, and Ezek 33:10–11, where God urges the wicked to turn from their ways. Whether one's actions are strictly predetermined, completely open, or some combination or parallel of the two, human beings act and think as if they are free to make choices. You may believe that God directs your actions, but that does not relieve you from the necessity of performing them. Consider how Martin Luther denies free will on the one hand[4] and yet asserts *The Freedom of a Christian* on the other.[5]

---

3. Ellul, *Sources and Trajectories*, 116.

4. Luther writes, "For if we believe it to be true that God foreknows and predestines all things, that he can neither be mistaken in his foreknowledge nor hindered in his predestination, and that nothing takes place but as he wills it (as reason itself is forced to admit), then on the testimony of reason itself *there cannot be any free choice in man or angel or any creature.*" Luther, "Bondage of the Will," 293. My emphasis.

5. Luther's two paradoxical "propositions concerning the freedom and the bondage of the spirit" are as follows: "A Christian is a perfectly free lord of all, subject to none. A Christian is a perfectly dutiful servant of all, subject to all." Luther, "Freedom of a Christian," 344. Cf. Jüngel, *Freedom of a Christian*, 47–87.

For the purposes of my discussion, it does not matter whether or not classical theism[6] is true, because (at least from a human perspective) God reveals himself as someone who interacts with human beings, responding to their acts and urging them to take the path of righteousness instead of the path of wickedness (e.g. Deut 30:11–20; Ezek 16; Rom 2:1–11). Whether or not God actually changes his mind in response to human action, from a human perspective on the human-divine relationship, he can and does. From the story of Hezekiah's pleading with God (2 Kgs 20:1–11) to James urging his readers to pray for God to act (Jas 5:13–18), Scripture portrays God as someone who is willing to respond to his people. Scripture appears to uphold the agency of God's creatures in choosing to do his will or in choosing their own way.

In my use of the term, "Christian freedom" first entails being liberated by God from the constraints of the self and the powers of this world into the constraints of the Kingdom of God. Second, it involves creatively improvising with the constraints of this kingdom. Among other things, these constraints include God's revelation and the continuing work of the Holy Spirit. Improvising with these constraints is the enactment of Christian freedom.

CHRISTIAN FREEDOM AND POLITICAL FREEDOM: A SECOND CAVEAT

A second caveat is that Christian freedom, while overlapping in certain respects with political freedom as it is thought of in the West, cannot be conflated with it. Political freedom in the West is closely associated with the rights (freedoms) which a person or a group of people is able to exercise in a political community.[7] Unlike Christian freedom, political freedom is synonymous with the legal right to "freedom of action" rather than the event of liberation or the act of exercising freedom.[8] In terms of the context of political freedom, Max Weber's definition of "political community" includes a "readiness to resort to physical force" in order to ensure the desired

6. In classical theism, God is, among other things, immutable (he cannot change) and impassible (he cannot suffer).

7. Zygmunt Bauman points out that "[i]n Old and Middle English, freedom always meant an exemption. . . . Exemption, in its turn, meant privilege: to be free meant to be admitted to exclusive rights." Bauman, *Freedom*, 9.

8. According to Tara Smith, the purpose of rights is to "protect one thing: freedom of action." Smith, *Moral Rights*, 5. See pp. 121–84 for her conception of "freedom of action." See chapters 2 and 3 for a defense and development of a conception of Christian freedom tied to liberation and the transgression of boundaries.

"conduct of the persons within it."[9] In other words, the political community that upholds the rights that constitute political freedom enforces these rights by the threat of force. By contrast, Christian freedom cannot be forced on anyone.[10]

Political freedom overlaps with Christian freedom because political communities have implications for Christians attempting to exercise their freedom. As the Apostle Paul points out, the government's use of coercive force in a state can be a positive counter to any who threaten the common good, checking oppressive forces and providing space for those within the state to choose a set of constraints in which to operate (Rom 13:4).[11] In other words, political freedom can provide an environment in which acts of Christian freedom can flourish. When political freedom is denied to Christians, exercising Christian freedom becomes much more costly.[12] In this respect, Christian freedom is not necessarily opposed to countering evil through coercive power, nor is it necessarily opposed to political structures as such.[13] Yet it cannot be grounded in coercive power; Christian freedom is grounded in the Kingdom of God, not any earthly kingdom. Exercising Christian freedom may entail challenging political structures, but the moment one exercises coercive power over another, one is no longer exercising Christian freedom.

For a Christian, belonging to this Kingdom must come prior to all other commitments and sources of identity (Matt 6:33). Christians cannot

9. Weber, *Economy and Society*, 2:901.

10. Alan Storkey, writing about the Kingdom of God, says, "To enter you repent and believe the good news about living with God; you agree to live life on God's terms. Entry is by choice, not by imposed rule." Storkey, *Jesus and Politics*, 114. Entry into this kingdom, as I show below, is a prerequisite to enacting Christian freedom. He continues, "Here is a kingdom without domineering, control, or defenses. God does not need to be assertive. We are created with responsive freedom, and we enter the kingdom or we do not" (114). While I would argue that by inaugurating his kingdom God is in some sense assertive, I agree with Storkey that Jesus does not provide an example of coercive behavior.

11. Douglas Moo writes, "For the purpose of his argument at this point, Paul is assuming that the laws of the state embody those general moral principles that are taught in the word of God. The 'evil' that the civil authorities punish, therefore, is evil in the absolute sense: those acts that God himself condemns as evil." Moo, *Romans*, 802.

12. For a sobering account of the historic destruction of formerly flourishing Christian communities outside of Europe, see Jenkins, *Lost History*. Jenkins writes, "The largest single factor for Christian decline [in the Near East] was organized violence, whether in the form of massacre, expulsion, or forced migration" (141). Clearly, political freedom can benefit expressions of Christian freedom.

13. See Skillen, *Good of Politics*, 27–29, 129–31, for a robust defense of this position. See also Studebaker, "Servants of Christ." For opposing views, see Hays, *Moral Vision*, 317–46; and Hauerwas, "Should War Be Eliminated?" and "On Being a Church."

afford to confuse their cultural and political loyalties with their prior commitment to the Kingdom of God. At the same time, Christians cannot rightly allege commitment to the Kingdom of God while being ignorant of racial, cultural, and social tensions and divisions that operate in the world in which they live.[14] Christians ought to be what Steven M. Studebaker calls "citizen sojourners," in that they are citizens of the world and have a vested interest in its well-being and are also simultaneously foreigners in that they have a prior loyalty to a kingdom that has a nature that is intrinsically different from the political communities of the world.[15] An informed commitment to the constraints of the Kingdom of God allows, and may even insist upon, acts of Christian freedom that transgress the laws and expectations of the world.

While affirming the importance of working out the implications of Christian freedom in and for a political community, the present work focuses primarily on Christian freedom as it is exercised in the local church.[16] To demonstrate the freedom that they have in Christ, Christians ought to begin by enacting that freedom when they meet together.[17]

THE INTERSECTION BETWEEN JAZZ AND THEOLOGY

The fertile space at the crossing between jazz and theology is quietly yielding its fruit. Jazz traces its roots in part back to African-American spirituals, and the influence of the black church was impressed into the music almost from its inception.[18] While I personally find the growing body of literature on jazz and theology fascinating, much of it is not directly related to my own project of using jazz as an analogy for a Christian theology of freedom. Those interested in exploring the literature on jazz and theology further can

14. Of course, people can believe they are putting the Kingdom of God first while dealing unjustly with others or unconsciously perpetuating unjust social structures. See, for example, Emerson and Smith, *Divided by Faith*, 69–91, for an analysis and assessment of the blind spots white Evangelicals have with respect to race relations in America. In chapters 4–6, a portion of the analogy between jazz and the Christian life is devoted to wrestling with this issue.

15. See Studebaker, "Servants of Christ," 61–67, for a fuller explication of his concept of "citizen sojourners."

16. See Heltzel, *Resurrection City*, for a work linking jazz to Christian social justice.

17. The principle of beginning with smaller units and expanding outward is found throughout Scripture. See, for example, Luke 16:10–12 and 1 Tim 3:4–5.

18. Commenting on the legend that jazz was birthed in the brothels of New Orleans, Ted Gioia writes, "Chastized [sic] as the devil's music, jazz may have even deeper ties with the house of God," and provides supporting evidence from the comments of early New Orleans jazz musicians. Gioia, *History of Jazz*, 29.

find my assessment of it in the appendix. Here, I briefly trace some early developments in the conversation between jazz and theology and then focus in on Jeremy Begbie's work on improvisation and freedom.

From Duke Ellington's *Sacred Concerts*, to Jimmy Smith's album, *Prayer Meetin'*, the influence of the church on jazz is easily discerned. In other words, the conversation between jazz and theology began outside of academic circles and inside the development of jazz itself. It eventually caught the ears of several theologians, including Hans R. Rookmaaker and James McClendon Jr., who were inspired to examine jazz from a theological perspective.[19] Then, beginning with Carl F. Ellis Jr., it became apparent that jazz had something to contribute to theology.

Ellis suggests that "jazz theology" is a way of doing theology that complements "classical theology."[20] The latter he sees as "the formal methods of arranging what we know about God and his world into a reasoned, cogent and consistent system," while the former is "not so much concerned with the status of theological propositions as with the hurts of oppressed people."[21] In other words, jazz theology is more concerned with engaging with contemporary situations than setting forth timeless truths. Ellis also provides an example of how the personal styles of different jazz musicians can contribute to an understanding of the inspiration of Scripture. He examines the similarities and differences between the four Gospels in the

19. See Rookmaaker, *Modern Art*; *New Orleans Jazz*; and McClendon and Murphy, *Witness*, 3:165–79.

20. A handful of scholars have made use of Ellis's distinction. John Piper approvingly cites Ellis's comments on presupposing God's existence (Ellis, *Free at Last?* 158), arguing that "the supremacy of God in all things" is a theme that "must be played by the black jazz preacher, and it must be played by the white classical preacher." Piper, *Bloodlines*, 250. He goes on to urge "these preachers [to] learn from one another, because there are more white people longing for the soul of jazz preaching and more black people longing for the substance of classical preaching than we ever dreamed" (250). Sidney L. Green uses Ellis's distinction to round off a symphonic analogy for the challenges faced by contemporary Anglicanism. For Green, "the jazz theology approach" provides a way of getting beyond "statements based on historical events and the history of theological and ecclesiological thought" by "encouraging that which does not obviously fit in to [*sic*] the accepted forms and in a revolutionary way raising questions about the way things are." Green, *Beating the Bounds*, 202, 203. See also the discussion on Robert Gelinas below.

21. Ellis, *Free at Last?* 174. These quotations are from the 1996 2nd edition; an earlier version was published in 1983 under the title, *Beyond Liberation: The Gospel in the Black American Experience*. Ellis may have theologians such as Charles Hodge in mind when he describes "classical theology." In the introduction to his *Systematic Theology*, Hodge writes, "The Bible contains the truths which the theologian has to collect, authenticate, arrange, and exhibit in their internal relation to each other." Hodge, *Systematic Theology*, 1:1.

following way: "Where the four Gospels share the same narratives, there are relatively few differences in the text. But like jazz musicians who have distinctive differences in their solos, the Evangelists have distinctive differences in the arrangement of their facts when they do not share the same narratives."[22] In Ellis's understanding of the inspiration of Scripture, the Evangelists express their unique perspectives within the bounds of being a faithful witness to the revelation of Jesus Christ just as jazz musicians operate within the bounds of harmony.[23]

Ellis's work marks the point where theologians began to view jazz not only as a cultural object of theological interest but also as a resource capable of informing theology. He finds in jazz improvisation an analogy for contextual theology and in diverse expressions of jazz a way of explaining the human aspect of Scripture. He does not flesh these analogies out or work through them in a systematic fashion, but they nonetheless serve to start the conversation, allowing others to work out what it means to be a "jazz theologian."[24]

Although he writes twenty-six years after Ellis, Robert Gelinas picks up where Ellis left off, endeavoring to embody Ellis's vision.[25] With Ellis, he focuses on theological praxis, asserting that, "Jazz says we *don't know*

22. Ellis, *Free at Last?* 179.

23. Ellis, *Free at Last?* 178.

24. At the heart of Ellis's work is his concern for the African-American people. Jazz provides him with useful analogies because it is closely tied to his people and culture. According to Ellis, the role of a jazz theologian (in an African-American context) is "to apply the revitalized and expanded theological dynamic to all aspects of our culture" so that "a practical righteousness will begin to emerge—an *intra*cultural righteousness to overcome our ungodliness, and an *extra*cultural righteousness to overcome oppression." Ellis, *Free at Last?* 196. By "theological dynamic," he is essentially referring to the Gospel in the experience of African-Americans (48).

25. Gelinas writes of *Free at Last?* "I read this book at least once a year. It is here that I was first awakened to the possibility of a jazz-shaped Christianity." Gelinas, *Finding the Groove*, 213n3. Between Ellis and Gelinas, an article and a book chapter address jazz and theology in a similar manner. William G. Carter's article, "Singing a New Song," touches on themes that Gelinas notes later in his book, *Finding the Groove*. Carter links jazz to a number of things in the Christian life, from the way jazz has as many "denominations" as does Protestantism, to the way jazz can express things when words fall short, to the parallels between a jazz ensemble and the church. Carter's published address provides a link between jazz and church practice in a direct and clear manner, which in turn critiques the bureaucratic organization of some Western churches. Also notable is the way it interacts with jazz musicians themselves, using Miles Davis, among others, as a dialogue partner. Bill Hall's chapter provides a first-hand account of performing jazz in a church setting. He concludes with some brief comments about using the play that occurs between the individual and the group in jazz as a way of considering God at play and, by extension, the play of those made in his image. See Hall, "Jazz."

until we *can do.*[26] His thesis is that "a jazz-shaped faith is worth pursuing because it balances freedom with boundaries, the individual with the group, and traditions with the pursuit of what might be."[27] He develops his thesis by drawing narratives from jazz history and the civil rights movement and applying what he gleans to the Christian life, especially in the context of the Church. Gelinas also suggests that the close link between practice and knowledge in jazz can enliven one's hermeneutical approach to Scripture. In addition to exegeting Scripture, one can also imitate the text, using its forms and subject material to reflect on one's relationship with God. For example, one can write Psalms and record the acts of God in one's life and the lives of others. While Gelinas writes at a popular level, his broad insights into the way the constraints found in jazz mirror the constraints of the Christian life make good starting points for an engagement with the question of Christian freedom.[28]

According to Samuel Wells, *Theology, Music and Time* by Jeremy Begbie is "the benchmark for treatments of musical improvisation and theology."[29] In the section of his book on "liberating constraint," Begbie delves into the relationship between improvisation and freedom. Particularly useful for my own project is his taxonomy of the constraints that shape improvisation (see

26. Gelinas, *Finding the Groove,* 125.

27. Gelinas, *Finding the Groove,* 14.

28. According to Jamie Howison, "Gelinas is actually most interested in mounting in a kind of Christian apologetic for listening to jazz," and goes on to bemoan this sort of writing as "the great Achilles' heel in much of faith-based writing about popular music." Howison, *God's Mind in That Music,* 31. The scope and content of Gelinas's work, however, suggest otherwise.

29. Wells, *Improvisation,* 222. Heidi Epstein provides a more critical reading of Begbie in Epstein, *Melting the Venusberg,* 84–87. For Epstein, "in Begbie's rereading of jazz's theological significance, the erotic lifeblood of jazz improvisation is, at best, only implied and thus given surprisingly short shrift" (86). Richard Stoltzfus challenges Begbie's methodology, asking, "will the development of [Begbie's] aesthetic tools lead to a constructive reassessment of theological method and reengagement with issues central to the tradition, such as the concept of God, or will it merely assist us in providing apologetic decor to previously articulated doctrinal positions?" Stoltzfus, *Theology as Performance,* 16. Begbie picks up the gauntlet, responding, "I see no inherent or prima facie reason—if theology is to retain a sense of primary responsibility to the self-revealing triune God of Jesus Christ, which in turn means according some kind of normative role to Scripture—why this orientation should be relativized or radically revised by musical experience." Begbie, *Music, Modernity, and God,* 214. I side with Begbie; using jazz analogically in the service of theology in the way I propose below requires a reasonable amount of stability within each domain in order to evaluate whether or not the analogy holds. If music is allowed to render doctrinal positions fluid, it will destabilize the target domain of my analogy. For further analysis of Begbie's work, see also Broadhead, "An Overview," 159–61.

chapter 4). He makes important connections between jazz and church tradition, beginning by observing the way certain songs have been adapted and rewritten by jazz musicians over time as they particularized their "cultural constraints" (in the case of jazz, such things as harmony and melody) in "relation to occasional constraints" (which are the physical, social, and psychological conditions in which the improviser plays).[30] Begbie suggests that jazz can remind Christians that church tradition developed in a similar manner to the way new melodies were written over old harmonic progressions by jazz musicians and that this tradition itself is often a particularization of a specific set of circumstances.[31] And just as jazz would "fall to bits without interacting deeply with tradition," church tradition remains indispensible for "an appropriate and fruitful response to our own context."[32] Jazz is also used in a discussion of gift-giving in which certain rules apply to the way musical ideas are given and received in an improvising jazz ensemble. Begbie uses this model to characterize God's relationship with humanity and goes so far as to apply it to the doctrine of election in Rom 9–11.[33] Begbie's theological discussion of freedom through the lens of jazz improvisation remains unrivalled.[34]

Yet space remains for a work that pushes the subject further and treats jazz in a more holistic manner. In the portions of Begbie's book that engage with jazz, he cites major writers and critics such as Theodor Adorno,[35] Derek Bailey,[36] Paul Berliner,[37] Leroy Ostransky,[38] Frank Tirro,[39] and especially David Sudnow,[40] but eschews engaging with significant jazz musicians on their art.[41] By contrast, he devotes an entire chapter to contrasting Pierre Boulez

---

30. Begbie, *Theology, Music and Time*, 215.

31. Begbie, *Theology, Music and Time*, 216.

32. Begbie, *Theology, Music and Time*, 217, 219.

33. Begbie, *Theology, Music and Time*, 255–69.

34. See in particular Begbie, *Theology, Music and Time*, 199–270. A more recent work by Begbie contains references to improvisation throughout, but does not address it in a sustained manner: see Begbie, *Resounding Truth*, 188, 200, 208, 241, 269.

35. Adorno, "Perennial Fashion."

36. Bailey, *Improvisation.*

37. Berliner, *Thinking in Jazz.*

38. Ostransky, *Anatomy of Jazz.*

39. Tirro, "Silent Theme Tradition."

40. Sudnow, *Ways of the Hand.* Begbie uses Sudnow's account of learning to trust his hands as a classically trained pianist learning to play jazz to discuss the constraint of embodiment.

41. Begbie *refers* to major jazz musicians such as John Coltrane and Ornette Coleman (Begbie, *Theology, Music and Time*, 200n77) but does not engage with what they

with John Cage. But it is silly to fault Begbie for playing to his strengths, and it should be kept in mind that his objective is using improvisation in the broad Western tradition to discuss freedom, rather than jazz in particular. He simply leaves the door open for further and deeper engagement with jazz on the topic of freedom.

ANALOGY

My work depends on an analogy between jazz improvisation and Christian freedom. Paul Bartha helpfully distinguishes analogy as "a comparison between two objects, or systems of objects, that highlights respects in which they are thought to be similar," from an analogical argument, which is an "explicit representation of analogical reasoning that cites accepted similarities between two systems in support of the conclusion that some further similarity exists."[42] Over the course of this work, I develop an extensive analogy between jazz improvisation and Christian freedom that I draw upon to make analogical arguments about what Christian freedom ought to look like. In addition to these arguments, the analogy provides the opportunity to rethink both domains, much like a parable or a metaphor can prompt one to re-examine apparently familiar circumstances.

Understanding How an Analogy Works

Unfortunately, unless you are working with a mathematical analogy in which relationships between variables can be calculated, analogy cannot provide definitive conclusions. In the realm of the sciences, analogy is used to suggest plausible hypotheses that can then be tested empirically. This presents a problem for theology because encounters with God do not typically lend themselves to rigorous empirical verification.[43] Analogy applied

---

say about their music beyond a couple of quotations found in Berliner, *Thinking in Jazz*, (see Begbie, *Theology, Music and Time*, 201n79, 209).

42. Bartha, *By Parallel Reasoning*, 1.

43. One could point to Gideon laying out the fleece as one of the few exceptions (see Judges 6:36–40), but even in this case, God initiated the dialogue and accommodated Gideon's test in order to accomplish his goal of delivering Israel. God is not a force bound to operate in a predictable way under specific stimuli; he has a will all his own. Theology addressing ecclesiological concerns could conceivably be tested by working out the implications of this theology, applying it to a church setting, and evaluating the outcomes of its implementation. Difficulties with such an undertaking include creating a set of criteria to evaluate the success of the project, objectivity in this assessment, and controlling the multiple variables at play in a church setting.

to the realm of theology finds a better parallel in how it operates in law: in case law, judges use "the mechanism of *analogia legis*" to work out a "specification or an extension of a category that is implicit or not explicitly defined by law."[44] Unlike science, the object of analogy in theology is not to provide a hypothesis for an experiment but to a) provide fresh perspectives on old problems and b) to suggest solutions for contemporary problems based on precedent.[45] Jesus, for example, employs analogies that rely on things already accepted as true. Douglas Groothuis observes that Jesus commonly employed *a fortiori* arguments in his discourse. These arguments have the following underlying structure:

> The truth of A is accepted.
>
> The support for the truth of B (which is relevantly similar to A) is even stronger than that of A.
>
> Therefore, if the truth of A must be accepted, then so must the truth of B.[46]

Analogy comes to play in the second point of the structure where the "truth of B" is "relevantly similar to A." What this means is explicated below, but the important thing here is that Jesus sets a precedent for using analogical reasoning in theology.[47]

The first objective of an analogy in theology, which is to provide a new perspective, is best exemplified in Jesus' use of *a fortiori* arguments and parables that rely on a similar structure, such as Nathan's parable of the lamb (2 Sam 12:1–15). When Nathan tells the parable to David, David's sympathies are aroused over the plight of the poor man who had his sheep taken and slaughtered by the rich man. He pronounces judgment on the rich man. Then Nathan reveals to David that his adultery with Bathsheba is analogous to the actions of the rich man. As a result of seeing his actions through the lens of Nathan's parable, David repents. The second objective,

44. Macagno, "Analogy and Redefinition," 84. Cf. Holyoak and Thagard, *Mental Leaps*, 149–54.

45. A related discussion concerns the way analogy is used to talk about God. See, for example, White, *Talking about God*, 1–10. This discussion, while important, falls outside of the range of my own project.

46. Groothuis, *On Jesus*, 29.

47. Groothuis uses John 7:21–24 as an example of Jesus' use of *a fortiori*. Jesus argues that, since it is acceptable for a male to be circumcised on the Sabbath, it should be even more acceptable to heal the entire body of a man on the Sabbath. See Groothuis, *On Jesus*, 30. In *Talking about God*, Roger M. White uses Luke 11:11–13, which is also *a fortiori*, as an example of alternation in analogies, "[t]hat is to say, if A:B::C:D, then A:C::B:D" (179).

to suggest new solutions for contemporary problems based on precedent, can, I believe, benefit from the ongoing discussion on analogy that is taking place in the realms of cognitive science and philosophy.[48] I begin with the multiconstraint theory, as set forth by Keith Holyoak and Paul Thagard,[49] as a model for the structure of my analogy as a whole. It is valuable on at least two levels: first, it is easily grasped and, second, it accommodates multiple analogues and different levels of relations between them.

Cameron Shelley's concise reading of the multiconstraint theory begins with the division of "the analogy into two domains, the *source* and *target*. The source domain is that set of concepts that the analogy draws upon as the basis for a conclusion" and "the target domain is that set of concepts about which the analogy is going to make a claim."[50] My source domain is jazz and my target domain is the Christian life. Within each of the domains lie the elements from which they are formed. These elements are called analogues. For instance, the jam session is an analogue in the domain of jazz and the gathering of the local church is an analogue in the domain of Christian life.

The interaction between analogues is called a "mapping." According to the multiconstraint theory, there are three types of mappings: attribute mapping, relational mapping, and system mapping.[51] The first "is a mapping between the simple or 'atomic' elements of the analogy."[52] For instance, a

48. Bartha's preface to *By Parallel Reasoning* (vii–x) provides a brief introduction to this discussion. He credits Mary Hesse with raising "fundamental questions about the importance of analogies in scientific thought" (vii) in Hesse, *Models and Analogies in Science*, and cites the essays in Gentner, Holyoak, and Kokinov, *Analogical Mind,* as examples of computational models of analogy that have arisen in the past three decades thanks to "the efforts and interests of AI researchers, psychologists, and cognitive scientists" (vii). One of the two theories that I employ below, the multiconstraint theory, is derived from a computational model of analogy. See Holyoak and Thagard, *Mental Leaps*, especially 237–65. Bartha's critique of the multiconstraint theory is that the "soft constraints" (in contrast to "sharp principles") that it operates on become defects "if our project is to articulate a clear normative account of analogical arguments" (*By Parallel Reasoning*, 74). I hope to take advantage of the flexibility of the multiconstraint theory for the overarching analogy between jazz and Christian freedom, while using Bartha's articulation model to demonstrate the validity of the analogical arguments I make within it.

49. Holyoak and Thagard, *Mental Leaps*, 19–38.

50. Shelley, "Analogy Counterarguments," 226. Cf. Holyoak's and Thagard's use of these terms in describing proportional analogies. Holyoak and Thagard, *Mental Leaps*, 28.

51. Shelley, "Analogy Counterarguments," 237.

52. Shelley, "Analogy Counterarguments," 226. According to Holyoak and Thagard, this mapping involves "just one pair of objects considered in isolation from any other objects, which can be done on the basis of the semantic similarity between the attributes that apply to each object in the pair." Holyoak and Thagard, *Mental Leaps*, 26. This

jazz musician from the jazz domain can be mapped onto the Christian of the Christian life domain. The second, relational mapping, maps the relationships between analogues in each domain.[53] A jazz musician goes to a jam session in order to hone her craft, while a Christian goes to a local church to strengthen his faith.[54] The relationship between the individuals and gatherings is relevantly similar. Finally, system mapping maps "between relations of relations in the analogy" and therefore brings "all the relevant information together."[55] It would take more mapping between the domains of jazz and Christianity to come up with a system mapping. The closer the analogy is to an isomorphism, the more plausible are any suggestions made based on the similarity between jazz and theology.[56]

Understanding How an Analogical Argument Works

Bartha provides four types of analogical arguments in his articulation model,[57] but only two of them pertain to my present endeavor: predictive and explanatory arguments.[58] A predictive analogical argument begins with known facts P in the source domain that have an observed result Q. It finds analogues for these facts P^* in the target domain,[59] and posits an analogous result Q^*. For instance, if a person playing an instrument with a traditionally-defined role in a jazz combo switches roles with another instrument P, the audience is observed to pay closer attention to the music Q. Similarly, if a person who has fulfilled a certain role in a given church for a long period of time switches roles with someone else P^*, it may serve to draw the

is not to say that an analogy in this model must be limited to two objects but rather that attribute mapping "takes one pair of objects at a time" (26).

53. Holyoak and Thagard use proportional analogies to illustrate what they mean by relational mappings. They supply the mathematical example "2:4::3:6." Holyoak and Thagard, *Mental Leaps*, 28. The relationship between 2 and 4 is analogous to the relationship between 3 and 6.

54. Throughout this work, I endeavor to balance my use of gendered pronouns in order to be inclusive without being cumbersome.

55. Shelley, "Analogy Counterarguments," 226. Holyoak and Thagard define system mapping as "mappings based on similar higher-order relations coupled with a high degree of one-to-one mapping and structural consistency." Holyoak and Thagard, *Mental Leaps*, 31. Cf. Gentner, "Structure-Mapping," 157.

56. Holyoak and Thagard discuss isomorphism in *Mental Leaps*, 31–34.

57. See Bartha, *By Parallel Reasoning*, 95–98.

58. Bartha makes a further distinction between these two types of arguments in particular: they can be deductive or inductive. Since my analogy is neither mathematical nor syllogistic, it is inductive.

59. This process is called attribute mapping in the multiconstraint theory.

attention of the church to what is being said or done Q^*. An explanatory
analogical argument begins with an explanation Q for known facts P in the
source domain. Since analogous facts are observed in the target domain P^*,
they may be accounted for by an analogous explanation Q^*. For instance, if
a certain aspect of jazz tradition Q helps to explain how jazz musicians can
create exceptional music together at a jam session without working things
out beforehand P, then perhaps the operation of certain congregational
churches P^* can be explained in a similar fashion Q^*.

A LEAD SHEET[60]

To demonstrate that jazz is an effective analogy for a Christian theology of
freedom in a postmodern context, I 1) describe the problem of freedom in
the postmodern West; 2) consider the contributions of systematic theology
to a theology of freedom; 3) construct a biblical theology of freedom; 4)
describe the domain of jazz; 5) employ jazz improvisation as an analogy for
Christian freedom; 6) apply this analogy to the Christian life (including the
Church) in the postmodern West; and 7) evaluate the analogy.

Chapter 1 describes the contemporary problem of freedom with reference to two opposing poles of thought with respect to self and freedom and
to an impersonal force that mitigates human expressions of freedom. One of
these poles is the postmodern-self, illustrated by Ornette Coleman. It seeks
liberation from all traditional constraints. The other pole is authoritarian-
fundamentalism, illustrated by Wynton Marsalis. It seeks to multiply constraints in order to counter the relativism of the postmodern-self. I show
that the postmodern-self and authoritarianism are in fact intimately related
to one another as products of modernity. Encompassing both ends of the
spectrum is the alienating force that Jacques Ellul calls technique, illustrated by contemporary problems in jazz pedagogy. The problems inherent
in the way the opposing poles of the postmodern-self and authoritarian-
fundamentalism deal with freedom call out for a conception of Christian
freedom that escapes their impasse. Similarly, the seductive appeal of technique requires a rejection of its premises. For a jazz-shaped conception of
freedom to be effective in the contemporary West, it must provide a way of
addressing these issues.

Chapter 2 surveys the approach of a selection of recent theologians
and biblical scholars to the practical matter of Christian freedom. I compare
their different starting points, differences in defining Christian freedom,

60. A lead sheet is a rough sketch of the melody and chord changes (harmonic
structure) of a song.

approaches to the concept of freedom in Scripture, conception of freedom in relation to ecclesiology, and, finally, how they apply their concepts of freedom to their contemporary situations. I situate my approach in relation to theirs, marking out my own approach to each of these topics.

Having set the stage by examining the contemporary problem of freedom in the West and surveying salient contributions to this issue in the realm of systematic theology, I begin to move towards a solution by constructing a biblical theology of freedom in chapter 3. This chapter grounds my understanding of Christian freedom in Scripture, setting limits on the scope of the analogy I develop in the following chapters. I trace the notion of freedom and liberation from the first chapters of Genesis, through the central narrative of the Exodus in the Old Testament to the freedom found in Christ in the New Testament. In the process, I set forth the importance of willingly choosing to carry out God's will and the link between God's constraints and human flourishing.

Chapter 4 opens by defining, explaining, and illustrating the art of jazz improvisation. It then proceeds to its two main objectives. The first is to describe the domain of jazz in terms of its constraints and to show how these constraints can serve as constructive resources for improvisation. The second is to show how jazz provides a way of resolving apparent contradictions in navigating these constraints, such as assertiveness and openness. Begbie provides a taxonomy of constraints and Paul Rinzler shows how to come to terms with seemingly contradictory values in jazz. Finally, I examine the connection between mistakes and risk-taking that is inherent in jazz improvisation. Having laid out the various analogues in the domain of jazz and worked out their relationships, the stage is set for mapping these onto the domain of the Christian life.

Chapter 5 is taken up with performing this mapping from the source domain of jazz onto the target domain of the Christian life. Retaining Begbie's taxonomy and Rinzler's approach to navigating apparent contradictions, I find analogues and relationships in the domain of the Christian life that correspond to the ones I lay out in chapter 5. I draw upon examples from Scripture and Christian thought and history. In particular, I focus on the areas of physical spaces, tradition (especially Scripture), the other, self, and risk taking, making analogical arguments to both expand the biblical notion of Christian freedom and to aid in explaining it. The result is a fresh perspective on the nature of Christian freedom and a few suggestions for enacting it.

Chapter 6 returns to the contemporary problem of freedom as described in chapter 1. In this chapter, I focus particularly on the church, building on Kevin Vanhoozer's insight that Evangelicals have slid from an approach to the Christian life rooted in God's revelation into an approach rooted in culture.[61] I chart a course that, against the postmodern-self, affirms the foundational nature of God's revelation and the need for community, and that, against authoritarian-fundamentalism, affirms the worth and value of each member's contribution to not only the operation but the direction of the community. I further show the alienating effects of technique on the church in North America and suggest ways the church can move towards enacting the freedom described in Scripture.

Chapter 7 evaluates the analogy as a whole. I also reflect on the implications of the insights gleaned through the analogy for the contemporary church.

61. Vanhoozer, *Drama of Doctrine*, 26.

1

The Problem of Freedom
in the Postmodern West

ENACTING CHRISTIAN FREEDOM IN the Western world is like Christian's journey through the Valley of the Shadow of Death in John Bunyan's *The Pilgrim's Progress*, a journey in the dark on a narrow path bounded by a ditch on one side and a mire on the other. In the ditch one plummets into the situation of the postmodern-self as it abandons tradition and overt authority in favor of self-discovery and formation.[1] In the mire, one sinks under the morass of the multiplied constraints found in authoritarian-fundamentalism.[2] And the "discouraging clouds of confusion" are the alienating forces of technique and capitalism that overshadow the Western horizon. Unlike Christian, I must pause to consider these pitfalls, dangling a lantern over each side of the path to expose their danger and their appeal (not everyone has the same perspective as Christian).[3] To help shed this light I draw on two influential figures in the world of jazz and the challenges faced by contemporary jazz pedagogy.

1. By the "postmodern-self," I refer to the Western self that continues to be shaped by modern forces while it simultaneously wrestles with postmodern questions. See below for further details.

2. See below for my definition of authoritarian-fundamentalism.

3. I am not suggesting that this is the only way to view the contemporary West. Neither am I suggesting that my description is exhaustive; it is not my goal to produce a totalizing metanarrative. My aim is to describe in general terms the polarities in the West, along with the alienating forces that often exacerbate them, in relation to the concept of freedom.

For my purposes, Ornette Coleman and Wynton Marsalis represent a bifurcation of dealing with freedom in the jazz tradition: Coleman
pushes aside the governing constraints of the jazz tradition, while Marsalis
valorizes the tradition to the point where he has to form a protective hedge
around it. Naturally, neither musician can be reduced to being merely the
type of what I employ them for; life is always more subtle and complex
than categories allow. Furthermore, both musicians have had an undeniable and substantial impact on the history of jazz. Yet certain aspects of
their diverging approaches to music can be productively used to illustrate
the postmodern-self and authoritarian-fundamentalism respectively. I see
a parallel between Coleman's emancipation from the constraints of the
jazz tradition and a similar endeavor on the part of the postmodern-self
to be liberated from all constraints, especially the authority found in traditional communities and religious faith. I see another parallel between
the endeavors of Marsalis and authoritarian-fundamentalism. This form of
fundamentalism is an attempt "to recover the pristine message of the Messiah or the Prophet"[4] and to impose "uniformity of belief and practice"[5]
via unassailable contemporary leadership in reaction to undesired developments in the dominant culture. It reacts to the relativism espoused by the
postmodern-self with strong assertions of tradition, authority, and order.
With a tightly clenched fist, it attempts to minimize freedom. The conflict
between the desire of the postmodern-self for liberation on the one hand
and the desire of the authoritarian fundamentalist to adopt constraints that
will shield them from this liberation on the other is deeply felt; abandoning one often entails embracing the other.[6] Meanwhile, hanging over this

4. Almond et al., *Strong Religion*, 18. Almond et al. provide examples of the way
fundamentalist leaders can "reject all previous interpretations" of sacred scriptures,
clearing the way for their own apparent recovery of the unadulterated message of a
given founding religious figure (18). The result is that the leader gains authority and
power at the expense of tradition.

5. Almond et al., *Strong Religion*, 17. Almond et al. argue that "fundamentalisms
equate 'strong religion' with 'purity' and purity, with uniformity of belief and practice"
(17). This non-negotiable imposition of uniformity by a charismatic leader is part of
what separates what I call "authoritarian-fundamentalism" from being convinced of
the veracity of the Bible.

6. Berger writes, "For reasons that may not be immediately obvious, relativism and
fundamentalism as cultural forces are closely interlinked. . . . In every relativist there
is a fundamentalist about to be born, and in every fundamentalist there is a relativist
waiting to be liberated. "Introduction," 1–2. He goes on to show how a relativist, confronted with "what they are quite certain is a moral outrage" such as rape, "may become
a convert to this or that version of fundamentalism" (2). Likewise, a "fundamentalist,
looking at the shambles of an intended utopia, may lapse into relativism" (2).

bifurcation are the ubiquitous forces of technique (as described by Jacques Ellul)[7] and alienation (as described by Karl Marx).[8]

Jazz is shaped by the same forces of modernity that gave rise to the postmodern-self and the reaction of authoritarian-fundamentalism.[9] As such, it provides an instructive analogy for the contemporary problem of freedom. In the succeeding chapters, I show that it can also aid in the quest for a solution. I begin by describing the plight of the postmodern-self with reference to Coleman, and the nature of authoritarian-fundamentalism with reference to Marsalis. I then show the mutually reinforcing nature of these two opposing poles and conclude with a discussion of technique and alienation in the light of contemporary struggles in jazz pedagogy.

ORNETTE COLEMAN AND THE POSTMODERN-SELF

Ornette Coleman's rise to fame marks a turning point in the history of jazz. According to biographer John Litweiler, his approach to improvisation served "to overturn the very foundations of jazz for its entire previous existence."[10] What separates Coleman from prior innovators in jazz are the ways he downplays, or even tries to sever, ties with traditional approaches to playing an instrument, improvisation, and music theory. Many of those who first heard him when he began to gain some notoriety in the jazz world complained that he was out of tune.[11] Coleman responded that he played the way he did deliberately.[12] In his self-taught approaches to the trumpet

7. See below.

8. See below.

9. In his essay, "Jazz and American Modernism," Jed Rasula argues that jazz was "a conspicuous feature of modernity as it was manifested during and after the Great War. . . . Jazz unquestionably informed modernism as intellectual challenge, sensory provocation, and social texture" (157).

10. Litweiler, *Ornette Coleman*, 15–16.

11. In an interview with jazz critic Leonard Feather, bassist Charles Mingus said of Coleman, "Now aside from the fact that I doubt he can even play a C scale in whole notes—tied whole notes, a couple of bars apiece—in tune, the fact remains that his notes and lines are so fresh." Feather, "Another View," 21. Trombonist Bob Brookmeyer was on the faculty of the School of Jazz at Lenox, Massachusetts, when Coleman was a student. He is quoted as saying, "I used to scream out of my window, 'Damn it, tune up!' as these cats would play evenings downstairs," in Adderley, "Cannonball," 20.

12. Valarie Wilmer recounts an interview of Coleman by Richard Williams in which Coleman "was worried at the suggestion that by basing his playing on the 'natural' pitch of the instrument, he was playing 'out of tune.' Then he realized, 'My emotions were raising my tone to another level. . . . I could still hear the centre of what I was reading.'" Wilmer, *As Serious as Your Life*, 65. The quote from Coleman is from Williams, "Ornette and the Pipes," n.p.

and violin, he goes even further. He completely disregards developed ways of playing these instruments. According to Litweiler, "He had no teachers or guides to show him how to play trumpet and violin and *purposely avoided* learning standard techniques, for his objective was to create as spontaneously as possible."[13] Jazz improvisation prior to Coleman was based on improvising with the chords that accompany a given melody. Coleman threw this out the window, insisting that soloists and accompanists negotiate tonality in real time.

His struggle with conventional theory is illustrated in the difficulties he encountered in the lessons he took from composer Gunther Schuller. Schuller relates that, "I think what happened was, he caught a glimpse of what I was talking about in terms of accurate reading and notation and it was . . . disturbing because it meant everything he had learned up to then was 'wrong.'"[14] In place of conventional theory Coleman devised his own theory, harmolodics, but never ended up writing an authoritative account of it; Coleman's comments on his theory are notoriously cryptic.[15] All of these factors combined leads to an approach to making music that places "attention on the musician's powers of subjective expression above all else," mirroring the postmodern-self's turn to subjective evaluation.[16] A determined individualist, Coleman pursued his own course through discouragement and persecution. Decades after his most influential recordings, he continues to represent the avant-garde of jazz. His attempts to construct a de novo approach to music mirror the self-construction of the postmodern-self.

The self-constructed nature of the postmodern-self is necessitated by what it desires to be free from. In Dale S. Kuehne's reading of John Ashcroft, contemporary Western societies desire "freedom from nature," "freedom from authority," and "freedom from want."[17] Describing the liberation of the postmodern-self from these constraints (with the exception of liberation from want, which is, ironically, something many desire, but few attain) necessitates a brief look at the emergence of this self in Western history. According to Peter Berger, the Christian synthesis of "Hellenic and Israelite traditions" marks the point at which the latent roots of individuality in each tradition came together and began to be worked out "in earnest."[18]

13. Litweiler, *Ornette Coleman*, 117. My emphasis.

14. Gunther Schuller, quoted in Litweiler, *Ornette Coleman*, 94.

15. According to David Ayers, "Coleman has never succeeded in being verbally articulate about his methods." Ayers, "Jazz," 415. For an overview and assessment of Coleman's writings and statements on harmolodics, see Litweiler, *Ornette Coleman*, 147–50.

16. Gebhardt, *Going for Jazz*, 127.

17. Kuehne, *Sex and the iWorld*, 64.

18. Berger, "Western Individuality," 330.

In particular, Berger points to Paul's declaration in Gal 3:28—"There is no longer Jew or Greek, there is no longer slave or free, there is no longer male and female; for all of you are one in Christ Jesus" (NRSV)—as an antecedent to the notion that the "accidents of birth and biography" do not determine the true nature "of the unique individual" that lies behind the labels.[19] While he acknowledges that Paul "was speaking only of the unity of all Christians within the body of Christ," he draws a connection between this formulation and the modern notion "of the individual who has inalienable rights" regardless of "accidents" such as race, religion, or sexual orientation.[20] The philosophers of the modern era, such as René Descartes and Immanuel Kant, gradually stripped the notion of individual autonomy from its Christian context.[21] This process culminated in Frederich Nietzsche, who rejects Christian morality as a slave morality and instead holds up the will to power.[22] The subsequent atheistic strain of existentialism embodied in Jean-Paul

19. Berger, "Western Individuality," 328.

20. Berger, "Western Individuality," 328.

21. Descartes, searching for something that cannot be doubted, writes his famous dictum, "*I am thinking therefore I exist.*" Descartes, *Discourse on the Method*, 28 (32). Emphasis in original. In spite of the fact that Descartes is a Catholic believer, this dictum, along with related passages in his work, show that "the existence of the 'I' is known to be certain, and the certainty coincides with truth, before we know anything of the existence of God." Schouls, "Descartes," 308. In other words, Descartes places the starting point for thinking about the self with the existence of the self, prior to seeing the self in relation to God. As Peter A. Schouls argues, "in a very basic sense, reason is autonomous for Descartes" (308). If reason is autonomous, so is the self that reasons.

Kant writes,

> Natural necessity was a heteronomy of efficient causes, since every effect was possible only in accordance with the law that something else determines the efficient cause to causality; what, then, can freedom of the will be other than autonomy, that is, the will's property of being a law to itself? But the proposition, the will is in all its actions a law to itself, indicates only the principle, to act on no other maxim than that which can also have as object itself as a universal law.

Kant, *Groundwork*, 52 (4:446–47). If the will is indeed "a law to itself," it appears that Kant does not require a Christian foundation for the self, or even for morality.

22. In *Beyond Good and Evil*, Nietzsche compares "noble morality," by which he means a morality created by a certain type of people independently of their actions, to "slave morality." He writes, "The noble type of person feels that *he* determines value, he does not need anyone's approval, he judges that 'what is harmful to me is harmful in itself,' he knows that he is the one who gives honor to things in the first place, he *creates values.*" Nietzsche, *Beyond Good*, 154 (260). Emphasis in original. By contrast, "slave morality" arises from resentment of "the virtues of the powerful," and elevates the "qualities that serve to alleviate existence for suffering people" leading Nietzsche to conclude that "[s]lave morality is essentially a morality of utility" 155–56 (260). In *On the*

Sartre and Albert Camus found in the idea of God a threat to individual freedom.[23] Whatever its point of origin, Western individuality exists comfortably outside of a Christian context.

Sociology corroborates the emergence of the postmodern-self in philosophy.[24] Berger identifies at least six propositions about the Western conception of the self.[25] First, the self is unique, regardless of whatever similarities it shares with others or however close it is to them. The collective does not subsume the self. Second, as per Sartre, the self asserts that it is capable of acting independently of external forces. The third follows consequentially: the self is responsible for its own actions and not the actions of others. And vice versa. Fourth, the self constructs its perception of the world based on how it understands itself. Berger holds up Don Quixote as

---

Genealogy of Morality, Nietzsche traces "a reversal" in which slave morality triumphs over noble morality:

> It was the Jews who, rejecting the aristocratic value equation (good = noble = powerful = beautiful = happy = blessed) ventured, with awe-inspiring consistency, to bring about a reversal . . . saying, "Only those who suffer are good, only the poor, the powerless, the lowly are good . . . salvation is for them alone, whereas you rich, the noble and powerful, you are eternally wicked, cruel, lustful, insatiate, godless, you will also be eternally wretched, cursed and damned!" . . . We know *who* became heir to this Jewish revaluation.

Nietzsche, *On the Genealogy*, 19 (7). Emphasis in original. This heir, of course, is Christendom. It is not difficult to see how Nietzsche's sympathies with noble morality lead him to assert the will to power. For his discussion on the will, see Nietzsche, *Beyond Good*, 15–24 (13–23).

23. "Indeed, everything is permissible if God does not exist," writes Sartre, "For if it is true that existence precedes essence, we can never explain our actions by reference to a given and immutable human nature. In other words, there is no determinism—man is free, man is freedom." Sartre, *Existentialism*, 29. In a similar vein, Camus writes, "I cannot understand what kind of freedom would be given me by a higher being" (51), and, "If God exists, all depends on him and we can do nothing against his will. If he does not exist, everything depends on us." Camus, *Myth of Sisyphus*, 108.

24. Walter Anderson describes the shift from the modern self to the postmodern-self. The consensus of modern psychologists was the imperative to "[g]et your act together; be consistent, integrated, authentic, whole." Anderson, *Future Self*, 34. Yet, with the advent of the postmodern era, "[m]any psychologists now claim that the way to health and happiness in today's decentralized, pluralistic world is to *be* decentralized and pluralistic" (34). Emphasis in original. Both approaches appear to be compatible with Berger's observations of the Western conception of the self, but the postmodern approach appears to be the outcome of this conception (see below).

25. Graham Ward appears to be thinking along similar lines when he observes the contemporary "rampant individualism of the I am, I want, and I will" that grounds "today's social atomism." Ward, *Cities of God*, 70.

an example of the modern self: Quixote constructs his own reality. Fifth, the self has rights that can override the ties of community. The sixth combines the previous propositions into the radical notion that the self claims the right and the capacity to choose its own life, world, and very self.[26] These views are certainly neither compatible with certain Western philosophical positions (e.g., materialistic determinism), nor are they necessarily accurate descriptions of reality.[27] But they do provide insight into the perceptions and experiences of Western people.[28] Coleman, for instance, exemplifies a concern with acting independently of external musical forces in his rejection of conventional tuning and instrumental technique. His musically (and at times physically) violent clashes with other musicians when he first gained an audience in New York represent his independence in relation to the larger jazz community and his independent construction of his own music theory is essentially a construction of his own musical reality.[29] In these respects, at least, he musically mirrors the concerns and objects of the postmodern-self.

It seems evident from Berger's analysis that the postmodern-self is very concerned with autonomy. The question of autonomy, as Isaiah Berlin sees it, is, "'What is the area within which the subject—a person or group of persons—is or should be left to do or be what he is able to do or be, without interference by other persons?'"[30] The area in which the individual exercises autonomy is inversely proportional to the interfering acts of others. *Habits of the Heart*, a sociological study of American individualism, describes the implications of attempting to maximize this area:

> to be free is not simply to be left alone by others; it is also somehow to be your own person in the sense that you have defined who you are, decided for yourself what you want out of life, free as much as possible from the demands of conformity to family, friends, or community. From this point of view, to be free psychologically is to succeed in separating oneself from the values

26. Berger, "Western Individuality," 326–27.

27. Jerzy Jedlicky, responding to Berger's description of "the spiritual experiences of the autonomous individual," notes that "our world hardly resembles a stage on which individual actors, free from social ties, play roles of their own choice and give account only of their performance." Jedlicki, "Heritage," 59.

28. Berger, "Western Individuality," 326. Admittedly, Berger's study is a little dated, but, as I show below, these propositions continue to describe the outlook and experiences of contemporary Western life.

29. See Litweiler, *Ornette Coleman*, 82–83.

30. Berlin, *Four Essays*, 121–22.

imposed by one's past or by conformity to one's social milieu, so that one can discover what one really wants.[31]

When all of these constraints—including "family, religion, and calling as sources of authority, duty, and moral example"—are set aside, the self is liberated to pursue what it truly desires.[32] Yet finding what one really wants is often more complex in practice than in theory. In the film series, *The Pirates of the Caribbean*, the character Captain Jack Sparrow carries with him a compass that helpfully points towards the thing he truly desires. Unfortunately for Sparrow, his indecisiveness at times prevents the compass from steadily pointing in one direction. Furthermore, the self is vulnerable to the insidious effects of more subtle external forces.

Being liberated from traditional sources of overt authority does not necessarily entail being liberated from more subtle (but no less powerful) influences. In the West, former expectations of a stable career, stable relationships, and a stable community have been replaced with uncertainty. Beverly Southgate describes the impact of this shift on the self:

> Freed from the constraints of any need for enduring commitment (in matters personal and public), postmodern men and women prefer to keep their options open. . . . And that openendedness applies, of course, not only to their professional or working lives, but also to their private selves—their own identities. So a definition of self, in the past so closely identified with work (with what one did in life), can now be indefinitely postponed; or rather, with the uncertainties of work's availability, indefinitely postponed it must be.[33]

Escaping traditional authority, then, is not just an existential assertion of freedom, but a response closely related to the socio-economic climate of the West. Instead of being an existential act of transgression, this rebellion against commitment is actually a reflection of trends beyond the control of the individual. It is not that individuals cannot choose; it just happens that some choices are easier than others.

If identity based on what one does is consistently being deferred, identity based on consumption ends up merely trading traditional masters for capitalist ones. According to Benjamin R. Barber, "Much of [the] strategy for creating global markets depends on a systematic rejection of any

31. Bellah, *Habits of the Heart*, 23–24.
32. Bellah, *Habits of the Heart*, 79.
33. Southgate, *Postmodernism in History*, 8.

genuine consumer autonomy."[34] The apparently infinite variety of products and services "means at best someone else's product or someone else's profit, but cannot be permitted to become no product at all and thus no profit for anyone."[35] Selecting to consume one thing rather than another still leaves one bound to consumerism.[36] I take a closer look at the forces of technique and capitalism below.

Rejecting traditional authority not only entails finding a new master, but an entirely different ethical system; it ultimately leads to the rejection of any claim to universal values. Values are existentially chosen rather than received. Sharon D. Welch, for instance, asks, "What is the foundation of moral action, of individuals and groups acting with courage, insight, and vision to end some form of systematic injustice?" and answers, "There is none."[37] Actions are not objectively right or wrong; the morality of a given action is determined solely by how one feels about it.[38] According to Zygmunt Bauman, in postmodernity "individual freedom reigns supreme; it is the value by which all other values [are] evaluated, and the benchmark against which the wisdom of all supra-individual rules and resolutions are to be measured."[39] All value judgments must be measured by the self in relation to its own freedom from external influences. Yet ironically, as in the case of pursuing what one desires, choosing one's own values makes one very susceptible to external influence. Choosing values based on feeling allows one to put on different "social masks" for different social situations.[40] The field is open for interest groups to shape societal values through whatever means they have access to, as they see fit. Once a certain idea gains enough traction and support, it becomes convenient for those who select their own values to adopt it. Selecting one's own values (or at least believing that one does) ends up affirming Nietzsche's notion of the will to power.

---

34. Barber, *Jihad Vs. McWorld*, 116. Graham Ward adds, "The citizen is customer, catered for by both the state and the commercial world, but it is a customer who, on the one hand, seems to be given a vast freedom to choose and, on the other, is heavily directed toward what to choose." Ward, *Politics of Discipleship*, 112.

35. Barber, *Jihad Vs. McWorld*, 116.

36. William T. Cavanaugh defines consumerism as "a way of seeing the world: one that argues or assumes that we have been liberated by being able to choose what we want." Cavanaugh, "'What Do I Want?,'" 25.

37. Welch, *Sweet Dreams*, 132.

38. Bellah, *Habits of the Heart*, 77–79.

39. Bauman, *Postmodernity*, 2–3.

40. Bellah, *Habits of the Heart*, 80. Bauman sees "rejoicing in the chance of putting on and taking off identities" as a requirement for navigating the postmodern milieu. Bauman, *Postmodernity*, 14.

The privatization of values has a significant impact on relationships; the postmodern-self is situated differently to others than the traditional self. In eschewing the bonds of duty and obligation, even intimate relationships are subjected to a cost-benefit method of evaluation. Francis Fukuyama observes that "the Anglo-Saxon version of liberal theory on which the United States was founded" gives individuals "perfect rights but no perfect duties to their communities."[41] Communities are only necessary insofar as they protect the rights of individuals, not vice versa. Relationships are contractual; they function to promote the self-interests of all parties involved. When a person feels that their self-interests are not being served by the relationship, the terms of the contract are void. The problem is that certain communities—families in particular—cannot function properly on such principles. As Fukuyama points out, "Raising children or making a marriage work through a lifetime requires personal sacrifices that are irrational, if looked at from a cost-benefit calculus. For the true benefits of strong family life frequently do not accrue to those bearing the heaviest obligations, but are transmitted across generations."[42] Without being bound by some sense of duty and obligation, the postmodern-self creates inherently unstable relationships. Evaluating the cost-benefit of a given relationship is necessarily subjective; the only means of measurement are the feelings of the participant. And feelings are both unstable and far from invulnerable to external persuasion.

On a more abstract level, postmodernism is closely linked to the collapse of universal values and the proliferation of subjectivism. In fact, postmodern theory plays a role in legitimizing and aiding the self in its pursuit of freedom from traditional constraints. Just as Coleman so dramatically called into question the legacy of the jazz tradition, postmodernism calls into question metanarratives—the overarching stories that make sense of all else.[43] From a postmodern perspective, these explanatory systems are inherently unstable and problematic. Religious texts can no longer provide justification for adopting one set of ethics over another. Neither can philosophy or science. On the one hand, postmodern "incredulity" towards metanarratives provides a set of useful tools for uncovering abuses in authoritarian systems; it uncovers assertions of power cloaked in the language of morality and cracks open previously unquestioned dogmatic assertions. On the other hand, it cannot provide a workable alternative.

41. Fukuyama, *End of History*, 323.
42. Fukuyama, *End of History*, 324.
43. Lyotard, *Postmodern Condition*, xxiv.

The postmodern-self is not content to be liberated from traditional values and sources of authority; it seeks also to be liberated from nature. In fact, liberation from authority paves the way for this final act of liberation. David Walsh identifies the endgame of "the modern project": "to liberate humanity from the shackles of traditional morality in order to expand limitlessly our power of subordinating the whole of existence to our fulfillment."[44] Whether altering one's appearance with respect to sex or race or, looking to an ever closer horizon, the very genetic makeup of one's offspring, human beings are moving ever closer to complete control over "the nature and development of human life."[45] In *The Abolition of Man*, C. S. Lewis suggests that "conditioners" may ultimately determine what sort of human life ought to be produced.[46] And, as Jacques Ellul shows, these conditioners will not likely be an exception to the contemporary principle that "everything which is technique is necessarily used as soon as it is available, without distinction of good or evil."[47] The liberation of humanity from nature entails the liberation of humans from their humanity.[48] Once again, little is left aside from the will to power.

In summary, the freedom and autonomy of the postmodern-self is "conceived exclusively as the emancipation of the individual from all constraints and as unlimited freedom of choice" and is "constructed as the only absolute in a radically relativistic culture."[49] The postmodern-self above all else is dedicated to pursuing unconstrained freedom from authority, nature, and want. And yet freedom from these constraints does not entail freedom from all constraints. Liberation from certain constraints entails bondage to the less overt, but no less powerful, constraints of socio-economic forces governed by technique (see below). The postmodern-self is left vulnerable to the external influences of marketing and the agendas of various interest groups. The "radically isolating individualism" practiced by the postmodern-self (or determined by technique and capitalism) does not even provide a viable defense from authoritarian manipulation.[50] In fact, someone seeking to escape the vertigo of the sort of freedom experienced by the postmodern-self is inevitably drawn to authoritarian-fundamentalism.

44. Walsh, *After Ideology*, 15.
45. Walsh, *After Ideology*, 15.
46. See Lewis, "The Abolition of Man," 721–28.
47. Ellul, *The Technological Society*, 97.
48. See Lewis, "Abolition of Man."
49. Bauckham, *God and the Crisis*, 3.
50. Bellah, *Habits of the Heart*, 162.

WYNTON MARSALIS, WERKTREUE, AND
AUTHORITARIAN-FUNDAMENTALISM

Wynton Marsalis appeared in the 1980s as the long-awaited jazz-messiah; he had the right pedigree, credentials, and unquestionable command of the trumpet and the jazz tradition. Yet in spite of the accolades he has garnered and the influence he wields, few jazz critics are arguing that he has earned a place in the jazz pantheon next to greats such as Louis Armstrong and Charlie Parker. In contrast to Coleman, Marsalis has firmly entrenched himself in the past. Under his direction, Jazz at the Lincoln Center continues to look back at select luminaries of the jazz tradition. In fact, Marsalis appears to be adopting the classical ideal of *werktreue* in a jazz context.[51] In other words, Marsalis appears to be a consummate traditionalist.

Critic Stuart Nicholson writes that "when music—or any art form—becomes a refuge from the present, from facing up to the world today, then its force is diminished; it becomes an embalmed corpse, beautiful to behold but ultimately inert."[52] He is concerned about the powerful influence exerted by Marsalis and the critics that back him on the development of jazz in the United States. In reaction to the fracturing of jazz into various subgenres, some of which strayed from traditional acoustic instruments, Marsalis went back to certain key figures in early jazz to inform his own playing. He proceeded from his recordings and interviews to define jazz in such a way that it excluded many of these subgenres along with repertoire drawn from the contemporary world of pop. As director of Jazz at the Lincoln Center, Marsalis recreates the compositions of past masters in a way that mirrors the classical idea of *werktreue*, that is, fidelity to the intentions of a given composer. Bruce Ellis Benson observes,

> The ideal of *Werktreue* has proven so hegemonic that it has even spilled over from classical music into other genres. For instance, in the last decade, both Wynton Marsalis (with the Lincoln Center Jazz Orchestra) and William Russo (with the Chicago Jazz Ensemble) have provided us with painstakingly historically accurate performances of Duke Ellington compositions—along with Ellingtonian performance practice.[53]

He goes on to note that this practice contrasts starkly with Marsalis' explanation of what separates jazz from classical music, namely, that jazz

51. For a discussion of the impact of classical ideals on Marsalis, see DeVeaux, "Constructing the Jazz Tradition," 551–52.

52. Nicholson, *Is Jazz Dead?*, 38.

53. Benson, *Improvisation of Musical Dialogue*, 14.

musicians—like classical composers—create the music while classical musicians strive to reproduce the composer's intentions.[54] In other words, in his desire to be faithful to the jazz tradition, Marsalis undermines the freedom of the musicians in his ensemble to participate in creating the music. Ironically, in seeking to preserve the essence of jazz he loses it.

A principle similar to *werktreue* appears at work in fundamentalism as it is described by sociologists. Harriet A. Harris argues that "[f]undamentalists are primitivists, meaning that they wish to live in accord with the beliefs and practices of the earliest followers of their faith."[55] Like Marsalis, they seek to live a life of fidelity to the intentions of the composer and conductor of their faith—to God. From an orthodox Christian perspective—which I am adopting—, this is a laudable goal. My concern is whether certain forms of fundamentalism undermine Christian freedom as they seek to preserve and maintain the Christian faith.

Before proceeding, it is necessary to clarify what aspects of fundamentalism with which I am especially concerned. The term "fundamentalism" can be traced back to *The Fundamentals: A Testimony of the Truth* in 1909. The goal of this publication was a scholarly defense of the historic tenets of the Christian faith. According to George M. Marsden, the tone of *The Fundamentals* was "relatively moderate," but "[a]fter 1920 conservative evangelical councils were dominated by 'fundamentalists' engaged in holy warfare to drive the scourge of modernism out of church and culture."[56] Liberal theology and evolution were the primary enemies. In the 1960s, fundamentalists reacted to the sexual revolution and in the 1970s began to be involved in politics. Since then, the domain of the word has been expanded to include movements in any major world religion that "*attempt to arrest the erosion of religious identity, fortify the borders of the religious community, and create viable alternatives to secular institutions and behaviors.*"[57] In rhetorical exchanges, "fundamentalism" is often used pejoratively, "as a word to describe believers more orthodox than oneself when one is displeased with them."[58] Many evangelical Christians do not wish to be labeled as fundamentalists, while many critics insist that they are.[59] But my object is not to quibble about what qualifies as fundamentalism. I am not

54. Benson, *Improvisation of Musical Dialogue*, 14.

55. Harris, *Fundamentalism and Evangelicals*, v.

56. Marsden, *Fundamentalism and American Culture*, 141.

57. Almond et al., *Strong Religion*, 17. Emphasis in original.

58. Pinnock, "Defining American Fundamentalism," 42.

59. See Guinness, "Pilgrim at the Spaghetti Junction," for an example of an evangelical taking exception to the fundamentalist label. See also Harriet A. Harris' discussion of the issue in Harris, *Fundamentalism and Evangelicals*, 1–18.

concerned with how fervently central tenets of a faith are upheld, but rather with attempts to tightly regulate aspects of daily life and to enforce uniform interpretation of sacred texts on the basis of alleged fidelity to them. I am concerned with *authoritarian-fundamentalism*. In relation to the notion of freedom, authoritarian-fundamentalism is the multiplication of constraints in reaction to the iconoclastic attitude towards undesired constraints held by the postmodern-self.

While *Strong Religion: The Rise of Fundamentalisms around the World* paints with a rather broad brush (it is not at all careful to distinguish between evangelicals and fundamentalists), it does identify certain traits of fundamentalist movements that serve to multiply constraints.[60] Organizationally, authoritarian fundamentalist movements are governed by a charismatic leader, numerous behavioral requirements, and sharp boundaries between insiders and outsiders. Such movements also tend to be reactive, selectively emphasize aspects of their respective religious traditions, have a heightened sense of darkness and light (especially in cases where others share their religious tradition but eschew the movement's distinctives), and oppose competing hermeneutical approaches to their religious texts.[61]

Turning again to the impact of Marsalis on the development of jazz, it is interesting to note his role in policing the tastes and musical expressions of the "young lions" of the 1990s. Christian McBride, a respected bassist who emerged as a prominent voice in this movement says, "I think why a lot of us did what we did, I think some of us were kind of scared to do other things, because we were scared that Wynton Marsalis or Stanley Crouch would do a big interview in *The New York Times* and blast us, you know?"[62] While the coercive nature of the forces that act on the postmodern-self only appear upon careful reflection, in authoritarian-fundamentalism authority has a face. Participants trade their freedom for the security of conforming to a system held together by someone they trust implicitly. As Fyodor Dostoevsky's Grand Inquisitor says, "They will bring us their most tormenting problems of conscience—everything, they will bring everything to us and we shall resolve everything, and they will accept our judgment with joy, because it will spare them the great burden and terrible torment of personal and free choice that they suffer today."[63] Dostoevsky understands

---

60. In fact, one gets the impression that religious orthodoxy in any meaningful sense is tantamount to fundamentalism. I take the liberty of selecting and reorganizing the traits that it lists.

61. Almond et al., *Strong Religion*, 90–115.

62. Christian McBride, quoted in Nicholson, *Is Jazz Dead?*, 46–47.

63. Dostoevsky, *Karamazov Brothers*, 325.

the discomfort and disorientation that comes with freedom and rightly observes that human nature is more inclined to lean towards authoritarianism. Continuing with the theme of the charismatic leader, it is important to note the role of such a leader in shaping the past and tidying the present. In a revealing analysis of a Marsalis album, David Ake shows that the accompanying liner notes scrupulously avoid referring "to the nonjazz histories of the tunes," preferring instead to "invoke specific jazz performers and their recordings."[64] Instead of referring to a song from a musical in terms of the musical, it is detached and placed within a constructed history of jazz, essentially creating a barrier between jazz and the culture it drew upon. In his playing, Marsalis' ideal is not risk, but accuracy, of having complete mastery over his instrument and the notes he plays.[65] In other words, Marsalis sands away the rough edges of jazz, separating it from its context and from its exploratory and risk-taking aspects. According to *Strong Religion*, in order for a movement to be strong, a charismatic leader "must be unassailable in their authority over contemporary belief and practice."[66] They provide definitive interpretations of scripture for their communities, select aspects to emphasize, and help to fill in areas of conduct not specifically addressed in Scripture. Like Marsalis, they offer a tailor-made version of the past and aim for certainty and security in the present.

Behavioral requirements place limits on where participants can go and what they can do and say. Such restrictions prevent them from interacting with certain people and mark them "as a distinctive people."[67] For example, Marsden notes that certain American Christian fundamentalists are expected to avoid "the barroom vices, such as smoking, drinking, dancing, card playing, immodest dress, and any sort of sexual license."[68] Note that while this list is consistent with some of the activities prohibited in the Bible, it also goes beyond it. For instance, although many have tried, it is difficult to make a substantive case that the Bible bans the consumption of alcohol. But instead of leaving certain activities to conscience or requiring moderation or discretion, it is simpler to ban them outright. When a biblical prohibition is not explicitly spelled out in detail, certain fundamentalist groups have resorted to arbitrarily determining what counts as modest dress or proper hair length among themselves. Getting all participants to conform to the same pattern of behavior reinforces the identity of the group, especially in

---

64. Ake, *Jazz Cultures*, 153.
65. Nicholson, *Is Jazz Dead?*, 42–43.
66. Almond et al., *Strong Religion*, 18.
67. Marsden, "Defining American Fundamentalism," 25.
68. Marsden, "Defining American Fundamentalism," 25.

relation to outsiders. It also serves to simplify social interactions; there is no need to negotiate with the internal convictions and preferences of each individual member. A clear code of conduct also makes behavior easier to regulate. It creates a sense of role and function within the community that is stable and secure. It can also be unforgivingly rigid.

Behavioral requirements dovetail naturally with a heightened sense of separation from secular culture and even from believers who do not abide by the same requirements. For instance, Harris observes that "[m]ost self-proclaimed fundamentalists in the States today are strict in their separation from non-fundamentalist Christians."[69] Once again, Marsalis' actions illustrate this mindset: when his brother, saxophonist Branford Marsalis, and his pianist at the time decided to tour with Sting, a rock star, it spelled the end for a promising ensemble. Wynton Marsalis was incensed; he saw it as a personal betrayal and an attack on African-American culture.[70] While it is true that the Bible calls on Christians to be separate from the world around them (e.g. 2 Cor 6:14–18), it also emphasizes Christian unity and the necessity for Christians to act in the world. Authoritarian-fundamentalism emphasizes the former while neglecting the latter.

Authoritarian-fundamentalism also has a rigid stance towards roles within the faith community. North American evangelicalism is still caught up in a struggle between complementarianism (clearly defined roles for the sexes in the church and the family) on the one hand, and egalitarianism (where defined roles do not exist) on the other.[71] While a full engagement with this controversy is beyond the scope of this work, I will observe that authoritarian-fundamentalism casts gender roles in a very rigid fashion that steps beyond what is warranted in the biblical text.

Randall Balmer traces the rigid division of gender roles in American fundamentalism to an ideal of femininity that emerged in the nineteenth century. Alexis de Tocqueville, a French observer of American society writing in 1835, notes that Americans "have taken the most continual care to draw cleanly separated lines of action for the two sexes" and goes on to show that women were barred from "directing the external affairs of the family, conducting a business, or indeed entering the political sphere," being bound rather to "the peaceful circle of domestic occupations."[72] Balmer shows how this state of affairs emerged as the workplace separated men from the farm and the home, causing women to assume "responsibility for

69. Harris, *Fundamentalism and Evangelicals*, 7.
70. Nicholson, *Is Jazz Dead?*, 30.
71. For an introduction to this debate, see Beck, *Two Views*.
72. Tocqueville, *Democracy in America*, 574.

domestic life, especially the religious instruction of the children."[73] In other words, according to Balmer, the gender roles championed by American fundamentalists are rooted in a nineteenth-century construct shaped by the sociological factors of its own time. If Balmer's analysis is correct, then authoritarian-fundamentalism, perhaps in spite of its best intentions, can end up grounding itself not in Scripture, but in cultural memory. In other words, when cultural tradition expands constraints in an area not fully delineated by Scripture, these traditions can easily form the presuppositions of authoritarian-fundamentalism.

In summary, authoritarian-fundamentalism is concerned with *werktreue*, but the needs of the participants for stability and certainty inevitably taint this goal with unexamined presuppositions.[74] Its reactionary nature often takes it beyond the grounds of Scripture as it pursues a haven from the relativism of the postmodern-self. Like the postmodern-self, it is vulnerable to external forces; authoritarian-fundamentalism does not hesitate to use technique for its own ends.[75] Once a participant uncovers unquestioned presuppositions and the too-often abused power of charismatic leaders, it is not uncommon for them to be drawn to the liberation promised by the postmodern-self.

THE RELATIONSHIP BETWEEN THE POSTMODERN-SELF AND AUTHORITARIAN-FUNDAMENTALISM

According to Slavoj Žižek, "today's ideological constellation is determined by the opposition between neoconservative fundamentalist populism and liberal multiculturalism—both parasitizing each other, both precluding any alternative to the system as such."[76] Like other secular scholars, Žižek does not appear to distinguish between those with strong beliefs about Scripture and authoritarian-fundamentalism. Nonetheless, his observation that "neoconservative fundamentalist populism" and "liberal multiculturalism" (which he also calls "liberal hedonism") feed off one another is a valuable insight. The former corresponds roughly to authoritarian-fundamentalism and the latter to the postmodern-self. In Charles Well's reading of Žižek, "what bothers the liberal tolerant multiculturalist about the fundamentalist and what bothers the fundamentalist about the liberal tolerant multiculturalist is essentially the same thing: The Other is imagined to have access to a

73. Balmer, "American Fundamentalism," 52.

74. In chapter 4, I discuss in detail the particular challenges of pursuing *werktreue*.

75. See Almond et al., *Strong Religion*, 11.

76. Žižek, *Parallax View*, 349.

kind of (excessive, self-destructive) enjoyment which the subject longs for and envies on the one hand and hates and fears on the other."[77] Provided this is the case, it is not difficult to imagine how wrongful desire (in the context of the perspective of each group) produces shame, which only serves to reinforce fear and hatred.

Both the postmodern-self and authoritarian-fundamentalism have emerged from modernizing forces. In fact, these forces continue to operate unabated and warrant a discussion of their own (see below). Pluralism emerges with urbanization; people holding traditional beliefs and values that were unquestioned in the regions they came from are uprooted and thrust together. The result is that "no belief is protected from the claims of alternative beliefs; no conviction is left unchallenged by other equally held convictions."[78] Confronted with plurality, the postmodern-self concludes that objective truth does not exist, or at least it cannot be discerned. As Southgate writes, "postmodernists assert that there is—there can be—no one privileged position from which to view that world, or from which to draw any meaningful conclusions about it. A slight shift of position—a slight adjustment of the centre—and it would all look very different; and who is to deny that shift? Relativity rules."[79] And if relativity rules, truth itself is relative. The vertigo of uncertainty this produces gives way to "an often-desperate quest for certainty, and where there is a demand, someone will proffer a supply."[80]

Authoritarian-fundamentalism offers an apparent solution. Bauman argues,

> The allure of fundamentalism stems from its promise to eman- cipate the converted from the agonies of choice. Here one finds, finally, the indubitably *supreme* authority, an authority to end all other authorities. One knows where to look when life-decisions are to be made, in matters big and small, and one knows that looking there one does the right thing and so is spared the dread of risk-taking.[81]

Authoritarian-fundamentalism selects and upholds a certain, narrow perspective. It claims direct access to the truth. In a show of strength authoritarian fundamentalists exude certainty, direction, and purpose, and yet "[t]he brutality of their power plays and violence (when we see it) is not a

---

77. Wells, *Subject of Liberation*, 103.

78. Hunter, "Fundamentalism and Relativism," 25.

79. Southgate, *Postmodernism in History*, 11.

80. Berger, "Introduction," 6.

81. Bauman, *Postmodernity*, 184. Emphasis in original.

demonstration of strength but a compensation for their own weak defenses against the terror that they may be wrong."[82] They cannot escape the function of reason in postmodernity to "negate necessity, introduce doubt, and uncover subjectivity."[83]

Instead of being confident, assured of the truth it possesses, authoritarian-fundamentalism falls into the problem laid out by Dostoevsky's Grand Inquisitor:

> man seeks to worship only what is indisputable, so indisputable that all men will agree unanimously to worship it universally. For these pitiful creatures yearn to find not only that which I or someone else could worship, but something in which we all believed and before which all bowed down, and indeed necessarily *together*. It is this demand for a *universality* of worship that has been the chief torment of each and every man individually and of the whole of humankind from the beginning of time. For this universality of worship, men have put one another to the sword.[84]

The Inquisitor goes on to chastise Christ for not taking the opportunity to make everyone worship him, choosing instead to allow people the choice of whether or not to believe. The impulse for universal worship is not wrong; what is wrong is working out the fear and insecurity arising from being confronted with another view in outward violence and/or inward tyranny. Such a reaction is a rejection of the freedom that Christ insists upon.[85] Authoritarian-fundamentalism reaches for certitude in human authority, looking for the security found in uniform consensus. But Christian freedom is grounded in faith and hope in Christ, not a system or intermediary. It can trust in God and his revelation in Scripture while embracing diverse improvisations within a set of constraints, as I show in chapters 4–6.

The postmodern-self and authoritarian-fundamentalism are the mutually reinforcing children of modernity. Neither knows how to enact responsible freedom because they are too busy defining themselves in opposition to one another. When combined with a growing trend of geographical

82. Hunter, "Fundamentalism and Relativism," 34.

83. Hunter, "Fundamentalism and Relativism," 23.

84. Dostoevsky, *Karamazov Brothers*, 318. Emphasis in original.

85. *The Grand Inquisitor* is a composition by Ivan Karamazov contained within Dostoevsky's *The Karamazov Brothers*. As such, it is difficult to be certain that this view of freedom is Dostoevsky's or only a view that he puts in the mouth of Ivan. Although I disagree with Ivan's conclusions, I agree with him insofar as this view of the freedom Christ gives to humanity.

segregation based on social-political beliefs, both camps become increasingly radicalized and it becomes more difficult to voice a moderate opinion.[86]

JAZZ PEDAGOGY, TECHNIQUE, AND ALIENATION

In its formative years, jazz developed on the street. Paul Berliner describes an environment marked by numerous venues open for jam sessions and a thriving community of musicians and listeners.[87] Musicians learned organically from one another in community. With the decline of widespread support for jazz, jazz pedagogy moved off the street and into the classroom. The shift from a casual to an institutional setting necessitated a corresponding shift in approaches to teaching. In this setting, jazz ended up being taught and evaluated in a way analogous to other subjects. Naturally, postsecondary jazz educators tend to gravitate towards teaching jazz in a way "that is Explainable, Analyzable, Categorizeable, [sic] [and] Doable."[88] Many jazz band directors focus on aspects that can be easily quantified, such as "centered and stable intonation, correct note reading, [and] section balance" while overlooking the riskier area of improvisation.[89] When improvisation is taught, Ake laments, teachers emphasize approaches to playing such as the "chord-scale system" that reduce "'clams' (notes heard as mistakes) and building 'chops' (virtuosity)" but downplay aspects of improvisation such as "musical interplay" between musicians, developing a unique sound, and idiomatic "rhythmic conceptions."[90] Ake goes on to show how institutional pressures to develop a way to measure and evaluate student progress ultimately place individual practice above developing in a group context.[91] In the process of being institutionalized, jazz pedagogy also became a commodity, something to be bought and sold. In order to put a price on pedagogy, it must be measured, and the easiest thing to measure is virtuosity. Virtuosity is developed by technique. Technique is a potent force at work within modernity that results in alienation, overshadowing all paths in the postmodern West.

Neither the postmodern-self nor authoritarian-fundamentalism are immune from the force of technique. In spite of the freedom from authority that the postmodern-self pursues, it cannot help being caught up in the

86. See Bishop and Cushing, *Big Sort*, especially 39.
87. See Berliner, *Thinking in Jazz*, 36–59.
88. Levine, *Jazz Theory*, vii.
89. Ake, *Jazz Cultures*, 114.
90. Ake, *Jazz Cultures*, 123.
91. Ake, *Jazz Cultures*, 142–44.

depersonalizing forces of modernity's fixation with production and efficiency. Nor does embracing authoritarian-fundamentalism offer a means of escape (aside from radical isolationism). Technique, as it is described by Ellul, is a powerful but impersonal force also at work in contemporary society. It fits snuggly into the capitalist drive to maximize profits. While the twentieth century may have demonstrated that communism is impractical economically, Karl Marx's analysis of the alienation endemic to capitalism still rings true for those who find themselves at its mercy. Technique breaks down and replaces traditional sources of authority. In fact, it works in tandem with the postmodern-self to break them down.

According to Ellul, technique is even more powerful than the greed and competition that drive a capitalist economy. The object of technique is to discover "'the one best way' to achieve any designated objective."[92] In fact, "[t]echnique refers to any complex of standardized means for attaining" this objective, with the result that "it converts spontaneous and unreflective behavior into behavior that is deliberate and rationalized."[93] Traditional behavior does not escape from the ravages of technique because "[t]echnique no longer rests on tradition, but rather on technical procedures; and its evolution is too rapid, too upsetting, to integrate the older traditions."[94] Ellul portrays technique as an irresistible force; once "a desired result is stipu-

92. Merton, "Foreword," vi.

93. Merton, "Foreword," vi. Ellul's own definition is a little more cumbersome: "*technique* is the *totality of methods rationally arrived at and having absolute efficiency* (for a given stage of development) in *every* field of human activity." Ellul, *Technological Society*, xxv. Emphasis in original. *The Technological Society* remains controversial. Critics contemporary with Ellul charged him with pessimism (e.g., Ferkiss, *Technological Man*, 87), but his defenders argued that the critics had misunderstood Ellul (e.g., Menninger, "Politics or Technique?," 110–12). More recently, Evgeny Morozov parodies Ellul's views: "technology, acting in its usually sly and autonomous fashion, can only compromise morality," and then dismisses them: "Such grand rhetoric, for all the quasi-religious fervor it used to generate, is long past its expiration date. It's time to give up this talk of 'Technology' with a big *T* and instead figure out how different technologies can boost or compromise the human condition." Morozov, *To Save Everything*, 323. His reading misses Ellul's point (as David Menninger points out) that Ellul was not just concerned with technology, but with technique. The issue is not technology, but the consequences of relentlessly pursuing the most efficient way of achieving a given end. A recent edited volume, Jerónimo, Garcia, and Mitcham, *Jacques Ellul and the Technological Society*, provides a deeper engagement and critique of Ellul's thought. George Ritzer, for instance, suggests his own theory of McDonaldization as a refined successor to Ellul's concept of technique "as a general theory." Ritzer "Technological Society," 35. Although Ellul's concept of technique may require refinement, "so as to incorporate the idea that some techniques are less of a problem than others" (Jerónimo, Garcia, and Mitcham, "Introduction," 7), it will suffice for my purposes as a way to describe an alienating force (or forces) working in opposition to Christian freedom.

94. Ellul, *Technological Society*, 14.

lated, there is no choice possible between technical means and nontechnical means based on imagination, individual qualities, or tradition. Nothing can compete with the technical means."[95] Whenever and wherever a competition emerges, those who employ technique will emerge victorious. For Ellul, technique is a universal force, forcing its way into every aspect of life.

A confluence of several factors was necessary for technique to gain ascendency in the West, but now technique is strong enough to create for itself the environment in which it thrives. It forces "social plasticity and a clear technical consciousness" everywhere it goes.[96] For instance, the formerly inextricably related matters of social and economic life are ripped apart by industrial plants. The strong guilds of the Middle Ages, that once provided a community for the individual from birth to death, have been completely dismantled. Technique "dissociates the sociological forms, destroys the moral framework, desacralizes men and things, explodes social and religious taboos, and reduces the body social to a collection of individuals."[97] The overlap between the objects of the postmodern-self and the effects of technique are remarkable. Technique reduces traditional authority to rubble and offers numerous comforts and distractions. And yet the self is stripped of all mystery and sacredness. All that remains is an object to be manipulated by Lewis's conditioners. These are the very factors that lead to protest in the form of authoritarian-fundamentalism. Yet authoritarian-fundamentalism happily (though selectively) employs technique for its own ends. Time will tell whether the use of technique will ultimately undermine fundamentalist ideals.

A capitalist economy is a way of perfecting technique; it is a way of discovering the one best way to accomplish a singular goal: maximizing profits. In theory, competition is supposed to benefit the consumer, resulting in the best products and services. But the goal of capitalism is not producing the best of anything; it is to produce a profit. This solitary goal weeds out the weak or swallows them up into corporate conglomerates. Even the most beautiful works—even the most useful products—will not survive in a market economy unless they can be reduced in some way to profit.

Marx connects the alienation of human beings to capitalism. Workers are dehumanized by being reduced to a means by which to produce capital: "[t]he worker has become a commodity, and it is a bit of luck for him if he can find a buyer."[98] The capitalist is alienated from workers because the

95. Ellul, *Technological Society*, 84.
96. Ellul, *Technological Society*, 126.
97. Ellul, *Technological Society*, 126.
98. Marx, *Economic and Philosophic*, 65.

workers are reduced to the labor they provide; their interests are opposed to one another. The capitalist seeks to maximize capital at the expense of the worker while the worker seeks to maximize wages. If work is scarce, workers must compete for it amongst themselves and are therefore alienated from one another. Furthermore, "[t]he more they wish to earn, the more must they sacrifice their time and carry out slave labor, completely losing all their freedom in the service of greed."[99] Workers are alienated from themselves as they sacrifice themselves on the altar of material gain.[100]

The effects of capitalization do not end even here; people begin to "relate to each other not directly, but through *commodities*. This means that relationships between human beings come to look like relationships between objects."[101] The example Dan Swain provides is the commodification of sexuality.[102] Pornography and escort services take "an undeniable aspect of our humanity, our sexuality," and sell it for a profit.[103] Sexualized imagery—primarily involving women—is in turn used to sell various products, encouraging men to view women's bodies as objects for consumption. Sex, even when it is not explicitly being commodified, "becomes understood through the form of value and commodities."[104] This notion dovetails neatly into the contractual nature of the relationships experienced by the postmodern-self. Just as the value of commodities is socially negotiated, so the value of other human beings can be negotiated based on performance in a desired area.

Marx's theory of alienation helps to explain the notion of the autonomous self. When the self is alienated from others by competition and intrinsically opposed interests its only recourse is to become autonomous. If traditional sources of authority are identified with (legitimately or otherwise) capitalists who exploit the labor of their workers, rejection of this authority is given an emotional ground. Marx uncovers the loss of freedom that those in a capitalist economy experience in their ability to relate to one another and their enslavement to this economy. Reducing human interaction to the level of exchanging commodities is a debilitating constraint.

99. Marx, *Economic and Philosophic*, 67.

100. William T. Cavanaugh, drawing upon Max Weber's *The Protestant Ethic and the Spirit of Capitalism*, argues that, prior to the advent of consumerism, "[p]eople had to be taught to think of themselves primarily as consumers of goods, and to see consumption as an end to work for, rather than a means to support the life to which they were accustomed." Cavanaugh, "'What Do I Want?,'" 27.

101. Swain, *Alienation*, 47. Emphasis in original.

102. Cf. Traina, "Commodifying Sex."

103. Swain, *Alienation*, 52.

104. Swain, *Alienation*, 53.

If enacting Christian freedom did not have enough difficulty in avoiding the polarizing dialectic between the postmodern-self and authoritarian-
fundamentalism, the shadow cast by the ubiquitous force of technique with
its accompanying alienation make the journey thoroughly harrowing. The
very structures of many Western churches are already arranged in terms of
commodities and technique.[105] The power these forces offer is tempting, but
the price they come at may prove too high.

CONCLUSION

The postmodern problem of freedom has two aspects. The first is determining what set of constraints to adopt and how much play can be negotiated within them. In other words, what are the appropriate sources for
constructive improvisation? The second is finding a way to escape, or at
least to re-negotiate, the ubiquitous constraint of technique. In other words,
how does one re-sacralise collective improvisation? The postmodern-self,
arising under the relativising influence of pluralism, finds in itself a lack
of constructive constraints. It is at the mercies of its desires—to get what it
wants and to appear amiable to others. It trades the constraints of tradition
and overt authority for more subtle—though no less powerful—forces. Authoritarian-fundamentalism multiplies constraints to create an illusion of
certainty and security. It narrows the tolerance level for any deviation from
the determinations of those holding power. Both must come to terms with
alienation: the apparent autonomy of the postmodern-self is threatened by
alienation and alienation often proves more powerful than authoritarian-
fundamentalism in spite of its best efforts. Both are also easily enslaved by
technique because both find it to be such an invaluable tool.

An alternative to the dilemma posed by the first aspect of the postmodern problem of freedom is difficult to articulate. As a Christian, I am
convinced that it is possible to ground a viable expression of freedom in
the Church as the body of Christ that charts a course between the pit and
the mire. Escaping the second aspect of this problem entirely may not be
possible, but if the Western church reconsiders its structure and methods, it
may be possible to mitigate the corrosive effect of technique. In this chapter,
I borrowed from jazz to illustrate the postmodern problem of freedom; in
later chapters, I show how it can be also used as a resource in the search
for a solution. However, I am hardly the first to identify this problem; the
next chapter looks at Christian freedom as it is articulated by contemporary
theologians and biblical scholars.

105. See Maddox, "'In the Goofy Parking Lot.'"

2

Theology on Christian Freedom

CHRISTIAN FREEDOM IS A perennial topic of interest among theologians.[1] It is closely tied to soteriology and sanctification, themes that lie at the heart of the Christian faith. Jesus died to free human beings from enslavement to sin and the powers of evil. Christians are to work out their salvation with fear and trembling (Phil 2:12) and in freedom (Gal 5:1). This chapter surveys and analyzes works of biblical scholars and theologians across the theological spectrum that engage directly with Christian freedom or the topic of freedom from a Christian perspective. Since the goal of my project is to articulate a conception of Christian freedom that engages with the problem of freedom in the contemporary West, I engage primarily with recent efforts along similar lines. I bring these works into dialogue with one another along the following topics: 1) where to start the discussion, 2) how to define freedom, 3) how to use Scripture, 4) how freedom functions with respect to ecclesiology, and 5) how Christian freedom relates to contemporary circumstances. Instead of attempting to give each author equal space in each section, I opt instead to focus on the works that best represent a certain

---

1. See the introduction for a discussion of the scope of the phrase "Christian freedom." Even though my focus is not on debating the subject of human free will in relation to Providence, the issue of one's understanding of divine Providence colors one's perception of God, and, as Michael St. A. Miller argues, affects one's understanding of Christian freedom. In other words, Christian freedom necessarily involves examining certain aspects of God's interaction with humanity. See Miller, *Freedom in Resistance*, esp. 163–98. Since a full treatment of this issue is not within the scope of my project, I go no further than interacting with the scholars below on how understandings of God affect understandings of Christian freedom.

perspective on a given topic. After assessing and evaluating the content of these works, I situate my own project in relation to them.

COMPARING DIFFERENT STARTING POINTS

The first question is where to locate one's notion of freedom. Two key perspectives emerge from the literature that I examine here. The first argues that freedom is a concept that can exist outside and apart from theological concerns. This perspective contends that freedom is something innately human. Theology can contribute something to it, or it can become a source of oppression that stifles it. In direct opposition to the first, the second insists that "true" or "real" freedom exists only in relation to God. Attempts at finding freedom apart from him are ultimately futile.

A Meeting between Christianity and Secular Freedom

Delwin Brown exemplifies the first perspective by making it his objective to determine "whether a Christian analysis can provide a basis for, and can strengthen, a secular understanding of freedom and the pursuit of that freedom's realization."[2] He argues that defining freedom in terms of "whatever it is that Christianity is thought to provide, e.g., eternal salvation or bondage to Christ, is to betray from the start that freedom which concerns human beings as such."[3] For Brown, in the dialogue between Christianity and secular freedom, the latter sets the terms of the conversation. His objective is not to explicate a Christian theology of freedom, but rather to provide "a theology *for* freedom."[4] According to Brown, freedom can be viewed entirely apart from "theistic or religious sympathies," making it possible to "confront the problem of relating faith and freedom in its most extreme form."[5] In effect, he attempts to pull the notion of freedom away from any associations with faith before bringing them back together. Freedom is a universal human concern that Christianity can speak to as one among many other perspectives.

Michael St. A. Miller's judgments on Scripture and certain theological conceptions of God using external criteria suggest that he shares Brown's perspective. For example, he insists that "[w]e need to question the

2. Brown, *To Set at Liberty*, xv.
3. Brown, *To Set at Liberty*, xv.
4. Brown, *To Set at Liberty*, xv. My emphasis.
5. Brown, *To Set at Liberty*, 21.

explicit theological considerations. With John Stuart Mill one can seek out "the nature and limits of the power which can be legitimately exercised by society over the individual"[22] and then turn to Isaiah Berlin's negative and positive concepts of freedom (as Miller does)[23] in which one experiences freedom from coercion and freedom to be one's own master respectively.[24] Afterwards, one may fall into Jean-Paul Sartre's existential burden of total freedom where nothing is determined.[25] Bauckham argues that "the meaning of freedom is unstable, because it necessarily varies with the context of world-interpreting or life-directing meaning to which, in any instance, it belongs."[26] His solution is to restore freedom "to a context of other values and beliefs."[27] Finally, Miller seeks to "explicate a kind of freedom that is finite, realistically libertarian, and relational."[28] I evaluate the strengths and weaknesses of each definition of freedom in relation to Christianity according to three criteria: first, the usefulness of the definition; second, its comprehensiveness; and third, the plausibility of the methodology on which it rests.

The Emergent Definition—Jacques Ellul

Ellul's definition of freedom is complex and takes time to explicate adequately.[29] Yet the scope of his project and the uniqueness of his insights justify the time and space necessary to tease it out. In particular, his discussion of the relationship between freedom and transgression sets his work apart from the work of many other theologians.

Freedom, 9–290.

22. Mill, *On Liberty*, 7.

23. See below.

24. See Berlin, *Four Essays*, 118–72.

25. See Brown, *To Set at Liberty*, 21–36, for his discussion of Sartre and freedom.

26. Bauckham, *God and the Crisis*, 2.

27. Bauckham, *God and the Crisis*, 3.

28. Miller, *Freedom in Resistance*, 1.

29. Ellul's primary work on the topic, *The Ethics of Freedom*, is in a rather raw state that leaves something to be desired. In his preface to the book, G. W. Bromiley unravels the history of the manuscript and Ellul's intentions. *The Ethics of Freedom* was to be the second of a four-volume study on ethics. The first book, functioning as a prolegomena to what was to follow, remained incomplete at the time of the English publication but is referred to in *The Ethics of Freedom*. Furthermore, *The Ethics of Freedom* was not first published as a unified whole: a portion of the book was published in French prior to the entire book being released in English, which was itself prior to a French book covering the latter chapters. See Bromiley, "Editor's Preface," 5.

In his opening remarks, Ellul mentions "a philosophical concept of freedom" that "will emerge as the work proceeds.[30] He then suggest that his readers begin with "the classical distinction between freedom defined as freedom of choice, which rests on a static conception, on the existence of a clearly established nature, or good and evil, in which freedom is to choose (the good), and freedom viewed as the coming of something new into the world with a creative and inexhaustible good."[31] In other words, Ellul's conception of freedom is not neutral; it presupposes a good to be chosen and an evil that entails bondage. This is a fine place to start, but it does not do justice to the freedom that Ellul takes such pains to explicate over the course of *The Ethics of Freedom*. A fuller understanding of Ellul's conception of freedom is achieved by pulling together his comments on freedom scattered throughout the book and integrating them into a coherent whole.

Ellul sets his understanding of freedom against the notion of freedom as the unconstrained ability to choose between a number of objects or orientations. This appearance of choice, especially for a consumer in a technological age, has already been conditioned by other factors. In fact, Ellul argues that an increase in means (which entails an increase in options) negates freedom because proliferation of means entails mediating relationships, stripping them of their immediacy. Power is gained at the expense of love and freedom.[32] A well-meaning check given to a charity or the workings of a committee defer the need for a person to directly interact with those they are affecting. Underlying this observation is Ellul's frank observation that servitude to self is not freedom, rejecting the equation of personal independence with freedom.

Slavery, which Ellul equates with the Marxist notion of alienation in his own era, is the antithesis to Ellul's conception of freedom. For Ellul, humanity "is the slave of sin and ultimately of nothing else"; this slavery is the determinative aspect of the human condition to which Christ is the sole

---

30. Ellul, *Ethics of Freedom*, 11.

31. Ellul, *Ethics of Freedom*, 11.

32. Ellul most often portrays power negatively throughout his work. He writes about power in terms of coercion or as a use of "[m]eans such as money, technology, and politics" that negates "the immediacy of love" by taking away the need "to act as a free man in relation to another free man." Ellul, *Ethics of Freedom*, 268. When he writes about the power of God, he takes pains to point out that God does not exercise this power coercively, but rather through the lordship of Jesus Christ, which "is exercised only through the mediation of man" (85). In my view Ellul does not present an understanding of power nuanced enough to account for its positive aspects. Furthermore, his comments on the negative aspects of the use of means, while insightful, are overstated. A more detailed consideration of Ellul's view of power is beyond the scope of this work. Finally, note that Ellul uses "man" as a term that includes all of humanity.

exception.[33] Independence, by itself, can never lead to freedom because it leads straight into the trap of slavery to oneself. Moreover, the desires of the self are shaped by spiritual, sociological, and biological forces, compromising the very notion of human independence. Linked to a desire for independence (not necessarily wrong in and of itself) is a desire for power and even conquest. Power is incompatible with freedom; those who employ it to gain control over others themselves become enslaved by it because "[p]ower is under the necessity of becoming absolute and totalitarian."[34] The dominion of sin in humanity infallibly undermines and destroys all unaided human effort to escape from it.

For Ellul, Christian freedom is not a possession, a state of being, a quality, or a virtue. Rather, it is something that "may at each moment become an event."[35] It must be practiced in order to exist. Though liberated by Christ, a Christian may lay aside their ability to act freely. They can refuse to exploit or utilize Christ's victory in acts that are free in relation to the powers and authorities of the world. In doing so, Christians return power to them. These powers and authorities were broken through the death and resurrection of Christ insofar as their future destruction is sure and that followers of Christ are now enabled to act freely in relation to them. But the work of Christ does not immediately alter what is ontologically the case on earth. It remains the responsibility of Christians to enact their freedom based on that work, mediating it to the rest of the world.

Although it is a notion that does not directly appear until late in *The Ethics of Freedom*, Ellul's association of freedom and transgression is central to the work. He boldly proclaims, "There is never freedom without transgression."[36] Freedom inherently involves transgressing limits. This means that limits are a corollary of freedom.[37] Transgression is not inherently good any more than submission is inherently evil; transgression in disobedience to God is "evidence of a greater bondage, namely, to evil, sin, and fatality"[38] while following the example of Jesus in transgressing powers such as social order and religious law are expressions of Christian freedom.

---

33. Ellul, *Ethics of Freedom*, 47–48.

34. Ellul, *Ethics of Freedom*, 38. See n32.

35. Ellul, *Ethics of Freedom*, 73.

36. Ellul, *Ethics of Freedom*, 344.

37. Even in an ideal situation where all oppressive and sinful constraints have been nullified, the self remains as a limit that can be transgressed through interaction with God and his creation. As long as one's self exists, the possibility exists for self-transgression.

38. Ellul, *Ethics of Freedom*, 348.

Transgression naturally involves risk. Pushing beyond a limit entails leaving behind "what is possible, immediate, and reasonable,"[39] although Ellul cautions that the risks and hazards one takes "must be oriented to love and the glory of God."[40] In other words, in order to risk transgression, one must have an objective consonant with serving and loving God and others. At the same time, Ellul holds that transgression cannot be calculated or turned into a principle. Instead, it should always be a present possibility that resists putting down roots that might prevent it from occurring. The daring required in an act of Christian freedom stands in stark contrast to the human tendency to desire comfort, happiness, stability, and the security of conforming to social norms.

In summary, Ellul's conception of freedom is antithetical to slavery, power, and sin. It is not something that is possessed, but rather is a possibility for Christians liberated by Christ from the powers of this world. When acts of freedom do occur, they take the form of unscripted transgressions that risk the unknown. They are enacted out of love for God and for others. For Ellul, freedom is the Christian transgression of limits enacted out of love of God and others and enabled by the liberating work of Christ.

Historical/Philosophical Definitions—Delwin Brown and James D. G. Dunn

Although Delwin Brown and James Dunn arrive at different definitions of freedom, they share a common approach to defining freedom.[41] They both adopt a history-of-ideas approach that entails looking back to the emergence of the concept of freedom and augmenting this with the insights of selected philosophers. Brown's *To Set at Liberty* antedates Dunn's *Christian Liberty*, but I begin with the latter because Dunn is more direct, and frankly, more lucid—examining how he arrives at his definition will aid in understanding Brown's approach.

Dunn begins with the ancient Greeks. Their notion of freedom is formed in opposition to slavery. Manumitted slaves were given the freedom to make independent decisions while being protected by the rights of citizenship. Freedom as the antithesis of slavery was applied metaphorically to political freedom and inner freedom. The former entailed being free from tyranny and the latter entailed being free from vices and passions. According

39. Ellul, *Ethics of Freedom*, 92.

40. Ellul, *Ethics of Freedom*, 356.

41. For a book-length treatment of the historical approach to defining freedom, see Patterson, *Freedom*.

to Dunn, "the emergence of the idea of *individual* liberty as a conscious *political* ideal" is a relatively recent development of the past two hundred years.[42] With John Stuart Mill, he contemplates the difficult relationship between liberty and authority. He concludes that *"the experience of liberation* [is] *the critical moment of liberty."*[43] Freedom *from* is only meaningful in relation to authority. In considering what freedom *to* means, Dunn turns once again to the Greeks and the Cynic and Stoic ideals of self-sufficiency and self-knowledge. However, these ideals do not hold up when he introduces the possibility of self-deception and the role of external forces. Turning to the individual and society, Dunn critiques Mill's myopic focus on individualism, arguing that "he does not seem to take sufficiently seriously that exercise of individual liberty can impinge on and restrict freedom of others in a whole complex variety of ways and degrees; no man is an island."[44] He goes on to suggest that "in the modern world the real test of liberty is not so much the liberty of the individual but the liberty of minority societies."[45] Having completed his survey, Dunn identifies three themes: 1) the relationship between freedom and authority, 2) freedom and self, and 3) freedom and community. These themes form the basis for his discussion of freedom in the New Testament. Dunn does not provide a comprehensive definition of Christian freedom. What he does provide is a concise treatment of the emergence of the notion of freedom and its historical development.

Brown's historical survey is not as concise, so I present a selected account of it.[46] Like Dunn, he notes that for the Greeks the concept of freedom emerged as the opposite of slavery. When political and social structures were discovered to be unstable, Stoic philosophers responded by grounding "the self in a more durable structure, namely, in the Reason or Logos that constitutes the orderly foundation of the cosmos."[47] These philosophers wrote about freedom not only from slavery, but also from institutions, norms, and even the body. The mind was constrained by the cosmic law, but since "individual reason is essentially at one with the cosmic Reason, bondage to Reason is also bondage to oneself."[48] Brown then turns to the Hebraic contribution to freedom, which he views as a notion of the freedom of God

42. Dunn, *Christian Liberty*, 10. Emphasis in original.

43. Dunn, *Christian Liberty*, 15. Emphasis in original.

44. Dunn, *Christian Liberty*, 22.

45. Dunn, *Christian Liberty*, 23.

46. For instance, he begins with "intimations of freedom" in Sumerian, Egyptian, and Minoan civilizations before coming to the Greeks and includes many references not directly related to the topic of freedom.

47. Brown, *To Set at Liberty*, 7.

48. Brown, *To Set at Liberty*, 7.

that is transferred to humanity by virtue of the "Hebraic claim that human nature mirrors or images divine nature."[49] The impersonal Greek cosmic law is replaced by a God on whom human beings can prevail. Brown holds up Job as an example of "*moral* rebellion against God" and goes so far as to call him a "Jewish heretic."[50] The corollary to Job's act of rebellion is a sense of self that is aware of the capacity of deciding. Instead of taking on the topic of freedom directly, as Dunn does, Brown seems more concerned with how various eras and philosophers understand selfhood. Undoubtedly, this is related to freedom, but at a certain point this concern begins to eclipse his main topic.

I resume where Brown once again directly engages with the topic of freedom. Staying clear of Mill and Berlin, Brown engages with Jean-Paul Sartre. Of Sartre's *Being and Nothingness*, Brown comments, "no one else has given so bold a picture of human freedom as creativity, the source of all meaning and value."[51] However, Sartre's notion of consciousness as "being-for-itself," as pristine freedom, was altered by his encounter with Marxism.[52] After this encounter, Sartre still maintains that one constructs one's self, but concedes that freedom emerges from "need" instead of *ex nihilo*. Acknowledging this allows Sartre to commit "to the construction of a philosophy of human freedom that recognizes both external conditioning and the individual's creative self-making."[53] Yet, according to Brown, Sartre cannot account for how a passive material world creates needs. True to his process roots, Brown turns to Alfred N. Whitehead to insist that nature is not in fact passive and that it cannot be reduced to mere materialism. Once this is accepted, Sartre's quandary is solved. Freedom, then, is both "inextricably dependent on and embedded in its material environment" and rooted in "the freedom and creativity of the self."[54] Creativity and context, then, are the two poles that govern freedom.

The Contextualized Definition—Richard Bauckham

Like Ellul's *The Ethics of Freedom*, the definition of freedom in Bauckham's *God and the Crisis of Freedom* is not all found in one place and must be

49. Brown, *To Set at Liberty*, 9.

50. Brown, *To Set at Liberty*, 10. Emphasis in original.

51. Brown, *To Set at Liberty*, 24.

52. For Sartre's discussion of being-in-itself, see Sartre, *Being and Nothingness*, 119–300.

53. Brown, *To Set at Liberty*, 26.

54. Brown, *To Set at Liberty*, 29.

pieced together.[55] Bauckham begins his work by first considering freedom as a contemporary value before moving on to a conception of Christian freedom. The benefit of his approach is that it addresses the freight that the word "freedom" carries in contemporary context. Much of his discussion is guided by contemporary concerns.

While acknowledging that "much of the traditional language of Christian formation—self denial, humility, self-control, submission to God—is easily associated with repressive authoritarianism,"[56] Bauckham nonetheless makes the claim that authority is a necessary aspect of Christian freedom. The collection of essays that form his book, *God and the Crisis of Freedom*, examines the topic of freedom in Scripture, wrestles with the authority of Scripture, the authority of tradition, establishes a Christian conception of freedom, and contrasts this conception with freedom as it is experienced in the postmodern West.

For Bauckham, a Christian understanding of freedom is comprised of seeming contradictions: it is given and appropriated; it entails independence and belonging; it has limits and allows for transcendence; and it includes freedom of choice—and a need to choose well.[57] Human existence is by nature finite and dependent; it is a gift of God. No one constructs or determines their own identity independently of this gift. Freedom is also a gift. External environments and relationships enable or stifle one's ability to make free choices. At the same time, "freedom cannot be passively received; it must be actively appropriated in the actual exercise of freedom."[58] Bauckham illustrates this through the achievement of becoming an outstanding musician. The musician must strive to achieve this state, but the achievement still depends on a musical tradition and talent along with the opportunity to develop it.

In his assessment of the western conception of freedom in the modern era, Bauckham acknowledges its positive aspects, such as "the affirmation of individual human dignity, the foundation of democracy in the equal right to freedom of all individuals, and the fundamental freedoms of individuals

55. The book is in fact a compilation of essays that he has brought together and rounded out with an introduction and an epilogue. That the result is still coherent is to Bauckham's credit. However, it still entails a certain degree of redundancy as he reintroduces the concept of freedom in several of his chapters.

56. Bauckham, *God and the Crisis*, 196.

57. See also the way Peter Richardson organizes his book, *Paul's Ethic of Freedom*. The first three chapters work out the rationale and the implications of Paul's revolutionary formula in Gal 3:28. The following chapters are arranged topically around the issues of firmness and flexibility, love and license, weakness and strength, and order and charisma. See below for a more in-depth discussion of Richardson's work.

58. Bauckham, *God and the Crisis*, 38.

over against the powers of state and church."[59] And yet, he argues that "the Enlightenment belief in the wholly self-sufficient and self-determining self has led to the asocial, amoral, and isolated individual of contemporary atomized society in the West."[60] This self pits the freedom of the autonomous individual against society, creates fear of commitment by internalizing the market economy, and ultimately sees the very idea of God solely in terms of limiting freedom.[61] This "wholly self-sufficient and self-determining self" is essentially the postmodern-self that I describe in chapter 1.

By contrast, in a Christian conception of freedom, freedom and belonging become reciprocal instead of contradictory when one distinguishes between belonging and being owned.[62] In unbalanced relationships, such as between a parent and a child, maturity can bring on new freedoms, but even in a changed state of affairs, mutual belonging can be reaffirmed. Liberation from all limits is a denial of human finitude, and it makes reciprocal relationships with others impossible. Instead, limits enable freedom when they are accepted in love instead of being abolished. Bauckham argues that others "do not restrict but enable my freedom when I receive my freedom from them and exercise my freedom as freedom for them."[63] Finally, freedom to

---

59. Bauckham, *God and the Crisis*, 197.

60. Bauckham, *God and the Crisis*, 197.

61. See Bauckham, *God and the Crisis*, 33–36. According to Walter Anderson,

> The modern self was—is—one of the noblest creations of the human mind. . . . It was a construction of thought that freed people from the tyrannies of popes and kings, expanded the horizons of life, opened the mind to the vast possibilities of science. It was a great evolutionary achievement, but evolution moves quickly these days, and *we begin to wonder now if the jailbreaking* [sic] *thoughts of past centuries did not create yet another prison for the human spirit.*

Anderson, *Future Self*, 31. My emphasis. Cf. chapter 1 for a brief history of the development of the modern/postmodern-self and its roots in Paul's assertion of the equality of Christians in Christ.

62. Bauckham's argument might appear to be contradicted by Paul's self-identification as a slave of Christ and his argument that Christians belong to God by virtue of having been purchased by him (1 Cor 6:19–20). In the chapter being discussed, Bauckham avoids these texts and appeals instead to Paul's comments in Rom 8:15, 21 to substantiate his contrast between belonging (child of God) versus being owned (slave of God). In another chapter he addresses the more difficult texts by arguing that "the analogy of servants' or slaves' obedience to their masters or subjects' obedience to their king is frequent but also transmuted by paradox: 'As servants of God, live as free people' (1 Pet. 2:16); 'the perfect law, the law of liberty' (Jas. 1:25)." Bauckham, *God and the Crisis*, 69.

63. Bauckham, *God and the Crisis*, 45.

choose is important, but not in an intrinsic sense. It is important because it enables one to choose good, thereby enabling one to become good.

The Co-opted Definition—Michael St. A. Miller

Michael Miller constructs a conception of freedom that rests on categories established by Robert Neville (a theologian), Orlando Patterson (a sociologist), and Isaiah Berlin (a political theorist). Neville divides freedom into cosmological and ontological dimensions. The cosmological dimension consists of the freedom of human beings that is naturally present in individuals and society. The ontological dimension is this natural freedom in relation to God as creator and to his creation, including people as his creatures. For Neville, human beings were created to be free. Patterson conceives of freedom in personal, sovereignal [sic], and civic realms, which are interrelated and yet distinct. Berlin sets forth the notion of positive and negative freedom. Positive freedom entails acting according to internal purposes instead of external forces; it is the wish to be one's own master. Negative freedom is being free from external coercion by another individual or group. Miller provides nuances and qualifications to these conceptions, but generally accepts and employs them as a framework for engaging with other perspectives on freedom. In order to secure his objectives, he believes he must begin with a "finite, realistically libertarian, and relational" view of freedom. In other words, Miller constructs his framework prior to engaging with Scripture. On the one hand, he is open and up-front about his presuppositions, but on the other, these presuppositions restrict his understanding of Christian freedom and bring to bear concerns (especially in the case of Berlin) that are alien to the biblical text.

Assessment

Given the differences in their starting points, a surprising number of correlations are found in the way these authors set forth their understanding of freedom. For example, Ellul and Dunn agree that "freedom from" comes into existence at the moment of the free act or liberation. Aside from Miller, who is suspicious of all external authority,[64] the other authors, especially Bauckham and Dunn, see authority as a necessary corollary of freedom. Yet even Miller's suspicion is affirmed to some degree by Ellul's comments

64. For instance, Miller writes, "I develop this project with a strong suspicion of rhetoric that promotes freedom through slavery to God and submission to church authority." Miller, *Freedom in Resistance*, 2.

on the way exercising power over others is necessarily oppressive. Miller's insistence that freedom be relational not only finds affinity with Brown's process thought[65] but also with Bauckham's identification of the "wholly self-sufficient and self-determining self" as the root of the contemporary crisis of freedom. Ellul and Brown identify creativity as an intrinsic part of freedom.[66] The philosophical distinction of "freedom from" and "freedom to" is employed by both Ellul and Dunn.

In terms of the method used to arrive at a definition, Ellul's approach is flexible, open, and provides the most daring and comprehensive understanding of Christian freedom. But he also requires the reader to synthesize the final definition for themselves, increasing his odds of being misunderstood. Its antithesis, Miller's bald assertion of what freedom must be, focuses his discussion and provides clear criteria for engaging with the question of freedom. None of his criteria necessarily conflict with a Christian understanding but his prior commitments rule out other possibilities. Such an approach, because it is ultimately self-referential, risks being self-marginalizing. Brown's and Dunn's historical approaches have precedents in the well-tried philosophical approach of examining the development of a certain concept over time.[67] Yet a practical discussion of Christian freedom ought to focus on tracing the development of this notion using biblical and theological sources rather than relying heavily on the development of the philosophical idea of freedom. The two are certainly not mutually exclusive at every level—for instance, Paul's use of freedom vocabulary in the New Testament rests on the development of the concept in Greek—but beginning with Christian presuppositions about what liberation entails is, as Brown points out, incompatible with secular formulations of freedom. Bauckham opens with an assessment of contemporary issues surrounding freedom, focusing on the need to delineate the relationship between authority and freedom. Beginning with contemporary concerns has the advantage of focusing the discussion and demonstrating the relevance of the topic. Using the tensions in freedom to organize his discussion broadens his conception of freedom.

---

65. Miller also acknowledges the influence of process thought on his theology. See Miller, *Freedom in Resistance*, 7.

66. I leave out Miller because, while he discusses creativity, it is not intrinsic to his definition in the same way as it is for Ellul (who includes it in his preliminary definition) and Brown (for whom it forms one of two poles necessary for freedom).

67. See, for example, Adler, *Idea of Freedom*.

ENGAGING WITH SCRIPTURE

Miller wryly observes that when Christians pursue freedom, they "cannot avoid exploring biblical sources directly to see what is being said about it."[68] Biblical scholars and theologians alike find in Scripture explicit, though more often implicit, instruction on freedom. They tend to treat the Old Testament as a whole and then divide the New Testament into the example of Jesus, the theology of Paul, and the rest of the New Testament. To the best of my knowledge, no one has yet devoted a monograph to constructing a biblical theology of freedom. However, Peter Richardson has written on Paul's theology of freedom, and Ernst Käsemann and Dunn have written on the New Testament and freedom. Bauckham and Miller each devote sections of their work to providing an overview of Christian freedom that extends across the entire canon.[69] Since For the sake of ease, I divide the discussion on Paul's writings into his conception of Christian freedom vis-à-vis slavery below and vis-à-vis ecclesiology in the following section.

The Old Testament

Discussing the Old Testament in relation to Christian freedom might initially appear anachronistic, but wrestling with freedom in the text reveals the larger trajectory of freedom in Scripture and helps to clarify the concept of freedom in the New Testament. Bauckham and Miller provide contrasting views of how to approach and interpret the Old Testament text.

Bauckham describes the tasks of the interpreter of Scripture as follows: to judge between what is central and what is peripheral; to differentiate between the provisional and the permanent; and to determine the trajectory of biblical narrative. He argues that the Bible does not provide a ready-made blueprint for freedom in contemporary society, but points instead to "the fundamental nature of God's will for human freedom."[70] So when Bauckham surveys Old Testament slavery he focuses on breakthroughs in principle instead of the inequalities that continued to exist under Mosaic Law. In other words, freedom ought to be understood in its relative context. In the ancient (and modern) world, some experienced freedom (in the sense of being a master instead of a slave) at the expense of others. When God

---

68. Miller, *Freedom in Resistance*, 99. Miller appears to have mixed feelings about what Scripture says on the subject of freedom.

69. I do not engage Miller and Bauckham in all sections though. My approach is to focus on the strongest or most distinct contributions to a given section.

70. Bauckham, *God and the Crisis*, 8.

delivered his people from Egypt, they became his slaves alone (Lev 25:42). The goal of the Old Testament is for all to come under the liberating lordship of God, which in principle liberates human beings in relation to one another. Subjecting one human being to another is ultimately "contrary to the fundamental will of God as the Old Testament reveals it."[71]

Miller comes to the text from a perspective shaped by the experience of the Caribbean peoples with slavery, along with the way the biblical text has been used historically to justify and reinforce that slavery. In approaching Scripture, he draws heavily from the work of Orlando Patterson, who shares Miller's concern for the people of the Caribbean.[72] Yet he identifies a lacuna in Patterson's work on Paul's conception of freedom and seeks to rectify it by examining the influence of the Old Testament on Paul's thought. Patterson claims that "[f]reedom, in fact, was never a central value among the ancient Israelites and Jews,"[73] but Miller finds a concrete (as opposed to abstract) notion of collective freedom rooted in the Exodus. He considers Bauckham's attempt at presenting the positive aspects of Israel's practice of slavery but ultimately concludes that the existence of any form of slavery in light of the Exodus and the unequal treatment of foreign slaves in comparison to Israelite slaves suggests "that Israel's preoccupation with freedom as a communal phenomenon did not allow sufficient attention to its significance for each individual on the basis of their humanity *per se.*"[74] Miller is unimpressed with scholarly attempts to justify the master-slave vocabulary used in the Old Testament of the relationship between Yahweh and his people. He claims that "in Hebrew Scriptures Yahweh is shown to be not unlike many worldly despots in that he secures the allegiance of his people both by tenderness and tyranny, and Israel is shown to be not unlike many other 'claimed' peoples as they relate to God with both deep attachment and great anxiety."[75] This communal sense of freedom that nonetheless tolerates slavery and extends the notion of slavery to Israel's relationship with God provides the other portion of the context that frames, according to Miller, "Paul's considerations on personal freedom."[76]

71. Bauckham, *God and the Crisis*, 13.

72. See Patterson, *Freedom*, 325–44.

73. Patterson, *Freedom*, 34.

74. Miller, *Freedom in Resistance*, 109.

75. Miller, *Freedom in Resistance*, 112.

76. Miller, *Freedom in Resistance*, 112.

Jesus

While Jesus, unlike Paul, does not make extensive use of freedom vocabulary in his recorded teachings, theologians and biblical scholars alike find in his actions expressions of freedom. For Käsemann and Dunn, these actions are marked by a liberal attitude towards authority. Like them, Ellul employs Jesus as an exemplar, but he goes beyond them to show how Jesus' exercise of freedom entails freedom for his followers.

In *Jesus Means Freedom*, Käsemann provocatively asserts that Jesus was a liberal. He goes on to say that "Jesus' liberal attitude" is "the authentic mark of right Christian doctrine" and practice since "what is true of him must also be true of his followers."[77] One of the first points he makes in his argument (and complains about having to do so) is that Jesus' liberal attitude is fully compatible with his devoutness as a Jew.[78] On certain matters, Jesus was more severe in his interpretation of the law than his opponents, but on others, according to Käsemann, he placed himself above Scripture. Jesus did the latter when the letter of the law and piety were set up in such a way that they conflicted with loving one's neighbor. Käsemann argues that God's will for one to love one's neighbor trumps the notion that a perceived command from God does not require justification. Rather, understanding and reason are superior to unthinking submission to the law. In support of this claim, he holds up Jesus' appeal to common-sense arguments and the clearness of his teaching in contrast to those who use casuistry or too readily appeal to mystery. Moreover, when Jesus exercised love and freedom by associating with the dregs of society, it was deeply offensive to those trying to live holy lives. According to Käsemann, they saw in this an "attack [on] God the Father himself."[79] Politically, Jesus was not a model citizen; his actions inspired revolutionaries. Käsemann uses this to indict the "German Christian people" for making Jesus "a bourgeois after their own image."[80] He goes on to elevate loving one's neighbor above any orthodoxy that does not take to task atrocities tolerated and even perpetrated by Christians. Writing under the shadow of Auschwitz makes his observations particularly poignant. In John, Jesus proclaims that "the truth will make you free" (John

77. Käsemann, *Jesus Means Freedom*, 19.

78. According to Käsemann, "But today it is unmistakably plain that there cannot be the slightest doubt of Jesus' devotion; and if the risk of omitting to say this means that one may be pilloried for teaching a blasphemous theology, it is better to make the point quite clear. I must, however, confess that what seems to be downright blasphemous is to have to endorse Jesus' devotion." Käsemann, *Jesus Means Freedom*, 18.

79. Käsemann, *Jesus Means Freedom*, 28.

80. Käsemann, *Jesus Means Freedom*, 29.

8:32) and later says "I am the way and the truth and the life" (John 14:6). Freedom means being continually bound to Jesus as his disciple. Freedom is not possible apart from him. For Käsemann, the Jews in John actually stand for orthodox piety. Throughout the book, he has defended liberal theology, but here he takes the offensive against conservatives for creating an idol out of dogma and thereby obscuring the central thing about the Christian faith: one's relationship with Jesus.

Although "freedom" and its cognates appear only twice in the gospels and it is not a topic that Jesus addresses directly, Dunn argues that the life Jesus lived in relation to the authorities makes him a model for the enactment of Christian freedom.[81] Dunn makes it clear that Jesus was not a violent revolutionary. In fact, Jesus often works willingly within the constraints of the authorities of the time—including secular and religious authorities and the Torah. At the same time, Jesus exercises "critical judgment" in relation to these authorities: he criticizes Herod, cleanses the temple, and employs fundamental principles from the Torah to deemphasize certain commandments (ex. Mark 7:14–23).[82] Finally, Jesus appeals to the foundational nature of God's relationship with humanity and the nature of human relationships to circumvent the societal norms of his time. According to Dunn, determining what fundamentals to employ and what norms to transgress "lies at the heart of [Jesus'] own experience and exercise of liberty."[83]

Instead of beginning with Jesus' freedom in relation to constraints, Ellul begins by discussing Jesus' choices. Unlike God the Father, in his life on earth Jesus was constrained by the finitude of being human. In other words, he faced the same choices that humans typically encounter in life. He even faced "subjection to the structure of a sinful world and subjection to sinful men."[84] This situation is played out in the temptations Jesus encounters in the wilderness. In the first temptation, Jesus demonstrates freedom in relation to bodily needs; in the second, it is in relation to power; and in the third, Jesus freely affirms complete dependence upon the Father. He even demonstrates freedom from "the necessities, the world, and Satan by refusing to accept the perspectives of Satan or to be caught by his dilemmas."[85] By refraining from using the power rightfully at his disposal, Jesus demonstrates freedom with respect to power. Instead of focusing on Jesus' freedom

81. Dunn notes the caveats of Jesus' uniqueness in both his person and situation, but notes that the New Testament witness, nonetheless, urges Christians to follow Jesus' example (1 Cor 11:1).

82. Dunn, *Christian Liberty*, 52.

83. Dunn, *Christian Liberty*, 52.

84. Ellul, *Ethics of Freedom*, 51–52.

85. Ellul, *Ethics of Freedom*, 61.

in relation to authority, Ellul focuses on the freedom Jesus exercises by obeying the will of God. Then Ellul steps beyond those considered above and refers to the liberating work of Christ. Christ liberates his people, who do not enter a state of freedom (which is not possible for Ellul), but rather experience "renewals, new interventions and commitments, each expressing both freedom and eschatological irruption."[86] Finally, the life of Christ demonstrates that Christian freedom is not freedom from the necessities and determinations of the world, but is rather a "freedom lived out within and by means of the determinations."[87]

Paul

Of all the authors in Scripture, Paul writes the most about freedom. Miller continues his critical approach to Scripture as he wrestles with the implications of Paul's slave metaphor. Peter Richardson provides a book-length treatment of *Paul's Ethic of Freedom*.[88] Bauckham offers a more generous reading and Dunn focuses in on slavery and the individual.

Miller: Paul Is Bound by Slave Imagery

Miller opens his comments on freedom and Scripture with the caveat that the Scriptures were written "in epochs generally characterized by acceptance of various forms of oppressive hierarchy."[89] He then engages with secondary sources to shed light on Greco-Roman influences on Paul's theology of freedom. Relying heavily on Patterson,[90] he situates Paul's conception of freedom and his soteriology in relation to the Roman law that regulated slavery and redemption. If a Roman citizen was captured by a hostile power, his rights as a citizen were lost. If someone paid a ransom to return him, his status as a citizen would not be fully restored until this ransom was paid off. Romans 5:10—"For if while we were enemies, we were reconciled to God through the death of his Son, much more surely, having been reconciled, will we be saved by his life"— makes sense when the reconciliation enacted by Christ's death is seen through the lens of a Roman being returned to the

---

86. Ellul, *Ethics of Freedom*, 73.

87. Ellul, *Ethics of Freedom*, 75.

88. See also Jones, *Paul's Message*, for a contextualized presentation of Paul's theology of freedom for the black church in America.

89. Miller, *Freedom in Resistance*, 100.

90. See Patterson, *Freedom*, 325–44.

Empire and the salvation enacted by Christ's life is viewed as the repayment of his ransom. Galatians 4:21–31, the allegory of Hagar and Sarah, becomes a way of undermining privilege according to descent: the natural son is a slave, while the son of promise is the one who inherits. The descendants of slaves would understand that they could be heirs to the promise of Israel; they have been freed and adopted.

Miller brings an Old Testament conception of freedom, including the idea that enslavement to God is freedom, to act as a corrective to Patterson's fixation on the primacy of Roman institutions on Paul's conception of slavery. He counters Patterson's suggestion that Christ's redemption ultimately culminates in the final identification of slave with master as Christians lose their identity in God by claiming that this is a denial of humanity and of human freedom. For Miller, human beings are, in fact, not designed for slave-like submission to God. Drawing from the Caribbean experience of slavery, Miller argues that encouraging slave-like submission to God or to others is detrimental to human flourishing. He proceeds to challenge the hierarchical language Paul uses in 1 Cor 11 by creating a proportional analogy between the enslavement of human beings to God as head with the enslavement of wives to their husbands as their head. Miller insists that master-slave vocabulary carries with it "the lingering effects of traditional attitudes" that often overwhelms the best of intentions.[91] He concludes that Paul's utilization of the vocabulary of submission, subordination, and slavery shaped Christian consciousness to the degree that when Christianity gained ascendency, it "could fashion forms of slavery, that in the West, were multiple times more savage than that which was present when Christianity first emerged."[92] In summary, Miller argues that conceptions of God that place human beings into a master-slave relationship with him and Paul's use of the language of slavery to describe relationships between human beings as well have born "strange fruit" in the course of Christian history.[93] At the same time, the message of freedom contained within Scripture remains compelling.

Peter Richardson: Paul Doesn't Go Quite Far Enough

Unlike the other authors in this section, Richardson works on elucidating Paul's theology of freedom before bringing contemporary concerns into play. While Käsemann leaps freely between Scripture and his defense of

91. Miller, *Freedom in Resistance*, 122.

92. Miller, *Freedom in Resistance*, 123.

93. "Strange Fruit" is a song written by Abel Meeropol and performed by jazz singer Billy Holiday. It refers to the lynching of African-Americans in America.

liberal theology and Dunn opens with comments on the development of extra-biblical conceptions of freedom, Richardson begins with the biblical text.

With respect to slavery and freedom, Richardson portrays a conservative Paul who is content to leave the institution of slavery unchallenged. The point is not the condition one is found in, but one's relation to Christ. The fact that Christian slaves and masters had one impartial Lord did not do away with institutional slavery; rather, Christian slaves were to do a better job of serving their masters. Richardson notes that slavery as an analogy for Christian service to Christ has proved more lasting than the Jew/Gentile distinction and may offer a partial explanation as to why the practice of slavery took so long to be abolished in the West. He sees Paul's conservatism as a glaring weakness in his theology of freedom, but also notes that "there was enough in Paul's letters to prod the church's conscience."[94]

Richardson sees a trajectory with respect to the relationship between the sexes through Paul's letters in which Paul begins with more radical ideas about the freedom women have to participate in the church and then, as he becomes more conservative, he places more restrictions on them. Richardson suggests that Paul was pressured on three sides to place limits on the role of women. First, Jewish custom placed restrictions on the role of women. Second, Paul did not want to associate with the version of emancipation for women provided by pagan mystery religions. Third, a radical party pushing for immediate emancipation may have compelled Paul to adopt a more gradual approach to emancipation in order to avoid confusion and error. Richardson's Paul walks a tightrope between promoting freedom for women to pray and prophesy and mutuality between men and women on the one hand, and affirming male priority on the other.

In his analysis of Paul's approach to freedom, Richardson focuses on the limitations that Paul's context placed on him. Like Miller, he is concerned with the slavery analogy for Christian service, though he is not as harsh. In terms of the emancipation of women, Paul ends up backing away into a more conservative position. He points in the right direction, but is unable to follow through with the implications of his theology of freedom.

Bauckham: Paul Extends the Scope of Freedom

In *God and the Crisis of Freedom*, Bauckham opts to weave various texts in the New Testament into a whole instead of treating various sections separately. Yet Paul in the main predominates on the discussion of freedom and

94. Richardson, *Paul's Ethic*, 55–56.

slavery that Bauckham traces from the Old Testament. Since Christ liberates the people of God in a new Exodus, Paul's declaration in Gal 3:28 amounts to the principle that "there can be no relationships of subjection among Christians."[95] While certain passages do not seem to do much to change the nature of relationships between masters and slaves, Paul's instructions to Philemon—to treat Onesimus "no longer as a slave, but better than a slave, as a dear brother" (Philem 1:16 NIV)—stands as a more consistent application of this principle. And the notion of mutual service runs contrary to first-century cultural norms in Eph 5:21–6:9. Bauckham observes that "the continuing outward order of freedom and subjection would be inwardly transformed by the new Christian principle of freedom in mutual service" and that "the way the master-slave relationship is here transcended is not by making everyone masters."[96] Voluntary service replaces involuntary subjection. Instead of criticizing Paul's use of the slave metaphor, Bauckham attempts to redeem it, arguing for its continued relevancy and ultimately liberating effect.

Dunn: Paul's Conception of Freedom in Relation to the Self

Dunn examines freedom in relation to self and others in Paul's writings. The latter belongs to the following section on ecclesiology. He begins the former with Paul's view of the powers that exert control over the self. Dunn does not seem comfortable with the notion of spiritual powers as such, arguing that, "The extent to which Paul actually believed in the real existence of such powers is a matter of debate. The very variety of his vocabulary suggests that he himself had no firm conceptuality of the powers of evil of which he speaks, and that his concern may have been largely *ad hominem*."[97] In addition to these powers, Paul shows how flesh (according to Dunn, Paul uses this term to refer to human mortality and weakness) and desire hand over the self to the personified powers of sin and death. Finally, the Law itself is hijacked by sin and turned into another means of enslavement. For Dunn, the Law marked Israel as "special to God" (Rom 2:17; cf. Eph 2:12). It functioned as a "guardian angel against sin and [a] talisman against death."[98] The link between Israel and the Law effectively tied ethnicity to righteousness. This in turn led to boasting and the presumption of Jewish privilege.

95. Bauckham, *God and the Crisis*, 14.
96. Bauckham, *God and the Crisis*, 14–15.
97. Dunn, *Christian Liberty*, 56.
98. Dunn, *Christian Liberty*, 61.

The Rest of the New Testament

Some of the authors in this chapter mention the concept of freedom in the remaining books of the New Testament, but few find anything substantially different from what can be found in Jesus' life and Paul's letters to add to their theology of freedom. Käsemann is an exception, but in a negative sense. He argues that the pastoral epistles tame Paul's message and emphasize order at the expense of freedom. For instance, James' mention of "the law of liberty" is dismissed as part of a "tendency to use pretty phrases instead of words expressing original and vigorous thought."[99] Loss of freedom is the price of hierarchy and stability. He similarly blames Luke for identifying the gospel with Christianity and thereby bringing the church into rigid subjection to tradition and creeds and under the control of the pious. For Käsemann, Luke's strategy bore fruit in the past, but a different approach is needed in the present.

The book of Revelation provides a vehicle for Käsemann to pursue a number of agendas, but most interestingly, he touches on political revolution and insurrection. The thinly-veiled hostile references to Rome combine revolutionary zeal with Christian freedom. On the one hand, he does not advocate making "revolution the gospel's means and aim,"[100] but on the other he argues that "[t]o keep clear of revolutionaries in order to help maintain the *status quo* is at least as discreditable as it is to rush into the arms of revolution."[101]

Assessment

The analogy of slavery for God's relationship with humanity and a liberal outlook are the two main themes that emerge from the way the above works engage with Scripture.[102] At one extreme is Miller, who does not hesitate to

99. Käsemann, *Jesus Means Freedom*, 86.

100. Käsemann, *Jesus Means Freedom*, 136.

101. Käsemann, *Jesus Means Freedom*, 137.

102. A third possibility goes back to the creation narrative in Genesis. J. Richard Middleton shows that God gives to human beings "the commission to extend God's royal administration of the world as authorized representatives on earth." Middleton, *Liberating Image*, 289. Ellul views Adam (representing humanity) as a vice-gerent who lost his position in order to dominate creation. Only those who willingly set aside their ownership by acknowledging the lordship of Christ can return to being stewards and mediators of God's power. See Ellul, *Ethics of Freedom*, 84–85. This view of divine-human relations is not fully fleshed out in the New Testament, though it is strongly implied in passages such as Rom 8:19–23.

call out the God of the Old Testament as a tyrant and to lambast Paul for creating a theology that led to a particularly vicious form of slavery once Christianity gained ascendency in the Roman Empire. In my opinion, Miller is dangerously close to Marcion; attempting to excise the bits in Scripture you disagree with is tantamount to a denial of the unity and cogency of Scripture and results in an arbitrary collage of scriptural phrases that spell out prior commitments. At the same time, Paul has been interpreted in ways that justify the terrible acts of oppression and abuse that concern Miller. A contemporary theology of freedom must repudiate such interpretations and provide safeguards against their renewal. Richardson is milder, but he still charges Paul with being overly conservative and thereby delaying the abolition of slavery in the West. Both Miller and Richardson fail to appreciate that the abolition of slavery in contemporary society has historical roots in evangelical Christianity.[103] It is not at all remarkable for a given religion or ideology to endorse slavery—many have. What is remarkable is that a religion, namely Christianity, contributed to the overthrow of an institution as powerful as slavery. On the other end of the spectrum, Bauckham endeavors to show how God's place as the master of all implies the equality of all. Ellul forthrightly addresses and condemns the use of power over others that provokes Miller's stinging critiques. Yet Ellul finds in Jesus an answer to the temptation of power, not in his inherent freedom as a human being, but rather in his submission to God *over and against the powers of the world*. Finally, Dunn is right to emphasize Paul's concern with liberating the Christian self from the powers of the world, notwithstanding his squeamishness over their spiritual nature.

Miller and Richardson have a sizeable portion of history on their side. The emergence of Christendom did not entail emancipation. Certain biblical texts and theological constructs used in tandem have been used historically to justify slavery and oppression.[104] Dostoevsky's Grand Inquisitor tacitly speaks on behalf of Christian rulers and slave owners. The freedom Christ gives is too much; its banishment makes humanity happy. Yet the point is that Christ offers freedom. Bauckham and Ellul are right to look for it and to argue that Scripture ought to be interpreted in a way that supports it. This is what Christian abolitionists did. Their efforts to wrest the biblical

---

103. According to John Wolffe, "the contribution of evangelicals—Wilberforce and the Clapham Sect above all—to the abolition of the British slave trade was a crucial one." Wolffe, *Expansion of Evangelicalism*, 199–200.

104. See, for example, Willard M. Swartley's overview of historical theological pro-slavery arguments in America. Swartley, *Slavery, Sabbath*, 31–36.

text from the grasp of oppressors and to demonstrate that it points rather to freedom are entirely consistent with this text's trajectory.[105]

FREEDOM AND ECCLESIOLOGY

This section interacts with both systematic theology and Pauline studies on freedom. Dunn and Richardson offer case studies in how Paul applied his conception of freedom to challenges that arose in the church. Miller ties a certain conception of God to the outworking of ecclesiology before taking on the more Pauline problem of working out the priesthood of all believers.

Dunn: The Strong and the Weak

Dunn employs Rom 14:1–15:16 as a case study in exploring freedom within community. His reconstruction of the historical context of this text pits those with Jewish identity or loyalty (in the case of proselytes) against Gentile believers in Rome. The return of Jewish Christians after being expelled from Rome brought to the fore the issue of distinguishing between clean and unclean food. For Jewish Christians and proselytes, keeping food laws was a way of being loyal to the covenant God of Israel. They are weak because they fail "to realize that the life of the Spirit need no longer necessarily be restricted within the limitations of traditional and distinctive Jewish customs."[106] Dunn goes further by labeling the weak as "conservative" and the strong as "liberal." The weak judge the practices of the strong because they assume that God does. But in fact, all conduct is judged by God "and acceptance by God is the measure of acceptable conduct—nothing less, but nothing more."[107] Each person is to decide for themselves what conduct is called for, even if it conflicts with the convictions of others. According to Dunn, the strong are not to be blackmailed by the scruples of the weak, but are also to avoid destroying the weak by coercing them to break their scruples. Love and respect must limit the freedom of the strong and curb the judgment of the weak. More broadly, freedom occurs in and for community; Christian freedom is not about the freedom of the individual to choose, but the freedom to love one's neighbor, along with their differences.

---

105. I defend this assertion in chapter 3.

106. Dunn, *Christian Liberty*, 90.

107. Dunn, *Christian Liberty*, 97.

Richardson: Love and License, Order and Charisma

The two chapters in *Paul's Ethic of Freedom* that deal most directly with ecclesiology also focus in on the Corinthian church. Richardson demonstrates that love and license are mutually excluding, staving off the threat of freedom falling into license. His treatment of order and charisma is conflicted; a certain amount of order is necessary, but Richardson ultimately concludes that Paul pushes too far in this direction, reneging on what was previously given.

In his chapter on love and license, he shows how Paul deftly navigates between the pressures from conservative and liberal groups alike, "often accepting the rationale of one side and the practice of the other."[108] With the liberal-minded he accepts the assertion that "all things are lawful" (1 Cor 6:12) while conservatively insisting on certain constraints and at times even appealing to tradition. Richardson sees a form of proto-Gnosticism at work in the Corinthian church, turning some into ascetics and allowing others to adopt a libertine attitude towards the body. He argues that, while practices of these radicals may be wrong, Paul has a broad vision of Christian freedom that needs to be qualified without restricting its scope or denying its basis. Freedom is based in Christ, not hidden wisdom. It falls under his lordship and demands that Christian action is governed by love, not self-interest. One should give way in non-essentials, but one should not allow one's convictions to be overthrown by the scruples of another.

Richardson sees tension between order and charisma in the Corinthian church. He traces a trajectory from Paul's bold statements of freedom in earlier writings to his more conservative views in later writings. He holds up the Corinthians as an example of *charismata* (spiritual gifts) being exercised by all. In order to counter those who exercise these gifts to exalt themselves over others, Paul employs the metaphor of the church as a body. The *charismata* must be "fully integrated into one organism so that each gift assumes its rightful place alongside all the others."[109] According to Richardson, the emphasis is on exercising *charismata* while maintaining order is secondary, "useful only to create a harmonious setting in which the gifts can be used."[110] He gives Ephesians a later date and notes that Paul's list of functions in Eph 4:11 seems to posit a church in which some minister while others receive

---

108. Richardson, *Paul's Ethic*, 99. Richardson gives the examples of accepting the rationale of the liberals and the practice of the conservatives concerning food and the rationale of the right and the practice of the left with respect to the role of women in worship.

109. Richardson, *Paul's Ethic*, 150.

110. Richardson, *Paul's Ethic*, 156.

instead of upholding the participation of all. The pastoral letters go even further, making order a primary concern by delineating authoritative offices with stringent requirements. Once again, Richardson sees bold freedom eventually giving way to conservative tendencies in Paul's writings.

Miller: Dismantling Hierarchy

As much as I would like to sever debates on the nature and sovereignty of God from expressions of Christian freedom, I cannot do justice to Miller's arguments without acknowledging the link he sees between the perception of God held by many in Christendom and the opposition of the church to expressions of freedom. He argues "that the church was able to move with ease toward the mode of domination and control because the early disposition of communitarian egalitarianism that reflected their perception of the way Jesus lived his life was probably incongruous with deep-seated convictions about the character of the God of Jesus Christ."[111] In Christendom, the church gave God the attributes of Caesar and established a strict hierarchy to carry out his will on earth. Those who perceived themselves to be God's chosen representatives on earth felt justified in using coercive means to achieve desired ends. Moreover, Miller asserts that the failure of ecclesiological ideas from major Christian thinkers to revolutionize problematic dynamics of authority and power in the church is linked to their traditional conceptions of God.[112] He believes that these ideas will be more productive in a theological structure that conceptualizes God as "infinitely temporal and imaginatively creative" and that bears a commitment to Miller's conception of freedom as "finite, realistically libertarian, and relational."[113]

111. Miller, *Freedom in Resistance*, 215.

112. In a similar vein, Sallie McFague advocates for "the metaphor of the world as God's 'body' rather than as the king's 'realm,'" going on to say, "If we experiment with this metaphor, it becomes obvious that royalist, triumphalist images for God—God as king, lord, ruler, patriarch—will be inappropriate. Other metaphors, suggesting mutuality, interdependence, caring, and responsiveness, will be needed." McFague, *Models of God*, 61. Cf. Johnson, *She Who Is*.

113. Miller, *Freedom in Resistance*, 254.

Since I do not think Miller's overly-nuanced conception of the church[114] or his questionable Christology[115] are essential for his later comments on ecclesiology, I pass them by in favor of his comments concerning hierarchy in the church and the priesthood of all believers. Miller draws upon Luther's *The Freedom of a Christian* and the work of Hans Küng to affirm the priesthood of all believers, who are equal in authority and require no "holy middleman" between themselves and God. Yet each is required to appear before God on behalf of others and to enact the works of God in the world. A balance between carrying one's own load and the burdens of others avoids "spiritual co-dependency" and "makes for fruitful partnership between members of the church."[116] For Miller, the fixed structure of hierarchy prevalent in many churches is incompatible with his vision of "freedom-oriented Christianity."[117] It produces a stratified priesthood in which those who are called to leadership positions often adopt a paternalistic attitude towards others in the church. They become God's special representative.[118] It is important to note that Miller does not reject church offices such as teacher and pastor. His objective is to educate future leaders to avoid "the controlling approaches church leaders so easily adopt" in favor of enabling congregants to serve the community to the degree that the welfare of local churches will no longer depend as heavily upon specialists as they have in

114. Miller, while assenting to the local use of "the body of Christ" metaphor in 1 Cor 12:12–26, argues that this metaphor also "easily fixes the church to Jesus as the Christ and limits emphasis on his claim that his purpose was to facilitate access to God," and that it can lead to overemphasizing the corporate nature of the church "and the supernaturalizing of its institutional character." Miller, *Freedom in Resistance*, 255. His issue with fixing the church to Jesus as the Christ may reside in his implicit Christology (see n115 below). But his charge that the body of Christ metaphor is linked to a "supernaturalization" of the church as an institution is worthy of further exploration (see below).

115. Miller argues that church councils underplayed the humanity of Christ. He then asserts that Jesus ought to be understood as "a human being born of man and woman, and who, as a result of choices made, developed such a relationship with God that God's presence in his life was evident in an especially vivid way." Miller, *Freedom in Resistance*, 257. While he does not explicitly deny the deity of Christ, he certainly does implicitly. However, I do not think his "ecclesiology of partnership" requires one to accept his Christology. Affirming Christ's deity does not necessitate denying his humanity.

116. Miller, *Freedom in Resistance*, 262.

117. Miller, *Freedom in Resistance*, 264.

118. In support of Miller's contention, consider Kenneth Alan Moe's assertion that "[p]eople who are ordained to pastoral ministry are by definition set apart to pursue . . . intimacy with God on behalf of the people of the congregation." Moe, *Pastor's Survival*, 18.

the past.[119] The goal is congregations who can make their own decisions regarding organizational structure and ministry while still taking into account the ecclesial system of which they are a part.

Assessment

When freedom and ecclesiology intersect, the focus seems to be on finding a proper balance between two seemingly opposed but necessary things or denouncing a practice as harmful. Dunn looks at the strong and the weak; Richardson tries to balance order and charismata; Miller attacks hierarchy while attempting to retain structure. Richardson and Miller locate the imbalance they are trying to rectify within Scripture itself. While I sympathize with their goals and observations, I find their approaches to Scripture to be inherently problematic.[120] Yet exploring places of tension is certainly a valid and biblically-based approach to working out the implications of Christian freedom for ecclesiology. It might be interesting to consider what might emerge from linking Christian freedom to Paul's body metaphor, perhaps via a fresh analogy.

CONTEXTUALIZING CHRISTIAN FREEDOM

As I point out above, conservatives and liberals alike agree that Jesus' life exemplifies freedom. It is only natural that theologians of every stripe and color want to claim Jesus for themselves. That Jesus acted freely in relation to the law, culture, and the powers of the world is not something any of these authors would want to deny. The question is whether or not Jesus' "liberal outlook" translates into contemporary liberalism; how should Christian freedom be contextualized? Each author's approach to contextualizing their theology of freedom follows naturally from their stated aims, definitions, and methodology.

---

119. Miller, *Freedom in Resistance*, 269.

120. If Scripture is viewed as imbalanced or self-contradictory, it cannot act as a consistently reliable source for theology and Christian conduct. In fact, external criteria are required to judge the points at which it is mistaken. These criteria, whatever they might be and whatever sources they may be derived from, act de facto as alternative scriptures.

Käsemann and Dunn: Christian Freedom and Liberal Theology

Both Käsemann and Dunn make direct connections between a liberal perspective and the concept of freedom in the New Testament. In the preface
to *Jesus Means Freedom*, Käsemann is clear that his purpose in writing is to
make "a contribution, of a polemical nature, to the present discussion of the
New Testament and modern theology."[121] Throughout the book, he refers
to the history of the German church and alludes to contemporary politics,
placing them side by side with his construction of Jesus as a liberal. His aim
is to justify his own theological views and to rebut those who are attack-
ing him. In his work, Christian freedom is fused to a certain theological
perspective and employed to discredit his theological opponents. Similarly,
Dunn opens *Christian Liberty* by associating liberty with liberalism. As
seen above, he exegetes Rom 15 in such a way that the strong are liberal
and the weak are conservative. He defends liberal theology against John
Henry Newman's charge of elevating human reason above revelation on the
ground that liberal theology forced theologians to admit their limited and
fallible understanding of the truth. Yet, unlike Käsemann, he provides a balance, considering the role of authority in freedom and admitting the danger
of sliding from liberty into license. He also engages more deeply with the
text than does Käsemann and his contextualization is more cautious. After
considering the speech of the Grand Inquisitor in *The Karamazov Brothers*
and the struggles of the former communist bloc with the fall of the iron
curtain, Dunn muses,

> How tragic that the precious gift of liberty should be so threat-
> ening that it gives such scope to renewed authoritarianism, and
> so undisciplined that it confirms those who fear it in their preju-
> dices. Christian liberty recognizes both dangers, and offers both
> the Spirit of liberty and the necessary checks and balances of
> community belonging and community obligation.[122]

Richardson: Paul Was Flexible; We Should Be, Too

For Richardson, Paul is not consistent; his views change according to various circumstances. Reality and applicability are weighted more heavily than
consistency. Just as Paul strove to be all things to all people, so Christians
ought to use "hermeneutical freedom" to emphasize aspects of Scripture

121. Käsemann, *Jesus Means Freedom*, 7.
122. Dunn, *Christian Liberty*, 107–8.

that speak to our particular circumstances. In fact, "the development and change in Scripture [is] indicative of the freedom to apply the word of the Lord to specific circumstances in different ways."[123] Selecting what to emphasize should not be arbitrary, but rather "analogous to Paul's use of Scripture."[124] Richardson points to the historical example of the abolition of slavery. Although abolition was not mandated by Scripture—Richardson goes so far as to say that those defending slavery "were more literally correct"[125]—abolitionary Christians were right to oppose slavery on the grounds that circumstances had changed since Paul's day. For Richardson, present circumstances determine how one interprets Scripture.

Ellul: Concrete Out-workings of Christian Freedom

In comparison to the other works examined here, Ellul's *The Ethics of Freedom* is the most thorough and comprehensive. He engages his contemporary world throughout and devotes his final chapter to working out the concrete implications of his conception of Christian freedom. Several topics, including politics, family, and sexuality, are each examined in turn. Contrary to Käsemann and Dunn, Ellul claims, "I have found no Christian reasons, based on Revelation, why I should be more right than left or *vice versa*. . . . No choice on Christian grounds can be made between justice, equality, and revolution on the left and liberty, tradition, and responsibility on the right."[126] And, contrary to Richardson, Ellul argues that shifting theological commitments in response to circumstances in the realm of politics (though presumably not limited to it) suggests the motive of self-vindication; "The Word of God was utilized to provide reasons for emotional choices already made."[127] Theology should not be used as a means to justify certain political positions; this only causes rifts between fellow Christians. Christians of all political stripes should enact their freedom by placing their loyalty to Christ above their political affiliation, enabling them to act as peacemakers in volatile situations.[128]

123. Richardson, *Paul's Ethic*, 168.

124. Richardson, *Paul's Ethic*, 167.

125. Richardson, *Paul's Ethic*, 168.

126. Ellul, *Ethics of Freedom*, 376. Emphasis in original.

127. Ellul, *Ethics of Freedom*, 376.

128. Ellul, while arguing against Christians dividing themselves according to their politics, also insists that "[t]he freedom to be uninterested, to turn aside, or to sleep is not Christian freedom. An a-political attitude in modern society is not an expression of Christian freedom but of fear and weakness." Ellul, *Ethics of Freedom*, 374. Ellul's comments need to be qualified; as I point out in the introduction, political freedom

Ellul is suspicious of attempts to grasp freedom by institutional means or by use of force. History demonstrates the failure of institutions and revolutions alike to provide meaningful freedom to those who partake in them. Again, for Ellul, true freedom is impossible without Christ. He observes that in family life the liberation of children from parental oversight merely means a transfer of authority from them to educational institutions, which are even more difficult (if not impossible) to prevail upon. The emancipation of women from home life again only entailed a transfer of authority from their husbands (Ellul wrote in the 1970s) to their employers. The sexual revolution deified sex and by doing so only recreated old forms of slavery. By affirming the intrinsic value of family and exercising restraint in sexuality, Christians exercise freedom over the constraints of the contemporary world.

Bauckham: The Crisis of Freedom

Bauckham is expressly concerned with contextualizing Christian freedom in contemporary discourse. The depth of his analysis of his contemporary situation is only equaled by Ellul, and, while many of his insights remain pertinent, much of Ellul's analysis is out of date. Throughout *God and the Crisis of Freedom*, but especially in the final chapter, Bauckham engages with modern and postmodern conceptions of freedom in the contemporary world. He uses the work of Michel Houellebecq and Francis Fukuyama to demonstrate the problem of freedom in modernity. According to Bauckham, the thesis of Houellebecq's novel, *Atomised*, is that the modern age displaced religion and in doing so did away with a worldview that encouraged community and set boundaries on individualism. In the absence of religion, competitive individualism makes utopia impossible. Fukuyama's optimism about the triumph of liberal democracy is an optimistic counter to Houellebecq. Bauckham contends that the problem is that Fukuyama's atheism prevents him from giving a plausible rationale for the notion that human beings have dignity, which is a foundational premise for liberal democracy.

---

has an impact on how Christians can exercise Christian freedom. If given a clear choice between a murderous dictator and a prime minister with a record of righteous actions, it will not be hard to find theological grounds to prefer the latter. However, the choice is rarely so clear; in many, if not most, cases, Ellul is right in saying that allowing the divisions between the right in the left in politics to divide Christians is scandalous.

Assessment

Dunn's contextualization suffers from the weakness of reading terms like liberal and conservative back into Scripture without first carefully defining them, risking dragging contemporary connotations into what a first-century text is trying to say. Käsemann's passionate defense of his liberalism is closely tied to his own circumstances, and, like Dunn, is in danger of importing contemporary liberal baggage into his view of Jesus. Richardson is at least upfront in his conclusion that Scripture be read through the lens of contemporary situations. Bauckham's broad view of the contemporary crisis of freedom is well-stated, but it is not quite as thorough as Ellul's movement from theory to concrete implications. Both avoid the overly polemical approach of Käsemann as well as Dunn's anachronisms.

CONCLUSION

My sources are disparate in methodology and definition. Even the stronger works have points of weakness that call out for improvement. I now turn to the task of setting out my own approach in relation to them. First, it seems clear to me that beginning with a secular approach to freedom is problematic. The previous chapter, as well as the strong critiques of Ellul and Bauckham, rule it out as a starting point for developing a theology of Christian freedom. Second, I believe that the best approach to constructing a definition of Christian freedom is a variation on Ellul's approach. Instead of expecting the reader to work out my definition over the course of my work, my aim is to construct a biblical theology of freedom and to provide a definition at its conclusion. Yet it is not practical to expect to work out a biblical theology of Christian freedom without some philosophical categories already in hand. After all, Paul used freedom vocabulary in his epistles, terms that were already loaded with certain connotations found in the history of the Greek language. Like Ellul, I must begin with a provisional definition. Third, my approach to Scripture is opposed to Miller's, though hopefully aware of his criticisms. With Ellul and Bauckham, I emphasize the consistency of Scripture, but I also affirm a trajectory of maturation and development within it. Without going as far as Richardson, I agree that context shapes the emphases placed on Scripture; different contexts will inevitably draw attention to different aspects of the text. Fourth and finally, I depart from the works above by offering an intermediate stage of contextualization. Jazz provides an analogy that takes up the salient points of a biblical theology of freedom and expands them in a contemporary context.

3

Constructing a Biblical Theology
of Freedom

THE PREVIOUS CHAPTER PRESENTED theologians and biblical scholars in dialogue on the topic of Christian freedom. Some of those authors, such as James Dunn, use specific portions of Scripture, especially from the New Testament, to construct their views on Christian freedom. Others, such as Richard Bauckham and Michael St. A. Miller, look at the bigger picture by considering both Old and New Testaments.[1] Here my aim is to follow in the footsteps of the latter by constructing a biblical theology of Christian freedom. By "biblical theology," I mean the goal of allowing "the biblical texts to set the agenda."[2] This goal does not entail an attempt to view the text in isolation from its context. In fact, biblical theology requires "the cooperation of various disciplines" in the same way that civil engineering requires the cooperation of disciplines as varied as mathematics, sociology, and metallurgy.[3] In other words, this project requires exegetical and philosophical tools and a clear delineation of presuppositions. I presuppose that the various texts of the Bible speak on freedom in ways that are compatible with one another. I therefore privilege interpretations that do not necessitate seeing irreconcilable contradictions between its various texts.[4]

---

1. Miller critically engages with Old and New Testaments in light of his own objectives in Miller, *Freedom in Resistance*, 99–128, and Bauckham devotes a chapter to "a synthesis of the theme of freedom in the Bible," in Bauckham, *God and the Crisis*, 7.

2. Rosner, "Biblical Theology," 5.

3. Rosner, "Biblical Theology," 3.

4. For a response to those who argue "that the diversity of the Bible's theological

My goal is to uncover what Scripture says on the topic of freedom prior to juxtaposing it with contemporary issues. A classical musician listening to jazz for the first time will be restricted by the way they are accustomed to hearing the music. However, with perseverance and study, they will eventually become acclimatized to its different forms and conventions. In a similar way, although my own interests undoubtedly influence what I perceive, I trust that the text shapes my perception.[5]

One approach to constructing a biblical theology of Christian freedom is to study every passage containing Hebrew and Greek words related to the English word "freedom." However, not all passages relevant to the notion of freedom necessarily contain freedom vocabulary.[6] Furthermore, I am more concerned with discerning the nature and characteristics of freedom in the Bible than cataloguing each reference to freedom.[7] Another possible method would be to adopt the concerns of a certain perspective, such as liberation theology, feminist theology, or postcolonial theology, as a means of approaching the biblical text.[8] But this would contradict my intention of allowing the text to set the agenda. I also hope to gain a broader understanding of freedom in the Bible than the use of such approaches allow.

---

ideas rules out any unified biblical theology," see Balla, "Challenges to Biblical Theology," 20.

5. For a discussion of whether or not "exegesis without ideology is possible," see Vanhoozer, *Is There a Meaning*, 381–407.

6. In any case, it is dangerous to confuse words with concepts. As James Barr writes,

> The attempt in much recent biblical theology to demonstrate the existence of a biblical lexical stock of words or "concepts" . . . which are semantically distinctive, that is to say, which have a semantic distinctiveness which can be set in close correlation with the distinctiveness of the faith and theology of the Bible, is in principle a failure. That it appears to work at certain points is because some words become specialized, but only in certain syntactical contexts; the case for a semantic distinctiveness of the words as made by biblical theology depends on a haphazard method which exploits these occasional specializations. But as a whole the distinctiveness of biblical thought and language has to be settled at sentence level, that is, by the things the writers say, and not by the words they say them with.

Barr, *Semantics*, 269–70.

7. By references to freedom I include both vocabulary related to freedom and to situations in the biblical narrative where freedom is being enacted or suppressed.

8. For an example of such an approach to the subject of Christian freedom, see Jones, *Paul's Message*.

Instead, I have opted to examine central narratives and didactic passages in Scripture that deal with freedom explicitly or implicitly.

Reading a definition of freedom nuanced by contemporary usage back into the biblical text is problematic, but it is also difficult to discuss something while waiting for a definition to emerge from the material at hand. Until it is refined and expanded by the following discussion, "freedom" will refer to "the state of being free from (or unfettered by) undesirable controls, or restrictions and especially from the state of bondage or slavery."[9]

FREEDOM IN THE OLD TESTAMENT

A biblical view of freedom begins at creation with God's acts of creation and formation. Since I am concerned specifically with constructing a biblical theology of Christian freedom, I leave aside questions concerning the nature and extent of God's freedom. I begin with the freedom of the first human beings and move from there to the Exodus, which is God's defining act of liberation that becomes the type for his other acts of liberation and the basis of much of Old Testament ethics. By the time of the prophets, it becomes evident that liberation from political oppression is not enough; Israel requires a change of heart.

The Beginnings of Human Freedom

Freedom can be inferred from the opening chapters in Genesis, where God creates humanity within a certain context—providing them with constructive constraints as opposed to absolute freedom—and provides them with directions to "be fruitful and multiply, and fill the earth and subdue it; and have dominion over the fish of the sea and over the birds of the air and over every living thing that moves upon the earth" (Gen 1:28b).[10] The only restriction was not to eat from the tree of knowledge of good and evil (2:17). At this point, humanity was free from oppressive forces to an extent that has not been matched.

9. Ciampa, "Freedom," 503.

10. In his study of the *Imago Dei* in Gen 1, J. Richard Middleton suggests that "given the portrayal or rendering of God's power disclosed by a careful reading of Genesis 1 . . . the sort of power that humans are to exercise [as God's image bearers] is generous, loving power. It is power used to nurture, enhance, and empower others, noncoercively, for *their* benefit, not for the self-aggrandizement of the one exercising power." Middleton, *Liberating Image*, 295. Emphasis in original.

At first glance, the only significant constraint present in the narrative is God's command to not eat fruit from the treat of the knowledge of good and evil (Gen 2:17). Coupled with Jacques Ellul's assertion that there is a necessary correlation between freedom and transgression (see chapter 2), one might conclude that the only way for humanity to be free was to transgress God's command. Yet God's choice to create humanity as male and female (Gen 1:27) provides a significant boundary that, paradoxically, the marital union described in Gen 2:24 both maintains and crosses. Graham Ward observes that God's decision to divide humanity into male and female destabilizes the self "because it is only completed by the other."[11] In other words, from the inauguration of humanity, human beings were *meant* to transgress themselves through encountering the opposite sex.[12] The self is a boundary that never entirely dissolves, but which one constantly needs to transgress in order to be free. A significant aspect of the freedom that Adam and Eve experience in the garden is transcending their limitations as selves in the act of constructively engaging with God and with one another as members of opposing sexes.

Then the Fall delivered humanity into bondage to sin. The Fall itself is an opportunity to reflect on the nature of human freedom in the rest of Scripture. Unlike most commentaries and works seeking to make sense of Gen 2–3, R. R. Reno's commentary sees in the narrative, when it is interpreted as a story of cosmological significance, an opportunity to "learn something about the large biblical vision of human freedom."[13] Contra commentators such as Claus Westermann and Victor Hamilton, Reno makes a forceful theological argument for identifying the snake in the garden with Satan.[14] Making this identification fits with the spiritual powers opposing

11. Ward, "Postmodern Version," 11.

12. I am not suggesting that the self can only be transgressed through an encounter between a man and a woman, but rather that this basic difference is a model, perhaps even a paradigm, for this kind of transgression. Scripture often uses marriage as a metaphor for God's relationship with his people (ex. Isa 62:5; Jer 2:2; Eph 5:23–32; Rev 19:7).

13. Reno, *Genesis*, 80.

14. Westermann, in agreement with Gerhard von Rad, argues, "We are not justified by the text in seeing behind these words a complete orientation of the serpent against God or a being at enmity with God." Westermann, *Genesis 1–11*, 238. Hamilton goes further, arguing that viewing the serpent as Satan veers toward dualism: "Regarding the serpent's origin, we are clearly told that he was an animal made by God. This information immediately removes any possibility that the serpent is to be viewed as some kind of supernatural, divine force. There is no room here for any dualistic ideas about the origins of good and evil." Hamilton, *Genesis*, 1:188. Coming between Westermann and von Rad on the one side, and Reno on the other, John Walton observes that there is no precedent in the Old Testament for identifying the serpent with Satan, but, arguing from a confessional standpoint (that I share), he concludes that "the New Testament

God in the New Testament and fits with the imagery of Rev 12:9. It also contextualizes human freedom: "As any mention of the devil reminds us, we are cast into a world already shaped by a creationwide [*sic*] history of resistance to the divine plan. Our freedom is not pristine, unaffected, and uninfluenced by prior events. We must decide and act in circumstances beyond our control."[15] As Reno goes on to explain, this does not remove human responsibility, but is rather a reminder that human freedom does not command, but rather reacts and responds; human beings can choose loyalties, but "cannot invent new armies and new objectives."[16] This understanding of human freedom is borne out by the rest of the biblical narrative. Human beings are too limited to make promethean acts of free choice; they must choose a side and improvise within its constraints to the best of their ability.[17] In choosing to be free of one set of constraints, they necessarily must adopt another.

The Exodus Narrative

The notion of freedom is perhaps clearest in the Exodus narrative of YHWH's deliverance of the Israelites from their enslavement to the Egyptians. James Plastaras calls the exodus "*the* crucial event"[18] and boldly asserts that "nothing that happened afterward in the Old Testament was of quite equal importance."[19] Goran Larsson claims that "at the center of everything is the deliverance of Israel from Egypt, a theme resounding throughout the entire Bible."[20] In short, the Exodus narrative is the definitive model for understanding bondage and liberation in the Old Testament.

---

views the serpent as related to Satan and so ought we." Walton, *Genesis*, 210.

15. Reno, *Genesis*, 80.

16. Reno, *Genesis*, 83.

17. Reno posits "free spiritual beings whose created free wills are not moved by their perception of other created realities" that can make originative choices—Satan is such a being. If the serpent was merely a part of God's creation, argues Reno, "then sin emerges out of the human encounter with the natural order," thus casting aspersion on God's character. Reno, *Genesis*, 81. Suggesting a prior fall gets past Hamilton's charge of dualism (see n14 above) because it does not deny the status of Satan as a created being. Reno's explanation goes beyond a strictly biblical theology, but it also supplies a plausible way of integrating the later revelation in the New Testament with the story of the Fall and it does not shy away from natural questions concerning theodicy.

18. Plastaras, *God of Exodus*, 6.

19. Plastaras, *God of Exodus*, 7.

20. Larsson, *Bound for Freedom*, ix.

The book of Exodus begins by referring back to the immigration of Jacob and his sons to Egypt. They flourished there, causing the Egyptians to fear losing their dominant position. The Egyptians, acting on this fear, imposed hard physical labor on the Israelites, who continued to multiply. The Pharaoh responded to their increasing numbers by decreeing the slaughter of newborn Israelite males.[21] An escalating pattern can be discerned in which a malevolent force progressively imposes its will on its victims, to the point of denying them their very lives.

God responds to the cries of his people, raising up Moses to speak and act on his behalf. Exodus 7–12 chronicles the contest between YHWH and Pharaoh, concluding in chapter 14 with the parting of the Red Sea and the drowning of Pharaoh and his army. Interestingly, the demands of Moses are not framed in terms of simply setting the Israelites free, but rather celebrating a festival to YHWH in the wilderness (Exod 5:1). YHWH has an end in mind beyond delivering the Israelites from slavery to the Egyptians; he desires to be in covenant with them. The Exodus does not climax with the destruction of Pharaoh and his armies, but rather with the covenant at Mount Sinai.[22]

Exodus 19:1–9 marks the time and place where YHWH and Israel "enter[ed] into the covenant freely and willingly, without hesitation or coercion on either side."[23] YHWH has delivered Israel, but, as John Durham observes, he "is not forcing these people to serve him, as some conquering king might do."[24] In other words, the Israelites, having been liberated from Egypt, freely choose YHWH, rather than another god, a king, or some form of self-rule. The Israelites now belong to YHWH and are obliged to keep the terms of his covenant with them. They have traded one master for another. Yet their circumstances have changed. Their status as slaves to Pharaoh was shameful, but YHWH tells his people, "I have broken the bars of your yoke and made you walk erect" (Lev 26:13b NRSV). Although they are now bound to YHWH, they can expect him to bless them, provided they keep

---

21. The Egyptian focus on Israelite males reflects the patriarchal attitudes of the time; descent was reckoned through the male line. It is therefore interesting to note the prominent place of women in the opening chapters of Exodus.

22. According to William J. Dumbrell, "With some justification we could point to the Exodus liberation as having established the relationship [between YHWH and the Israelites], but there has been no mention in the earlier Exodus material of a covenant as specifically established by the Exodus event itself." Dumbrell, *Covenant and Creation*, 81.

23. Janzen, *Exodus*, 132.

24. Durham, *Exodus*, 262.

his covenant. Constraints remain in place, but they are designed to bless, not to harm.

As much as it might interest a contemporary western audience, the notion of autonomy is not the primary concern of the narrative. In fact, when the Israelites are dissatisfied with their lot, they advocate a return to Egypt as slaves (Exod 14:11–12; 16:3; Num 11:18). Even after they have settled in Canaan, the Israelites express dissatisfaction with their state as a loose association of tribes and clamor for a king (1 Sam 8). Freedom in the narrative is not a matter of simply being liberated from oppression; freedom also entails a new set of constraints, of exchanging a malevolent master for a benevolent one.

The Liberating Implications of the Exodus Narrative

Among the many ways in which the Exodus narrative resonates throughout the experience of the Israelites is its implications for how they are expected to treat one another. Deuteronomy 5:14–15 ties the narrative to the observation of the Sabbath day for all the occupants of an Israelite household, including slaves, and even livestock. According to Daniel Block, "In ancient Israel it would have been tempting for the head of the household and his immediate family to observe the Sabbath while the rest of the household carried on as usual."[25] By including everyone else, the text "insists that in their right to Sabbath rest these were all on a par with the householder; the Sabbath was a gift for all."[26] In Deut 16:9–12 the Israelites are once again reminded that everyone, including "male and female slaves, the Levites resident in your towns, as well as the strangers, the orphans, and the widows who are among you" (11 NRSV) are to participate in the Feast of Weeks; the text once again makes its appeal on the basis of remembering "that you were a slave in Egypt" (12). Those with power and authority are reminded that they were once oppressed and needed liberation. The former state of the Israelites as menial slaves ought to enable them to empathize and to act with compassion towards those who occupy lower social strata. The constraints of labor, especially when combined with an unequal distribution of power and authority, can become oppressive. The Sabbath mitigates them by insisting that the strong and weak alike rest.

Deuteronomy 15:12–18 appeals to the Exodus narrative in dealing with Hebrew slaves, stipulating that they be set free after a period of six years. The former slaves are even to be provided with material goods, presumably

25. Block, *Deuteronomy*, 164.
26. Block, *Deuteronomy*, 164.

to help them establish themselves as free persons. Just as YHWH did not deliver the Israelites from Egypt to abandon them in the wilderness, so the freed person is not merely set free, but is given the means to an independent life. Alternately, a slave may choose to remain a slave for life.[27] According to the text, such a decision is made on the grounds of love for the family to which a slave is attached and to their well-being in their current state. In the world of the text, the slave is able to choose between the constraints of their master and the constraints of self-sustenance.[28]

Deuteronomy 24:17–18 links the narrative to the just treatment of the vulnerable. As Christopher Wright points out, "*When Israel forgot its history, it forgot its poor.*"[29] The reader is left to draw the implicit connection between depriving "a resident alien or an orphan of justice" (Deut 14:17) and the oppressive acts of Pharaoh. Verses 21–22 also cite the narrative as justification to go even further by demanding acts of charity towards such persons. YHWH's benevolence and mercy towards the vulnerable is the implicit model for one's desired attitude towards them. Freedom from oppression is not only for those strong enough to stand by themselves, but also for the weak. In fact, the strong are to uphold the freedom of the weak on the grounds that their own freedom has been (and is) upheld by YHWH.

Repeating the Exodus ad Nauseam

As Walter Brueggemann observes, "When Israel began telling of its subsequent history, about what happened in other times and places and circumstances, Israel characteristically retold *all* of its experience through the powerful, definitional lens of the Exodus memory."[30] A pattern of bondage

27. Becoming a slave for life entailed a ceremony in which the master pushes an awl through the earlobe of the slave into the door (Deut 15:17). Jeffrey Tigay points out that "[l]ater Jewish exegesis saw the ceremony as putative: the ear, which heard God say at Mount Sinai that Israelites are *His* slaves and may not be sold into permanent servitude (Lev. 25:42), is punished for ignoring God's declaration by electing to remain a servant to a human master." Tigay, *Deuteronomy*, 150. This resonates with Richard Bauckham's argument that the Old Testament teaches that human beings "are all equally subject to God" and that God is opposed to "[a]ll relationships of subjection that permit the exploitation of one human being by another." Bauckham, *God and the Crisis*, 13. For a more detailed discussion of Bauckham's views, see chapter 2.

28. The text appears to represent an ideal situation (aside from the fact that one person is enslaved to another); it does not mention the risks involved for a slave attempting to be self-sustaining or consider the possibility of a lazy slave taking advantage of a lenient master in life-long servitude.

29. Wright, *Deuteronomy*, 261. Emphasis in original.

30. Brueggemann, *Old Testament*, 177. Emphasis in original.

and liberation quickly emerges. The Israelites fall back into bondage on a regular basis throughout the rest of the Old Testament. Often it is YHWH himself who hands them over to a foreign power because they have (yet again) broken his covenant (e.g., Judg 6:1). Just as often, YHWH has compassion on his people, breaking them loose yet another time, recapitulating the Exodus once again, pleading with them to abide by his covenant. Though glimmers of light appear, the history of the Israelites is often grim and sordid, a catalogue of indecisiveness and ambivalence towards YHWH. An exasperated Elijah asks the Israelites, "How long will you go limping with two different opinions? If the LORD is God, follow him; but if Baal, then follow him" (1 Kgs 18:21). Yet even fire from heaven was unable to settle the question decisively, once for all. In the end, the consequences for breaking YHWH's covenant fell upon the Israelites as first Israel and then Judah went into exile.

Israel was unable to decide upon what set of constraints to adopt, or which master to choose. Yet this state of affairs had been anticipated in Deut 30:1–10: YHWH promised an end to the curse to be incurred by Israel for breaking the covenant.[31] Furthermore, YHWH promised to deal with the root cause of Israel's unfaithfulness by circumcising their hearts, causing them to love him. Jeremiah 31:31–34 expounds upon this theme, speaking of a new covenant and a law that is written on the hearts of Israel. Ezekiel, speaking to the exiles, promises that YHWH will replace the stone heart of Israel with one of flesh (Ezek 11:19; 36:26) and give them his spirit (36:27). These passages might appear to revoke the place of human agency/freedom that featured in the initial covenant, but as Steven Tuell points out, according to Ezek 11:21[32] "disobedience is evidently still a possibility."[33] Tuell suggests that instead, these passages mark "a shift in emphasis, from reliance on one's own will and effort to reliance on God's transformative power."[34] The self is itself a master when it attempts to act independently of God.

Physical bondage to a malevolent ruler was certainly an issue that YHWH took seriously, but the course of Israel's history laid bare a deeper form of bondage. The Israelites were simply unwilling to be governed by YHWH's liberating set of constraints. Instead, they continually sampled any

31. Whether or not Deut 30:1–10 was written during the exile is beside the point; in the world of the text, YHWH's promise precedes the history of Israel after Moses. Cf. Craigie, *Deuteronomy*, 364.

32. "But as for those whose heart goes after their detestable things and their abominations, I will bring their deeds upon their own heads, says the Lord God."

33. Tuell, *Ezekiel*, 60.

34. Tuell, *Ezekiel*, 60.

and all of the alternatives that they could find. But in order for a set of constraints to be liberating, one must adopt them fully and consistently.

Summary

The Exodus narrative provides the primary way of understanding freedom in the Old Testament. It highlights not only the sovereign act of YHWH in liberating the Israelites from Egypt, but also the agency of the Israelites in freely choosing YHWH in turn to be their Lord. They were liberated from an oppressive set of constraints and then freely entered into the constraints entailed by a covenant with YHWH. The shared experience of slavery and liberation provided first an experiential and then a historical basis for protecting the weak and vulnerable from oppression and exploitation. Yet the Israelites did not keep the covenant, choosing instead to break faith with YHWH by flouting its constraints through idolatry and oppressing the weak. They could not abide by the constraints of the covenant. As a result, they fell into a cycle of being oppressed, calling out for deliverance, being liberated and then breaking the covenant. They were slaves to sin and self. Yet YHWH promises to deliver them even from their own hearts.

FREEDOM IN THE NEW TESTAMENT

Freedom in the New Testament is primarily about deliverance from sin, self, and the powers of darkness. Yet it is also concerned with freedom in relation to the Torah. I trace these themes first through the gospels, then the Pauline epistles and conclude with the general epistles.

Freedom in the Gospels

Given the historical relationship between YHWH and Israel, it is unsurprising that the New Testament opens with Israel once again the subject of a foreign power. Nor is it surprising that, when Jesus appears and begins to teach about the impending kingdom of God, his followers expect a political insurrection through which Israel would regain her independence. In fact, after his death and resurrection, and just before his ascension, his disciples asked, "Lord, is this the time when you will restore the kingdom to Israel?" (Acts 1:6). But the expected deliverance from a political oppressor was to be delayed. Jesus' ministry, with respect to freedom, dealt simultaneously with more localized and farther-reaching acts of liberation.

In Luke 4:16–21, Jesus reads from Isa 61:1–2. In this passage, Isaiah writes about someone anointed by the spirit of YHWH to proclaim liberation for the vulnerable and the oppressed. Jesus claims to have fulfilled it.[35] In all of the gospels, Jesus performs miracles that release people from the oppression of various diseases and demonic forces. In Luke 13:10–17, for instance, Jesus specifically attributes a crippled woman's condition to being bound by Satan and argues that she should be set free, even on the Sabbath. Jesus takes the time to deal with bondage and oppression localized in the experience of an individual, fulfilling the intent of the Law towards the weak and oppressed. And while Jesus does not always make demands of those he heals, he does speak plainly about the cost of discipleship (e.g. Mark 8:34–38) and several of his parables indicate the responsibility he places on his listeners to use what they have in a purposeful manner (e.g. the parable of the talents in Matt 25:14–30 and Luke 19:11–27).

In addition to localized acts of liberation, Jesus puts his finger on the crux of the problem of the Israelites in the Old Testament narratives. In John 8:31–38 he uses the vocabulary of freedom (ἐλεύθερος), arguing that keeping his word reveals the truth, the knowledge of which sets one free. Jesus' insinuation that his listeners are enslaved earns him their ire. They respond by claiming that they have never been slaves. As J. Ramsey Michaels points out, "[t]heir answer conspicuously ignores Moses' repeated commands in Deuteronomy to 'Remember that you were slaves in Egypt.'"[36] Rudolf Schnackenburg suggests that the Jews "are not thinking of external, political freedom . . . , but of the denigration of their sense of freedom. In spite of political oppression they think of themselves as free sons of Abraham, who have never inwardly bowed to foreign rule."[37] In their pride, they forget their history, including the fact that the Israelites considered returning to Egypt and the voices of the prophets who confronted the Israelites about an inward heart of stone. And this is precisely what Jesus touches on when he responds by saying, "anyone who commits sin is a slave to sin" (John 8:34b). The underlying root of the problem of the Israelites is revealed to be not a matter of bondage to a foreign entity, but rather of bondage to sin, in its personal and social aspects. There is no denying the gravity of political oppression, slavery (in a physical sense), or of being bound by a crippling

---

35. As Darrell Bock puts it, "Jesus' ultimate role is not only to proclaim deliverance: he brings that release. In this description of his mission, he is seen as both eschatological prophet and Messiah." Bock, *Luke*, 1:410.

36. Michaels, *John*, 506.

37. Schnackenburg, *John*, 2:207.

disease and/or demonic power, but slavery to sin by virtue of committing sin takes precedence over them all.[38]

Jesus, Power, and Politics

The words and life of Jesus cannot be properly understood outside of the political context of first century Judea in the Roman Empire. While Jesus was not a violent revolutionary,[39] the titles he accepted challenged Roman imperial claims. Warren Carter points out that many of these titles were already claimed by Roman rule, such as "Shepherd," "Savior of the World," "King of the Jews," and "Lord and God."[40] In other words, Jesus countered the demands of worship and loyalty the Roman emperors demanded by audaciously asking his followers to give those things to him. And as Richard Bauckham points out, "the effect of divine kingship or fatherhood [Jesus and God the Father are one (John 10:30)] is not in the direction of legitimating or bolstering human hierarchical power but of relativizing it."[41] By accepting his titles, Jesus liberated his followers from the absolute claims of the Roman empire. Without resorting to violence, he planted seeds for the liberation of oppressed peoples.

Properly understanding Jesus' own freedom in relation to political power in particular requires examining the temptations Jesus encountered in the wilderness in light of their political ramifications. Considering how Jesus affirms his position as Messiah while refuting popular conceptions of the Messiah shows how Jesus refused coercive political power in favor of the power of the Kingdom of God. His refusal was an act of freedom.

Mark 1:12–13 briefly mentions Jesus' temptation while Matt 4:1–11 and Luke 4:1–13 flesh out the threefold attack of the devil. Jacques Ellul, following Luke's sequence of temptations,[42] focuses on Jesus' freedom to wait on God when tempted to miraculously meet his own needs by turning stones into bread, freedom from the temptation to seize political control of the world by might, and the temptation to put God's promises to the test by

38. By slavery to sin, I mean participation in unjust societal and political structures as well as "personal" sin. Unless one is stranded on a desert island, sin of every kind always has destructive results that go beyond the individual sinner.

39. See Hengel, *Was Jesus a Revolutionist?*

40. Carter, *John and Empire*, 185–97.

41. Bauckham, *God and the Crisis*, 127.

42. Matthew and Luke order the temptations differently: Matthew and Luke begin with the temptation of bread. Matthew moves next to the temptation for Jesus to reveal himself at the temple and concludes with the temptation of political dominion while Luke reverses these two temptations.

throwing himself off of the temple.[43] Alan Storkey follows Matthew, teasing out the political implications of Jesus' steadfast resistance. He points to the politics of bread and writes, "But Jesus will not give the people what they want and allow the material aspect to dominate."[44] Contra Abraham Maslow's hierarchy of needs,[45] God must take precedence even over the physiological. Referring to the gold eagle Herod the Great placed over the front door of the temple to appease Rome and the loss of life that accompanied its removal by zealous students, Storkey shows that the devil's temptation "is not just some private act of magic" but an assumption of the Messianic role the Jews so desperately were waiting for someone to assume.[46] Jesus also reveals that possessing worldly power, the final temptation, is actually an illusion, because "[g]rasping power is not real *power*, but weakness."[47]

Jesus accepts the title of Messiah (Matt 16:16–17; Mark 8:29–30; Luke 9:20–21), but he does not want it proclaimed until the right time (Matt 16:20; Mark 8:30; Luke 9:21). He demonstrates reticence to either join with established sects or to take advantage of revolutionary fervor (John 6:15). Unlike the Essenes, Jesus freely engages with the culture of his time. Unlike the Sadducees, Jesus does not sidle up to those who have political power; unlike the Zealots, he will not incite revolution to seize it. Unlike the Pharisees, Jesus is free to "do things honestly before God . . . without seeking popularity, applause, or the moral high ground."[48] As the one who inaugurates the Kingdom of God, Jesus openly claims to be the Messiah at exactly the right time in order to freely lay down his life sacrificially for the world.

The Constraints of the Kingdom of God

The Sermon on the Mount in Matt 5 "remains the greatest moral document of all time."[49] Although Jesus does not mention freedom directly, in order to enact the teaching of the Sermon on the Mount one must transgress the expectations of human nature. Jesus sets aside any possibility of reducing the law to following a list of rules. It is not even enough simply to be obedient; one must desire to do the will of the Father. The use of metaphor, hyperbole,

43. Ellul, *Ethics of Freedom*, 60.

44. Storkey, *Jesus and Politics*, 76.

45. Maslow, "Theory of Human Motivation."

46. Storkey, *Jesus and Politics*, 77.

47. Storkey, *Jesus and Politics*, 78. Emphasis in original.

48. Storkey, *Jesus and Politics*, 82.

49. McKnight, *Sermon on the Mount*, 3.

and other devices require the hearer to engage creatively with Jesus' words, working out their universal implications in particular circumstances.

Anna Wierzbicka distinguishes between a certain notion of obedience and Jesus' open call to do the Father's will willingly. She portrays obedience as "someone (A) thinks about someone else (B): 'if this person (B) wants me to do something I have to do it.'"[50] But from the beginning of God's interaction with his creation through the covenant that Israel freely entered into, God desires his creatures to do his will willingly.[51] Rather than perceiving following God's will as a sort of blind obedience required "regardless of the content of what [a] person wants us to do," it becomes apparent that "God's will is indistinguishable from God's love."[52] Doing God's will then, is acting in love towards God and others. The Sermon on the Mount shows the "heart of flesh" God promised to the Israelites, a heart of love towards God and neighbor. It shows what a life liberated from self and sin looks like.

Jesus and the Law

The gospels do not directly speak about being set free from the law. Paul is the one who develops this idea and attempts to work out its implications (see below). But in order to incorporate Paul's thought into a broader biblical context, it is necessary to examine the relationship between Jesus and the law.

In Matt 5:17, Jesus strongly affirms the law, saying, "Do not think that I have come to abolish the law or the prophets; I have not come to abolish but to fulfill." The opposition in this verse, though, "is not between 'abolishing' and 'obeying' but between 'abolishing' and 'fulfilling.'"[53] In light of what follows, fulfilling the law and the prophets does not merely involve obedience, but going beyond what is said to their "real meaning."[54] This is demonstrated as the text continues: Jesus employs the formula, "You have heard that it was said" (5:21, 27, 31, etc.)[55] and follows it with, "But I say to you" (5:22, 28, 32, etc.), filling out the intent of the law. As Elian Cuvillier concludes,

50. Wierzbicka, *What Did Jesus Mean?*, 216.

51. In his study of "variations in the literary pattern of Genesis 1," J. Richard Middleton suggests that "[t]here is a certain . . . incipient subjectivity or freedom granted to the cosmos by God, by which it is allowed, in response to the creator's call, to find its own pattern." Middleton, *Liberating Image*, 278, 285. If he is correct, God's gift of freedom extends to the whole of creation.

52. Wierzbicka, *What Did Jesus Mean?*, 216.

53. Cuvillier, "Torah Observance," 149.

54. Cuvillier, "Torah Observance," 149.

55. Some verses have variants on the formula, but the basic idea remains the same.

"it is no longer obedience to [the law's] commandments that regulates the life of the disciples, but rather Jesus' teaching which is characterized by the logic of excess."[56] This "logic of excess" is about the responsibility of the individual "before God and the neighbor," which exceeds merely keeping "general rules."[57] For Jesus, the law by itself is insufficient.

In Luke 16:16, Jesus says, "The law and the prophets were in effect until John came; since then the good news of the kingdom of God is proclaimed."[58] This implies a paradigm shift from the period of the law and the prophets to a new period under Jesus.[59] This is borne out in Mark 7:1–23, where Jesus engages in a dispute with the Pharisees about hand washing and concludes, "Do you not see that whatever goes into a person from outside cannot defile, since it enters not the heart but the stomach, and goes out into the sewer?" (18b–19a). Mark interprets this to mean that Jesus was declaring all foods to be clean. As Heikki Räisänen observes, "the saying looks like a radical if implicit attack on important parts of the Torah. If nothing that enters into a man from outside can defile him, then the biblical food laws are actually set aside."[60] It appears as though Jesus was not bound to all aspects of the Torah.

Tension exists between Matthew's account of the law and what is suggested in Luke and asserted by Mark.[61] While a synthesis inevitably smoothes over the distinctiveness of each account, it will also aid an understanding of Paul's thought on the law. Jesus' fulfillment of the Torah as it is explicated in Matthew not only shows the purpose of the Torah, but demonstrates its shortcomings as well. A strong case in point is found in Matt 19:8 where, in his response to the criticism of his opponents to his teaching on divorce, Jesus says, "It was because you were so hard-hearted that Moses allowed you to divorce your wives, but from the beginning it was not so."[62] In this

56. Cuvillier, "Torah Observance," 159.

57. Cuvillier, "Torah Observance," 159.

58. This is a particularly controversial passage. For a good bibliography, see Nolland, *Luke*, 811–12. See also Bovon, *Luke*, 2:464–67.

59. After considering the debate around where to place John the Baptist in the division between the periods Jesus mentions in 16:16, François Bovon concludes, "in point of fact, that is not what is important. What does matter, in Luke's eyes, is that, since the time of John the Baptist and Jesus, the history of salvation has entered its final phase." Bovon, *Luke*, 2:465.

60. Räisänen, *Jesus, Paul and Torah*, 131–32.

61. For example, compare Mark 7:1–23 with Matt 15:10–20 and note that Matthew refrains from drawing the conclusions that Mark does.

62. According to Ulrich Luz, "From the Jesus tradition [Matthew] took the idea of the distinction between God's will as creator and the law of Moses and used it in this special case to relate the pure will of the creator (or of Jesus) to an Old Testament

case, Jesus shows that certain allowances in the Torah are constrained by human hard-heartedness and in this respect, the Torah falls short of God's intentions for humanity. Jesus makes it clear that he is inaugurating something beyond the Torah capable of addressing these shortcomings without rejecting it outright. In order to avoid a contradiction, his comments on food and defilement cannot be taken as abolishing the Torah. On the other hand, while the Torah is not abolished, neither is it binding. This is consistent with Paul's argument that in Christ one is no longer under Torah.

Freedom for Paul

The boldest statement in Scripture on freedom is found in Gal 5:1: "For freedom Christ has set us free." It is the culmination of Paul's argument to this point against returning to circumcision as the way of joining the people of God. Paul returns to it again in 5:13: "For you were called to freedom." If Christ set his people free at the cost of his very life and if the purpose of this was their freedom, then freedom is inextricably linked to the heart of the Gospel. It is therefore of the utmost importance to discern what this freedom is and what it entails.

In his writings, Paul develops the notion of freedom more explicitly, and to a greater extent, than the rest of the New Testament combined. Paul takes up and expounds upon whatever notions of freedom were latent in the actions of Jesus and in the narratives of the Old Testament. His use of vocabulary associated with freedom (ἐλευθερία, ἐλεύθερος, and ἐλευθερόω) accounts for sixty-eight percent of the total occurrences of these words in the New Testament, in spite of the fact that his writings make up only a quarter of it.[63] While some might argue that Paul does not have an inherently unified sense of freedom,[64] it appears to me that he provides enough material on freedom to construct a theology of freedom that can accom-

---

Torah that openly contradicted it." Luz, *Matthew*, 2:492. I agree that Matthew makes this distinction, but it is not necessary to view this case as an open contradiction between God's will and the Torah. Craig Keener is closer to the mark when he argues, "Jesus challenges [his opponent's] actual knowledge of Scripture by showing that they are proof-texting rather than reading it in light of God's entire plan." Keener, *Matthew*, 465. Keener goes on to cite Exod 13:17 and 1 Sam 12:12–13 as examples of God allowing "what was less than ideal because people's hard hearts made the ideal unattainable" (465). In other words, a fuller knowledge of the whole of Scripture shows how the allowances in the Torah can fall short of God's intentions for humanity.

63. These statistics are based upon Peter Richardson's work. See Richardson, *Paul's Ethic*, 164.

64. See, for example, Coppins, *Interpretation of Freedom*, 162.

modate his various uses of freedom vocabulary. I organize his content as follows: first, Paul develops Jesus' connection between slavery and sin;[65] second, he expounds upon freedom from the law and upholds the law of Christ; and third, he provides examples of how freedom ought to be enacted under this constraint.

Slavery and Sin: Righteousness and Slavery

Romans 6:15–23 provides the most direct discussion of freedom and slavery in relation to sin and righteousness in Paul's writings. Paul presents his readers with an either-or proposition: either one is a slave to sin or one is a slave to righteousness. At the same time, Paul not only writes of being free from sin, but also of a former state in which his audience was free with respect to righteousness. Being a slave to one frees one from the constraints of the other. Paul does not leave the matter there, though; like Pharaoh, sin is a malevolent master whose wages are certain destruction and death. Being a slave to righteousness, which Paul conflates with being a slave to God, results in sanctification that ends in eternal life.

Earlier in the same chapter (6:1–14), Paul paradoxically links death with freedom from sin. Baptism is the means by which one is brought into the death of Christ. The death of the old self frees one from sin. The difference between this death and death as a result of sin is that the former is followed by resurrection to eternal life. Like Christ, one has died to sin and now lives to God. This, however, does not mean that a baptized believer is no longer able to sin; Paul uses an imperative to warn against becoming dominated once again by sin, implying that this is a possibility.

Freedom from the Law

Scholars are far from agreed upon Paul's teaching on the law; in fact, the quantity of material on the subject is staggering.[66] However, it is hardly possible to deal with the topic of freedom in Paul's writings without wrestling with what he says about the law. Paul uses the word "law" (νόμος) in different ways. On the one hand, he claims that he is not under the law (1

---

65. The Gospel of John was likely written after the letters of Paul. However, in the world of the text (in a canonical reading), Jesus' words with respect to slavery to sin are chronologically prior to Paul's. There is, in any case, no means of conclusively demonstrating that Paul developed this notion independently of Jesus.

66. For an introduction to scholarship on Paul's teaching on the law, see Koperski, *What Are They Saying*.

Cor 9:20), but on the other hand, he claims to be under the law of Christ (1 Cor 9:21). Those who are in Christ are no longer under the law, but under grace (Rom 6:14). In other words, Paul argues that there is a sense in which he is free from a certain law and bound to another. The law he is free from is the Torah (Gal 3:17) and the law he is under is the law of Christ. It is necessary to understand the nature of both laws in order to understand the manner in which one is constrained by each. In order to skirt aspects of the scholarly debate that do not directly concern my undertaking, I limit my discussion to a few key passages that specifically address these two laws.

In Gal 3:19–4:7, Paul directly addresses the purpose of the Torah.[67] Its first purpose was to "make wrongdoing a legal offence" (19).[68] This particular translation lines up well with Rom 3:20, 4:15 and 5:13. This phrase has also been understood along the lines of Rom 5:20 and 7:7–11: the law activates and increases sin.[69] Its second purpose is tied up in the first: "to confine all in the prison-house of sin, from which there is no exit but the way of faith."[70] Sin and the law are not identical (Rom 7:7), but they are interrelated: the law reveals sin and makes it obvious that one is enslaved to it. The law makes one painfully aware of the constraints of sin. In Rom 7:1–6, Paul makes it clear that one is set free from the law in the same way one is set free from sin: by dying to it in Christ. Christ fulfills the Torah and gives the law to which Paul considers himself bound.

To aid in understanding one's relation to the law, Paul draws an analogy between a pedagogue (παιδαγωγος)—a slave responsible for accompanying a boy to his school, carrying his books, protecting him from those who might harm him, and teaching him manners—and the Torah.[71] The coming of Christ makes this guardian superfluous. The boy has now reached puberty and is able to do what he ought. As Paul makes clear elsewhere, the Torah is not of itself an evil or antagonistic force (e.g. Rom 7:7), but it is inadequate to set one free from the power of sin (Rom 8:3). The implication of Paul's analogy is that the law served a purpose in protecting its charge from harm from internal and external forces, but now its *telos* has been attained in Christ. Paul is not refuting or rejecting the law, any more than a grown

67. Paul's use of νόμος may have an uncertain referent in other places, but here Paul is speaking about the Jewish Law. As such, I use this passage in particular as a starting point for grasping Paul's position with respect to this law.

68. See Ronald Y. K. Fung's translation and its justification in Fung, *Galatians*, 158–59.

69. See Betz, *Galatians*, 165; Fung, *Galatians*, 159.

70. Bruce, *Galatians*, 175.

71. See Betz, *Galatians*, 177–78, for discussion on the role of pedagogue in antiquity.

man in antiquity would turn his back on everything he had learned from his pedagogue. But neither would the grown man continue to live in subjection to his pedagogue. In other words, Paul is not asking the Galatians to act in a way that is in complete opposition to the Torah; in fact, the object of the Torah is fulfilled by the way Paul is exhorting the Galatians to live, just as the purpose of the pedagogue can be fulfilled by a mature man.

Paul only refers to the law of Christ twice (1 Cor 9:21 and Gal 6:2). Scholars offer several interpretations for its referent.[72] Equating it, as it occurs in Gal 6:2, with the principle of love is an attractive possibility that has many supporters.[73] Others argue that it is in fact another reference to the Torah, used polemically by Paul to maintain his argument that keeping the law is not necessary to join the kingdom of God while avoiding antinomianism.[74] The latter seems implausible in light of 1 Cor 9:20.[75] Another option is to equate the law of Christ with his teachings in the Gospel, a commonly held position among the church fathers.[76] Even if Paul has a limited meaning for the term "the law of Christ," in Gal 6:2,[77] his use of a similar term in 1 Cor 9:21 in contrast to the Torah is wide enough to encompass the new constraints under which Christians find themselves. These constraints certainly do include the principle of love, which is reinforced by Paul's own exhortations in his letters to live a godly life in opposition to sin. Moreover, the Torah continues to inform these constraints; Paul supports his instructions on compensating elders who preach and teach analogically from the law against muzzling "oxen treading out the grain" (1 Tim 5:17–18; cf. Deut 25:4). Finally, although the evidence seems to suggest that Paul did not rely on the teachings of Christ in formulating his ethics,[78] a canonical reading naturally brings these teachings into a broad understanding of "the law of Christ," understood as the set of constraints into which Christians are freed from the Torah.

---

72. For a survey of opinions on the law of Christ in Paul, see Adeyemi, *New Covenant*, 5–14.

73. F. F. Bruce, for example, asserts that, "the 'law of Christ' is not essentially different from the commandment of love to one's neighbour." Bruce, *Galatians*, 261. See also Barrett, *Freedom and Obligation*, 83.

74. Hong, *Law in Galatians*, 177.

75. See Adeyemi, "New Covenant Law," 441–42.

76. According to Graham Stanton, "The notion of Christ as the new lawgiver was all pervasive in the later tradition of the church." Stanton, "What Is the Law of Christ," 50.

77. See Hong, *Law in Galatians*, 176, for his argument against Gal 6:2 referring back to 5:14.

78. According to Frank J. Matera, "it is difficult to isolate a coherent body of Jesus' ethical teachings in Paul's writings." Matera, *Galatians*, 219–20.

Enacting Freedom Under the Law of Christ

Certain pericopes in Paul's first letter to the Corinthians and his letter to the Romans provide an opportunity to see how Paul attempts to guide the outworking of freedom in Christ by marking boundaries and delineating constraints.[79] While a few of the particular circumstances the Corinthians faced may seem foreign, many do not seem far removed from a contemporary context.

In 1 Cor 6:12–20, Paul responds to a Corinthian slogan claiming, "All things are lawful for me."[80] He does not refute it outright but instead qualifies it. All things might be lawful, but they are not all beneficial. And this freedom that the Corinthians thought they were employing was in danger of being lost to the enslavement of fornication (πορνεία).[81] Sex is not merely an appetite like hunger to be sated at will; it involves forging a sacred union between the participants. At the end of the pericope Paul reaches the governing principle of his qualifications and warnings, "For you were bought with a price; therefore glorify God in your body" (20). Paul does not attempt to take away the freedom the Corinthians are seeking to exploit; instead, he shows that it is incompatible with becoming enslaved to self-gratifying ends.

Paul responds to the same slogan in a different context in 1 Cor 10:23–33 (cf. 8:1–13). This time the emphasis is on how freedom works in the context of community. Paul urges the Corinthians to put the concerns of others ahead of their own. He affirms their freedom with respect to food because "'the earth and its fullness are the Lord's'" (26) but at the same time urges them to take into account the conscience of the other.[82] In other words, when interacting with others, their spiritual well-being ought to constrain one's own enactment of freedom. Romans 14:1–15:3 also deals with this theme, setting up a series of contrasts between those who are weak

79. The pericopes I address are certainly not the only ones that could be employed in a discussion of freedom. I have selected the pericopes that follow because they clearly and directly address the Corinthian and Roman notions of freedom that Paul is attempting to temper.

80. For a defence of interpreting this phrase as a Corinthian slogan, see Burk, "Discerning Corinthian Slogans."

81. For a provocative discussion on how πορνεία leads to enslavement, see West, "Sex and Salvation."

82. The questions in verses 29b and 30 are notoriously difficult to interpret. Duane F. Watson's rhetorical analysis yields the conclusion that Paul uses them to demonstrate "the weakness of the position of the strong." Watson, "1 Corinthians 10:23–11:1," 318. This interpretation has the advantage of fitting well into the verses immediately prior to and following them and with 8:9–13.

and those who are strong in their faith; the strong are those who understand their freedom in Christ and the weak are those who retain traditional misgivings about certain practices. Paul rebukes both sides and urges them not to judge one another, allowing the strong to eat all things freely and to see all days as the same and the weak to limit their diet and elevate certain days above others.[83] It appears that in certain cases, the strong may exercise their freedoms without fear of reproach, but they are simultaneously called upon to exercise restraint in relating to the weak to avoid causing them to stumble. By the monikers "strong" and "weak," Paul is implicitly urging the weak to grow in their faith so that they can join the strong,[84] but in the meantime, sacrificial love for the other takes precedence over exercising one's rights.

Freedom in the General Epistles

Freedom in the general epistles falls readily within the categories applied above to its treatment in Paul. I therefore address each passage according to topic rather than staying strictly to the canonical order. First, carrying on the theme of slavery to sin, Peter shows what happens to those who were once free from it and return to it. Second, James writes about the obligation that accompanies "law of liberty." Third and finally, Peter admonishes his audience to use their freedom constructively, not destructively. Freedom in the epistles is essentially a response to the misunderstanding/abuse of the freedom that Paul writes of in his letters.

Freedom from sin is approached from a decidedly negative angle in 2 Pet 2:10–22. Peter is railing against false teachers who appear to give full reign to sinful desires, promising freedom while being themselves "slaves of corruption" (19).[85] As Gene L. Green points out, "The irony of their promise is the fact that one cannot offer what one does not have."[86] In fact, they have gone so far in the opposite direction of freedom from sin that they actually have "hearts trained in greed" (14). Peter concludes that such teachers, having been freed from sin through knowing Jesus but now once

---

83. Even though Paul does not explicitly link the strong to viewing all days as the same and the weak to viewing some days as more important than others, Moo makes a convincing case for this on the grounds that the weak were likely concerned with the observance of particular days according to the Mosaic Law. See Moo, *Romans*, 841–42.

84. See Moo, *Romans*, 836.

85. While it is not pertinent to my argument, I assume Petrine authorship; I take the author at his word. As Gene L. Green observes, "The author intends that his readers will recognize this letter as an authentic work of the principal apostle, Peter." Green, *Jude and 2 Peter*, 139.

86. Green, *Jude and 2 Peter*, 299.

again entangled in it, are worse off than when they started. It is as though a virtuoso pianist took up bare-fisted boxing.

James makes two references to a "law of liberty" (1:25; 2:12) and refers to the command to "love your neighbor as yourself" as the "royal law" (2:8). His second reference to the law of liberty provides the most clues for its possible referent. James begins with the royal law, and then goes on to describe how showing partiality violates it. He then refers to the Torah, making the point that violating it at just one point makes one "accountable for all of it" (10). James Adamson loosely paraphrases James as follows, "I advise you to *choose* the law of liberty as God's law of life for you: but remember this—just as the old law (which a Christian Jew may still choose as God's law for his life) requires infallibility within its scope, so likewise there is an indispensable requirement in the law of liberty."[87] Adamson's interpretation has the advantage of being compatible with Paul's understanding of the law and sheds light on James' intent in verse 12; being judged by the law of liberty entails showing mercy since one is receiving mercy (13). James' "law of liberty" echoes the Sermon on the Mount.[88] As in the Old Testament law concerning the Sabbath, being liberated by God obliges one to pass on the effects of that liberation to others. Freedom is for the weak as well as the strong.

In 1 Pet 2:16, Peter urges his readers to "live as free people" but not to use their freedom "as a pretext to evil." This freedom belongs in the context of living at peace with the political authorities of the time (2:11–17).[89] Like Paul, Peter upholds the notion of freedom but places boundaries around it. Christian freedom is not synonymous with the political freedom advocated by the Zealots, nor with the thought of the Stoics, who attempt to master pain and pleasure alike, nor the antinomian, who lives for self-gratification (cf. 4:1–5).[90] The objective of Christian freedom is service out of love for God and others.

87. Adamson, *James*, 118. Emphasis in original.

88. After surveying possible ways of understanding "the law of liberty," Scot McKnight settles on "the Christian reinterpretation of the Torah through the Jesus Creed." McKnight, *James*, 158.

89. As Leonhard Goppelt observes, "It is not coincidental that the letter addresses the problem of freedom at the beginning of its message concerning the institutions of society and especially in view of the tense political situation." Goppelt, *I Peter*, 187.

90. Davids, *Peter*, 102.

SYNTHESIS

Scripture begins with humanity at the apex of freedom, with no de-habilitating constraints, from which it quickly falls.[91] The Exodus narrative introduces the pattern of bondage to a malevolent force and God's deliverance from it. The freedom that God gives his people is not a nihilistic abandonment of all constraints (an impossible feat in any case), nor is it merely an exchange of one tyranny for another, but rather, it is bounded by constraints that are intrinsically necessary for human flourishing. God's constraints are benevolent ones. In the ethical implications drawn from the Exodus narrative, for instance, the weak and the vulnerable are protected from being dominated by the strong. When these constraints are abandoned, the Israelites inevitably fall back into slavery.

The root of the matter is not external oppression (although this is by no means insignificant), but internal slavery to sin. The prophets begin the process of bringing this slavery to light and Jesus and his followers make it explicit. A new covenant is required, along with a new heart and the presence of God's Spirit. The incarnation of Jesus inaugurates this new covenant. Jesus links freedom with keeping his word. His fulfillment of the old law brings its strict observance to a close, but it also carries forward its intent. Paul uncovers the relationship between sin and the law and points to associating with the death and resurrection of Jesus as the only means of deliverance from both. God's deliverance continues to be linked to constraints; the law of Christ fulfills the intent of the Torah and goes beyond it.

The ethical teachings of Jesus and the writers of the New Testament serve to clarify what this looks like. One lives out of love for God and the other, going so far as to set aside freedoms for the sake of bearing with others. At the same time, one endeavors to be strong in freedom, living in the liberty Christ died to provide. James lays bare the link between living in the freedom of Christ and treating others as one has been treated by Christ. As Peter shows negatively and as Paul shows positively, adopting one set of constraints over another is a deliberate act that requires time and effort; a process of training and engraining binds one to freedom from an alternative set of constraints. Christian freedom is always linked to a purpose, a purpose for good and not for evil.

---

91. For a creative refutation of the notion that the Fall was a positive and/or necessary development, read Lewis's novels, *Out of the Silent Planet* and *Perelandra*.

CONSTRUCTING A BIBLICAL THEOLOGY OF CHRISTIAN FREEDOM

Thus far, I have traced the notion of freedom from its implicit origins at the beginning of Scripture to the rest of the canon, endeavoring to show in some measure the interrelationships between aspects of freedom in the Old Testament and the New, between Jesus, Paul, Peter, and James. What follows is my attempt to distill aspects of biblical freedom into a set of propositions. I do not intend these as a replacement for the biblical witness, but a way of bringing to light the various aspects of biblical freedom in a systematic as opposed to chronological or narrative fashion.

In sum, here are the central aspects of a biblical notion of freedom:

- Human freedom always involves adopting one set of constraints in place of another.

- Human beings must adopt constraints consistently or risk becoming bound to other constraints; therefore, freedom can be lost.

- God's constraints lead to human flourishing; all alternatives lead to bondage to a malevolent force.

- God does not coerce his creatures into doing his will; in order to do his will, they must choose it freely.

- In Christ, Christians are free from sin but are bound to the law of Christ.

- In Christ, Christians are free with respect to the Torah, but are bound to the law of Christ, which fulfills, and is consistent with, the ultimate intent of the Torah.

- Associating with Christ's death and resurrection is the only means of becoming free from sin and the law.

- The constraints of the law of Christ involve acting out of love for God and for others.

- God is concerned primarily with freeing people from their sin, but he is also concerned with their political, social, and physical freedom.

CONCLUSION

Freedom as it is portrayed in Scripture stands in contrast to contemporary understandings of freedom as something characterized primarily by self-determination and the rejection of all sources of authority. Scripture reveals that, in the absence of divine constraint, one is inevitably enslaved by one's own impulses and by the oppression of the strong. The freedom that Christ gives is precious because of the price he paid for it; it is something to be valued, defended, taught, and upheld. Moreover, it is something to be practiced; apathy inevitably leads to its loss.

The constraints given by God are the most conducive way of approaching the points of contact between a biblical conception of freedom and jazz. Moreover, a "strong" sense of freedom, such as Paul was implicitly urging the church in Rome to adopt, leads in the direction of Eden, back towards the zenith of human freedom. Only lives lived out of love for God and others that are free from sin and rigid obedience to the Torah can bring together the people of God to create beauty beyond what each can achieve alone.

4

Jazz Improvisation

An Enactment of Freedom

CONSTRAINTS PROVIDE LIBERATION FROM other constraints. Christian freedom in particular liberates Christians from the constraints of sin (in its individual and corporate manifestations) and the law into the constraints of love and righteousness (the law of Christ). Learning to live out Christian freedom in relation to these constraints requires working out the latent implications of Scripture in a contemporary context. This process of working out these implications finds parallels in the way jazz improvisers creatively navigate their own various musical, personal, and environmental constraints. In fact, this process is the essence of freedom in jazz. According to John Litweiler, "The quest for freedom . . . appears at the very beginning of jazz and reappears at every growing point in the music's history."[1] And as Jeremy Begbie observes, "Improvisation provides a powerful enactment of the truth that our freedom is enabled to flourish only by engaging with and negotiating constraints."[2] Examining the philosophy, mechanics, and social aspects of jazz improvisation provides a model of how to engage in this negotiation. The approaches that jazz improvisers use in exploiting and transcending constraints are used to suggest analogous approaches to Christian freedom in a contemporary setting. But first, it is necessary to understand what jazz improvisation is and how it works.

"Improvisation" is nearly as difficult a term as "freedom." As Jeff Warren notes, "Improvisation always includes excess to that which is given,"

1. Litweiler, *Freedom Principle*, 13.
2. Begbie, *Theology, Music and Time*, 199.

making the notion of defining it (delimiting or boxing it in) inherently problematic.[3] Furthermore, a Western approach to music that divides music production into composition and performance creates additional problems.[4] On the one hand, jazz improvisation does not appear to qualify as a performance in that it does not seek to reproduce something that already exists. The point is not to execute the directions of the composer carefully in every detail but rather to play something new, or at least to fashion something unique out of available materials. On the other hand, jazz improvisation does not appear to be composition in the Western tradition because it lacks its fully premeditated character. And while jazz certainly appears to some as an act of *creatio ex nihilo*—creation out of nothing—the reality is far more complex.[5] According to Bruce Ellis Benson, composition and performance—in fact, all aspects of music-making—are actually improvisatory acts. While improvisation is not an act of *creatio ex nihilo*, neither is composition. Neither is performance simply a matter of reproducing precisely what a composer writes; a certain amount of interpretation is inevitably involved. Improvisation exists on a spectrum from minimal interpretation to playing with the form and even the tradition of a given piece.[6] Jazz improvisation occupies the liminal space between composition and performance. It creatively engages with multiple constraints, such as the jazz tradition, fellow improvisers, etc., to make music in the moment with materials found in the past and the present. Yet my attempt at a definition requires expansion and explanation. The following fictional and somewhat idealized account of playing trombone at a wedding gig based on my experiences (conscious and unconscious) shows the integrated process of jazz improvisation. Following that account, I break it down into its various components.[7]

Our trio is on the final stretch of the gig at the reception. The guests are socializing. My lips are a little tired, but not too sore to play. Next in our set list is "Somewhere Over the Rainbow." I expect most people at the reception will recognize the song, which will give them something to hum along to (in contrast to the earlier Wayne Shorter tune). We begin just as we had practiced, with the verse. I mouth the count off while nodding my head

3. Warren, *Music and Ethical Responsibility*, 103.

4. Benson, *Improvisation of Musical Dialogue*, 24.

5. See Benson, *Improvisation of Musical Dialogue*, 24, and Berliner, *Thinking in Jazz*, 1–2.

6. Benson, *Improvisation of Musical Dialogue*, 39–46.

7. This approach is inspired by Warren's description of playing a corporate gig to show improvisation from the inside. See Warren, *Music and Ethical Responsibility*, 104–7.

to indicate the tempo. As I play the melody, I stretch, contract, and displace the written rhythms, counting on the rhythm section to maintain the pulse and perhaps to accentuate what I am doing rhythmically. The drummer has a very light touch. Not bound to merely keeping time, he uses his cymbals to color in my long notes and to accentuate and create crescendos and decrescendos. The bass player grounds the beat, clearly setting up the chord changes. The melody elicits some response from bystanders; one at least is humming along by the time we reach the chorus. I can stretch the melody and adorn it, but it still must be recognizable in order for our listeners to enjoy it. When the chorus is over, I jettison the melody in favor of playing off the chord progression. Liberated from the former, I am now free to explore what the latter offers. I draw from years of engraining chords, scales, and musical phrases to built tension and release it, reveling in the satisfying way my line outlines the chord progression. I switch to a double-time feel, playing sixteenth notes instead of the traditional eighth notes that make up the basic pulse of the bebop idiom. The drummer catches it, but the bass player stays in the same groove, which helps to build a sense of anticipation. When the bass player finally doubles up, I try to match the sense of excitement by moving into the upper register of my instrument. Unfortunately, my lips are no longer up to the task. The aborted note comes and goes in the blink of an eye and I try to leave it behind me, though my own recognition of my mistake causes me to fumble a few times before concluding my solo. Finishing, I step aside to listen to the bass solo.

CONSTRAINTS AND CONTRADICTIONS

My own subjective experience of playing trombone is one instantiation of jazz improvisation. It exemplifies how my own abilities, limitations, and mistakes, as well as the external factors of environment and my band mates all play a role in making music. These factors rightfully belong together as a whole, but each can be examined in turn. In *Theology, Music and Time*, Jeremy Begbie provides a useful taxonomy of constraints that improvisers engage with when they make music. Paul Rinzler provides a way to navigate these constraints. In *The Contradictions of Jazz*, he discusses how improvisers navigate four pairs of values that function like constraints and appear to be self-contradictory. Begbie's taxonomy provides a basic structure to my endeavor and Rinzler's methodology shows how to navigate the constraints within that taxonomy.

Finally, risk and mistakes play a significant role in jazz. I define mistakes as the unintentional transgression of an adopted norm, and risk as the necessary precursor to it. Risk is an inherent aspect of navigating the constraints listed below. Risk and mistakes could perhaps be described under the constraint of being embodied, but in practice, they intersect with all of the constraints listed below. In short, they warrant a discussion of their own.

Begbie's Taxonomy of Constraints

Begbie, borrowing from John Webster, asserts that constraint is not about being boxed in or confined but rather about "specificity" and "particular shape."[8] Constraints are something to push against. Without them movement is impossible.[9] Reacting to the notion that freedom requires no limits on "self-determination, self-constitution and self-expression," Begbie reasons, "if there were unlimited degrees of self determination we could not advance beyond chaos."[10]

Improvisation involves multiple constraints that cannot be exhaustively catalogued, but Begbie provides "three broad and overlapping types: 'occasional', 'cultural' and 'continuous.'"[11] Occasional constraints are further broken down into physical space, other improvisers, and the disposition of the improviser in question.[12] To these constraints, I add that of the audience, which tends to play a more active role in jazz than in some musical traditions. Paul F. Berliner's chapter, "Vibes and Venues: Interacting with Different Audiences in Different Settings," provides a rich resource culled from multiple sources that explores the implications of spaces and audiences for jazz improvisation.[13] Other improvisers present a dynamic constraint that typically exerts a more direct impact on what a musician plays in a given moment. Interaction between musicians is a central concern in Rinzler's work, providing an opportunity to expand on Begbie's listed constraint of other improvisers at greater length (see below). Begbie's next type, cultural constraints, encompasses what he sees as central factors in traditional jazz: meter, harmony, and melody. These are shaped by a given idiom, for instance: bebop, swing, or Dixieland.[14] The overarching constraint here is tradition—a way of doing things rooted in the past. Once again, Rinzler provides a helpful way of approaching the topic, especially in

8. Begbie, *Theology, Music and Time*, 198.

9. See Stravinsky, *Poetics of Music*, 87.

10. Begbie, *Theology, Music and Time*, 198.

11. Begbie, *Theology, Music and Time*, 200.

12. Begbie, *Theology, Music and Time*, 205.

13. Berliner, *Thinking in Jazz*, 449–84.

14. Begbie, *Theology, Music and Time*, 208.

his chapter, "Creativity and Tradition." Within tradition, I am also interested in the relationship between composers and improvisers, and recordings and jazz theory. I also include certain social factors that play into the history of jazz because they shape the tradition (and therefore cultural constraints) in significant ways and that they offer more points of contact between jazz and Christian freedom. Begbie's final type, continuous constraints, includes embodiment and sonic order.[15]

In addition to Begbie's categories of constraints, I add the category of "transcendental constraints." This category of constraints overlays the categories in Begbie's taxonomy rather than simply adding to it. Two constraints in particular operate within his taxonomy, but also stand out in a certain way. Hal Crook's understanding of the "*It*" factor is both an occasional constraint because it changes in relation to the improviser and a transcendental constraint because of its elusive, hard-to-define nature in relation to the more concrete constraints of venues and other musicians. Similarly, the intentions of a jazz composer are certainly closely tied to cultural constraints, but they also exercise a certain priority over tradition; tradition can be appropriated and/or discarded, but the constraints of a song must be operative in order for the song to be recognizable.

Rinzler on Contradiction

The Contradictions of Jazz is built around eight values that are grouped into four internally-opposing pairs: "individualism and interconnectedness"; "assertion and openness"; "freedom and responsibility"; and "creativity and tradition."[16] Rinzler develops each value separately and then discusses how the paired values interact with one another. Ideally all four come together in interaction between musicians, so that the "musicians have the opportunity to take advantage of the *freedom* that interaction offers and *assert* themselves as *individuals* to produce a new, *creative* musical idea, while remaining *open* to another's idea and responding to it by supporting it in a *responsible* manner, thereby creating a unified group sound and conception that *interconnects* everyone in the group."[17]

15. Begbie, *Theology, Music and Time*, 224.

16. Rinzler, *Contradictions of Jazz*, xiv. While Rinzler uses "freedom" as a value opposite to "responsibility," I am interested in freedom in a broader sense that is in fact operative in each of his pairs of values.

17. Rinzler, *Contradictions of Jazz*, 102. Emphasis in original. Rinzler is certainly not the first to realize the apparent contradictions in playing jazz. Ralph Ellison observes

Rinzler is, in essence, discussing how to navigate constraints. In addition to providing an expansion and extension of the constraints that Begbie lists, he provides a way of showing how they function, even when—especially when—they contradict. His approach can be appropriated to engage with constraints that he does not directly address.

Rinzler offers seven ways in which opposites can interact:

- mutual exclusion (one negates the other)

- perspective (different sides of an object or a situation)

- inverse proportion (a zero-sum game)

- gradation (a gradual blend)

- propagation (an offspring from parents)

- juxtaposition (two opposites side by side)

- dynamic tension (opposites fully present but clashing)[18]

These alternatives aid in understanding how jazz musicians navigate the constraints inherent in the music.

Rinzler's approach to dealing with the contradictory values present in jazz improvisation is not an easily packaged way of enacting freedom. In fact, a perusal of Berliner's chapter, "The Lives of Bands: Conflict Resolution and Artistic Development," reveals that jazz musicians deal with struggles that bear a strong resemblance to those that occur in the church.[19] Both the solutions to these difficulties and the failure to resolve them in a jazz context provide a mirror for the freedom of a Christian in relation to the church in chapter 5.

---

a cruel contradiction implicit in the art form itself, for true jazz is an art of individual assertion within and against the group. Each true jazz moment (as distinct from the uninspired commercial performance) springs from a contest in which each artist challenges all the rest; each solo flight, or improvisation, represents (like the successive canvases of a painter) a definition of his identity as individual, as member of the collectivity and as a link in the chain of tradition. Thus, because jazz finds its very life in an endless improvisation upon traditional materials, the jazzman must lose his identity even as he finds it.

Ellison, *Living with Music*, 36.

18. Rinzler, *Contradictions of Jazz*, xiv.

19. Berliner, *Thinking in Jazz*, 416–46.

OCCASIONAL CONSTRAINTS

Occasional constraints are constraints that change in relation to the improviser. For instance, a given space might remain constant, but the improviser
will perform in different spaces, requiring her to navigate the specific constraints of each.[20] When constraints take the form of other active agents,
such as an audience or fellow musicians, improvisers are caught up in reciprocal relationships with them. The unpredictable nature of these encounters
highlights the tension between Rinzler's pairs of values such as individualism and interconnectedness, and assertion and openness. Navigating these
constraints is a significant aspect of what it means for an improviser to act
freely.

Spaces and Audiences

A venue and an audience provide a set of constraints quite different in nature
from a practice room. In addition to potentially influencing the internal disposition of a jazz improviser, they can influence a number of variables from
song selection to dynamics (the contrast between loud and soft playing)
and even solo duration and content. The acoustics in certain rooms can be
exploited in certain circumstances but can also be detrimental in others.[21]
In a less tangible way, a concert hall provides a different social feel from a
club. Audience expectations and participation are often tied to the type of
venue in question and to the values held by management.[22]

Berliner observes that, "Performing on different parts of the stage and
projecting sounds in different directions alter pitch colors and patterns of
attack and decay."[23] One striking example of taking advantage of acoustics
is flutist Paul Horn's solo album recorded in the Taj Mahal.[24] The extended
decay of his notes allows him to create chords on what is typically a single-
note instrument. In a sense, the space the improviser plays into becomes
an extension of their instrument, its limitations providing otherwise un-
imagined opportunities. The acoustics of a room can also be detrimental
to musical performances, preventing musicians from hearing one another.
Extended decay can work against certain song choices, muddying intricate

20. Because I find using both gendered pronouns cumbersome, I alternate between these pronouns throughout.

21. Berliner, *Thinking in Jazz*, 450.

22. Berliner, *Thinking in Jazz*, 452.

23. Berliner, *Thinking in Jazz*, 450.

24. Horn, *Inside the Taj Mahal*.

passages. In such cases, improvisers must respect the challenges posed by a given space and position themselves to compensate for them.

Acoustics aside, certain spaces provide challenges and opportunities for improvisers in terms of the cultural and social expectations they implicitly hold for audiences. Concert halls create certain expectations. The start and end of the performance ought to be punctual, instruments ought to be in tune, and sound equipment ought to be operated by experienced professionals. At times large venues also create distance between the audience and the musicians.[25] In a smaller setting such as a club, the audience can spur on the performers. Knowledgeable audiences are aware of certain conventions rooted "in the African American cultural experience" comparable to "a church congregation's testimonial responses to an inspired sermon."[26] They know when to clap or even respond vocally to the music. At times audiences can create obstacles as well. One night at the Village Vanguard (a small but famous jazz club), trumpeter Wynton Marsalis was about to conclude an unaccompanied version of "I Don't Stand a Ghost of a Chance with You" when "someone's cell phone went off, blaring a rapid singsong melody in electronic bleeps."[27] David Hajdu describes what happened next:

> People started giggling and picking up their drinks. The moment—the whole performance—unraveled.
> Marsalis paused for a beat, motionless, and his eyebrows arched. I scrawled on a sheet of notepaper, MAGIC, RUINED. The cell-phone offender scooted into the hall as the chatter in the room grew louder. Still frozen at the microphone, Marsalis replayed the silly cell-phone melody note for note. Then he repeated it, and began improvising variations on the tune. The audience slowly came back to him. In a few minutes he resolved the improvisation—which had changed keys once or twice and throttled down to a ballad tempo—and ended up exactly where he had left off: "with . . . you . . ." The ovation was tremendous.[28]

Audience participation, even when unintentional, can shape the course of jazz improvisation.

25. At an outdoor concert in New York, saxophonist Sonny Rollins felt the need to get closer to his audience. He jumped five or six feet down the side of the stage (the stage and amphitheatre were made of stone). He fractured his heel, but kept on playing. Crow, *Jazz Anecdotes*, 19.

26. Berliner, *Thinking in Jazz*, 456.

27. Hajdu, "Wynton's Blues."

28. Hajdu, "Wynton's Blues." I should note that in spite of the critical outlook that I adopt to Marsalis' leadership in contemporary jazz in chapter 1, he remains an undeniably accomplished musician and performer. Cf. Gelinas, *Finding the Groove*, 34.

Community: The Constraint of Others

Historically, jazz bands usually take the form of a "big band," a group of sixteen or more musicians playing notated arrangements, or "combos," a group with fewer members that typically focuses more on improvisation than notated arrangements. Since I am here concerned with the interaction that occurs in improvised music between musicians, I focus on the combo. Combos typically include a rhythm section (percussion, bass, and a chording instrument such as a piano or guitar) and one or two horns (wind instruments, such as trumpet, saxophone, or trombone). They effectively demonstrate freedom in relation to roles, soloing, and conversing.

A traditional norm in jazz combos is that each musician is given an opportunity to solo, causing other musicians to change their accompaniment style to accommodate the instrument that is playing, or even dropping out altogether for the duration of the solo.[29] Such accommodation uses a strategy of inverse proportion to deal with the conflict between assertion and openness. Yet even though a musician may be functioning in a supportive role, they still may on occasion be assertive in their accompaniment. Robert Hodson provides the example of pianist Wynton Kelly influencing the direction of saxophonist Cannonball Adderley's improvised solo. After Adderley completes a phrase deriving from the bebop idiom, Kelly "punctuates" Adderley's phrase with a chord that contains blue notes that clash with the conventional notes in the chord.[30] Adderley responds to this by playing a line based off the Eb blues scale, even though this scale clashes with the Eb major chord in the tune being played. In this way, Kelly is assertive and Adderley is open, even though the solo belongs to Adderley. In other words, even though Adderley is in a leadership position with respect to the shape of his solo, he is open to the suggestions of his fellow musicians. Kelly naturally reciprocates, adopting a two-note motive introduced by Adderley into his accompaniment. For Adderley and Kelly, leadership does not necessitate a unidirectional movement of influence.

Seen again through the lens of Rinzler's pairing of individuality and interconnectedness, this musical exchange of ideas can serve to lift a solo beyond the original conception of the soloist. Later on in his book, *Interaction*,

29. While there is certainly a degree of overlap between switching roles and the practice of soloing, I distinguish between them because roles are often in effect for the statement of the melody and the solo section, and only shift to accommodate a member of the rhythm section who is taking a solo. I wish to distinguish between the freedom to play different roles and the practice of speaking and listening.

30. Kelly combines a Bb13 (Bb, D, Ab, G) with the "blue notes" Db and Gb. The D (the 3rd) clashes with the Db (the #9) and the G (the 13th) clashes with Gb (the b13). Hodson, *Interaction*, 7. Hodson notates Kelly's voicing on page 8.

Improvisation, and Interplay in Jazz, Hodson documents other examples of the way soloists and accompanists interact with one another to achieve musical goals. For instance, he shows how saxophonist Wayne Shorter and pianist Herbie Hancock collaborate to achieve a "metric superimposition" in relation to the "basic metric structure of the tune" (i.e., playing an idea in 3/4 time over 4/4 time).[31] In this case, propagation (the creation of something new) resolves the problem of individualism and interconnectedness; the soloist asserts their individuality, but in connection with the rest of the ensemble, their expression is enhanced and developed.

This dynamic interplay of assertion and openness, and individuality and interconnectedness, is not solely a conscious effort on the part of the improviser. Otherwise, "one's inner assertions must alternate with conscious attention to one's outer environment."[32] If the unconscious plays a role in being receptive to new ideas or creating them, then, in tandem with the conscious mind, these things may occur simultaneously, providing an example of dynamic tension as yet another way of resolving the contradiction between assertion and openness.[33] In other words, jazz shows that freely navigating the constraint of others entails the whole person, not just a conscious effort of the will. This connection with others takes time to cultivate; it requires conscious listening and awareness in order to make listening to others second nature.

At times, creating space for the other involves a more deliberate approach that entails inverse proportion to the point of mutual exclusion. Some instruments stop playing altogether to create space for others to be heard. This silence is not merely the practice of restraint; it also creates the opportunity to listen. It is precisely in this encounter that one is presented with fresh options for improvisation. This often happens in bass solos; melodic and harmonic instruments stop playing and the drummer plays less to allow the softer sound of the bass to be clearly heard. Another example of this is the practice of "trading fours" among musicians at a jam session, usually after the soloists have finished improvising through the chord progression of the piece being played. Players interact with one another in four-bar segments—this works best when their statements interact, much like in a good conversation or debate.

There is another sense in which a soloist is set against the rest of the band, "a contest in which each artist challenges all the rest."[34] If this oper-

31. Hodson, *Interaction*, 113.

32. Rinzler, *Contradictions of Jazz*, 111.

33. Rinzler, *Contradictions of Jazz*, 112.

34. Ellison, *Living with Music*, 36.

ates in a positive fashion, each participant is spurred on by their peers to do greater things. A prophetic voice can shake up a performance, lifting it above the familiar and the tried-and-true. Of course, it can also be used to intimidate and discourage others, turning the music into an expression of battling egos. The line between challenging others to do better on the one hand and attempting to assert superiority on the other is a hazy one. Some musicians relish the latter, but others are more concerned with something transcending the ego in their playing.

The "It" Factor: The Disposition of the Improviser in Relation to the Unknown

Hal Crook's introduction to the basics of jazz improvisation provides an "unscientific" view of the ego and how it relates to "*It*," a pronoun that plays the music once the ego is out of the way. For Crook, the ego plays a role in the early development of an individual and then becomes superfluous with respect to improvisation, but still active. The ego latches on to the rational analysis of a jazz musician's solo, causing them to feel superior when they play well and inferior when they don't. These emotions link the self of the jazz musician to their improvisatory skills. The jazz musician feels possessive of her solos, which in turn inspires competition, "which has questionable value at best for learning how to improvise, and nothing whatsoever to do with improvising, per se."[35] The ego demands to be responsible for whatever happens, good or bad. Thus, the jazz musician feels inferior when he does not achieve the musical results he was striving for, regardless of the merits of his work. Feeling superior at some moments is unavoidably tied to feeling inferior at others. According to Crook, one should aim to enjoy the process of attempting a good solo, even if it turns out poorly. One must let go of being bound to self. Yet if the "ego is not actually that which improvises the solo but that which interferes with and judges it, who—or what—then, does play it?"[36] His answer is worth quoting at length:

> Now, this may sound a little non-scientific at first, but I would say, quite seriously and for lack of a better term, that *It*—yes, *It*—plays the solo; and that *It* plays the solo *through* us, using our musical resources, i.e., our instrumental technique, musicianship, experience, understanding, etc. And, to the degree that *It* can play through us freely and without our ego's interference, to that degree is *It* the author and creator of the solo; to that

35. Crook, *Ready, Aim, Improvise!*, 313.
36. Crook, *Ready, Aim, Improvise!*, 315.

degree is *It* responsible for the results of the playing. Therefore, we cannot take the credit—or the blame!—when *It* plays. All we can ever do is take responsibility for continually preparing ourselves through practice and experience to become more fit vehicles for *Its* use.[37]

The mysterious nature of this *It* makes it a transcendental constraint as well as an occasional one; something indescribable takes over in the process of making music. Crook is not alone in his experience of the "*It*" factor; jazz trombonist Bob Brookmeyer describes something similar: "So, if it comes from somewhere, that means we are 'receivers' of music. The music god is out there saying, 'O.K., I think I'll visit Grantham today, and see what Brookmeyer's doing.'"[38] Granting that this is the case, Brookmeyer concludes that in order to be a fit vehicle for the music, "we have to keep our receivers in good working order," mirroring Crook's comments about being responsible for musical resources but not being the source per se of the music.[39]

Crook and Brookmeyer provide insight into one of Begbie's listed cultural constraints: the disposition of the improviser. This disposition is connected to the constraint of others; how should they be treated on the spectrum between collaborators and competitors? Jazz has a history of "cutting sessions"—jam sessions designed as competitions to determine who demonstrated the most prowess on their instrument on a given night. Many accomplished jazz performers are undoubtedly strongly connected to their egos. Yet for many improvisers in the tradition there is an apparent need to be liberated from the self in playing music, a need to be attuned to something outside of themselves. Ralph Ellison writes that "the jazzman [*sic*] must lose his identity even as he finds it."[40] Here the strategy is not to find a way to resolve a contradiction, but to be liberated from a constraint that gets in the way of improvisation.

---

37. Crook, *Ready, Aim, Improvise!*, 315.

38. From an interview with Bob Brookmeyer in Hudson, *Evolution*, xii.

39. Dana Reason argues the opposite, asserting that "you [the performer] are held responsible for a perceived failure or triumph—by you and by the audience" and that "it is not possible to claim that the music was not yours to begin with." Reason, "Navigable Structures," 77. It is possible that Crook and Brookmeyer simply present a more nuanced position; they acknowledge personal responsibility in terms of developing and maintaining musical resources but also acknowledge some sort of external agency when they improvise. It seems to me that personal responsibility is a factor, but claiming total ownership of the music—especially in light of the multiple constraints at work in improvisation—is problematic.

40. Ellison, *Living with Music*, 36.

CULTURAL CONSTRAINTS

Cultural constraints are essentially about tradition. Both Rinzler and Begbie provide apt analyses of the tension between tradition and creativity in jazz. Rinzler takes the contradiction on directly while Begbie analyzes the relationship between the two in terms of the emergence of bebop. Following a summary and analysis of their work, I consider particular constraints that fall under the umbrella of the jazz tradition.

Rinzler on "Creativity and Tradition"

Cultural constraints are bound up with tradition. Navigating them entails negotiating the contradiction between them and innovation. Engaging with Rinzler's chapter, "Creativity and Tradition," is a good way to set the stage before moving into discussions that are more particular. Rinzler highlights the contradiction in his chapter with a pair of quotations from a 1954 article by William Bruce Cameron. The second will suffice for my purposes: "The jazz esthetic is basically a paradox, tragic in that it is ultimately unrealizable. The comprehensibility of traditionalism and radical originality are irreconcilable."[41] This opening quotation, along with Eric Nisenson's book, *Blue: The Murder of Jazz*, provide Rinzler with a foil for his attempts to show how this contradiction can be brokered without resorting to mutual exclusion. Nisenson makes a few rash remarks about the place of tradition in jazz. For example: "The whole problem with this concept of the jazz 'tradition' is that the truth is, the only real tradition in jazz has been no tradition at all, or rather, the tradition of individual expression and constant change and growth,"[42] and "jazz is a form of art that is a blank slate the artist fills in out of the grist of his or her own life and experience."[43] On the other side of the spectrum are those who define jazz according to a narrow set of parameters.[44]

Rinzler sets about resolving this contradiction by first distinguishing stimulus freedom from stimulus-bound freedom. Stimulus freedom is being able to think outside of what is immediately apparent—"thinking outside the box." Stimulus-bound freedom is creativity within what is given,

41. Cameron, "Sociological Notes," 181. Quoted in Rinzler, *Contradictions of Jazz*, 124.

42. Nisenson, *Blue*, 16.

43. Nisenson, *Blue*, 47. Quoted in Rinzler, *Contradictions of Jazz*, 131.

44. See Nisenson, *Blue*, 15–16, for a pointed critique of the major players that hold this position. For a more balanced perspective on defining jazz, see Gridley, Maxham, and Hoff, "Three Approaches."

constructing something from designated materials. He then provides a taxonomy of how tradition and creativity can interact in jazz. The first type is conservative jazz that is squarely within the tradition and deemphasizes creativity. The second involves saying something new, but still within the boundaries of tradition. This approach is exemplified by the so-called "young lions" of the 1990s. In this type, "Tradition and creativity are juxtaposed in the sense that they are both present but coexist without any significant conflict."[45] The third type begins to break down "some of the fundamentals of the tradition" without completely abandoning it.[46] Rinzler frames it in terms of asking new questions as opposed to giving new answers to old ones. Here, tradition and creativity stand in dynamic tension with one another. He sees Miles Davis' quintet in the 1960s as exemplifying this approach. The fourth and final type stretches the very definition of jazz to the breaking point, as he uses Ornette Coleman's *Free Jazz* and Albert Ayler's *Bells—Prophecy* to demonstrate.[47]

Begbie on Tradition

In his chapter "Liberating Constraint," Begbie approaches the problem of tradition and creativity through an examination of how compositions that served as vehicles for jazz improvisation evolved historically. Bebop musicians in particular reshaped the tunes they used as vehicles for improvisation while remaining faithful to the harmonic structure of a given piece of music. After surveying the process of how bebop developed innovations over older forms, Begbie analyzes the relationship between tradition and the act of improvisation and considers the implications of this for the future. He suggests that, "In improvisation, *cultural constraints are particularized in relation to occasional constraints.*"[48] In other words, tradition moves from the past to the present when an improviser brings tradition into contact with constraints such as space, other improvisers, and the musician's own disposition. The improviser mediates between tradition and their contemporary situation.

Begbie also points out that tradition can engage in a negative zerosum game with freedom when it calcifies in a form that is universal and normative. In order to distinguish between negative and positive forms of tradition he makes a distinction "between tradition as process and tradition

45. Rinzler, *Contradictions of Jazz*, 128.
46. Rinzler, *Contradictions of Jazz*, 128.
47. Coleman, *Free Jazz*; Ayler, *Bells/Prophecy*.
48. Begbie, *Theology, Music and Time*, 215. Emphasis in original.

as the results ('deposits') of the process."[49] Jazz in the twenty-first century is struggling with how to relate to its tradition. In an essay that compares albums by trumpeter Wynton Marsalis and guitarist Bill Frisell respectively, David Ake is critical of Marsalis' attempts to situate himself in the jazz tradition.[50] Ake argues that Marsalis and his supporters actually reconstruct the jazz tradition in a way that ignores the contextualized nature of the music. For instance, in the liner notes to Marsalis' album, *Standard Time*, jazz critic Stanley Crouch entirely ignores the Tin Pan Alley roots of the songs on the album, choosing only to mention them in relation to famous jazz interpreters. By contrast, Bill Frisell's album pulls from American composers in the classical and contemporary pop traditions. Frisell even eschews the classic jazz combo that Marsalis prefers in favor of a more eclectic instrumentation that includes accordion. To treat them typologically (which appears to be Ake's intent), Marsalis represents the tendency towards attempts to formulate universal, normative versions of jazz, while Frisell's album serves as a reminder that jazz historically has borrowed liberally from contemporary sources.

Back to the Combo: Subverting Expectations

Traditionally, each instrument in a jazz combo has specific roles to play. For instance, the drums and the bass mark the time and the bass, in a second role, and the harmonic instrument (usually piano or guitar—but accordion could do) mark the chord progression while the horns play the melody. Each instrument is uniquely suited to its roles; the range of the bass is better suited for sounding the roots of the chords in the chord progression than the trumpet, just as the trumpet is better suited to clearly playing the melody than the drums. The nature of each instrument is in fact a type of continuous constraint (see below). Of course, one can modify to some extent the nature of an instrument—take Dizzy Gillespie's famous trumpet with the bell bent at a forty-five degree angle for instance—but such modifications can only be taken so far before a given instrument becomes an entirely different instrument. It's only natural that tradition and the nature of each instrument reinforce one another. Diverse instruments with different roles and accompanying traditions provide a shape that enables musicians who are strangers to each other to perform together.

These traditional roles create expectations that can be transgressed; they can be swapped and traded in any number of different permutations.

49. Begbie, *Theology, Music and Time*, 216.
50. Ake, *Jazz Cultures*, 146–76.

For example, trumpeter Tom Harrell's composition "Manhattan, 3 A.M." opens with the bass playing higher than the trumpet and the saxophone.[51] This unexpected change makes this piece stand out from others, drawing attention to what the bass—which usually functions in a supportive role—is doing. Such reversals are not permanent or normative, but reside as colors to be employed at the aesthetically appropriate moment. Tradition creates the boundary that makes the transgression possible.

Improvisation, Composers, and Their Compositions

The intentions of a composer are simultaneously closely related to tradition and at the same time operate on a higher level than tradition; the composition being performed is interpreted in relation to tradition, but it is the composition rather than the tradition that gives the performance its particular form.[52] These intentions therefore act as a transcendental constraint as well as cultural constraint. Benson's discussion of composition and performance provides a starting point for discussing the relation of the jazz improviser to the work that is being improvised upon. Even in the classical tradition, "A score is itself limited in terms of defining the limits of the musical work. What this means in practice is that a musical work can be interpreted (which is to say 'instantiated' or 'embodied') in various ways, none of which necessarily have any priority over the others."[53] In other words, the score does not and cannot contain directions for every aspect of a performance. But what of the intention of the composer? Is there any relationship between their intention and the performer/improviser or does the separate existence of the score make such concerns irrelevant? As Benson points out, composers have historically had conflicting views on how their pieces should be performed. Twentieth-century composer Igor Stravinsky, for instance, was so caught up in controlling all aspects of the performance of his pieces that he "felt the need to record his pieces (*ad nauseam*) in order to demonstrate to the musical world exactly how they were to be performed."[54] Popular tune

---

51. Harrell, *Live at the Village*.

52. In a musical context, tradition undoubtedly shapes the form and conventions used by the composer. Yet tradition cannot itself compose; a composition requires personal agency. Even software that "composes" music must be programmed.

53. Benson, *Improvisation of Musical Dialogue*, 82.

54. Benson, *Improvisation of Musical Dialogue*, 95. Italics in original. For a more in-depth look at Stravinsky's well-known concern for the performance of his scores and his antagonism toward performers taking liberties with written music, including a synopsis of one of his lectures on the topic, see Joseph, *Stravinsky*, 211–20.

writer George Gershwin, on the other hand, delighted in how pianist Art Tatum improvised on his compositions.[55]

Randall Dipert helpfully divides a composer's intent into three levels: 1) low-level intentions involve such things as instrumentation and instrumental technique; 2) middle-level intentions "concern the intended *sound*, such as temperament, timbre, attack, pitch, and vibrato;" and 3) high-level intentions "are the effects that the composer intends to produce in the listener."[56] He points out that attempting to be true to the low- and middle-level intentions of a composer may at times thwart the high-level intentions of the composer. For instance, when the clarinet was an instrument unfamiliar to an audience, its unfamiliar timbre could be used to draw their attention to a certain musical line. A composer who scored a piece of music with the intention of using the clarinet for its exotic qualities leaves an irreconcilable conflict for contemporary performers. Since contemporary audiences are now quite familiar with the clarinet, how will performers reconcile the composer's low-level intentions (the use of the clarinet) and her high-level intentions (drawing attention to the musical line)?[57] High-level intentions are more difficult to discern than middle and low-level intentions, but the composer's desired effect on the audience is arguably more important than attempting to preserve antiquated means.

Analogously, jazz musicians can conceivably bend or ignore altogether the low- and mid-level intentions of a composer while evoking their high-level intentions (at least in the case of a composer such as Gershwin). They can also go beyond the composer's intentions, translating the composer's work into unforeseen forms and contexts. In traditional jazz improvisation, the harmonic structure or chord progression of a given piece grounds the improviser's melodic improvisations. This structure can be negotiated through elaboration, simplification, or spontaneous reharmonization, but it must have points of contact with key resolutions in order to be recognizable.[58] A composer in the jazz tradition has intentions that can only be realized through improvisation; a performer who desires to respect those intentions will still produce something recognizable, but they will also bring their own voice to the composition. The question of fidelity to a composer's

55. Oscar Levant gives an account of Tatum impressing Gershwin with his improvisation on Gershwin's song "Liza" in Levant, *Smattering*, 196.

56. Dipert, "Composer's Intentions," 206–7.

57. Dipert, "Composer's Intentions," 210.

58. For instance, playing a "bird blues"—named after a progression used by jazz saxophonist Charlie Parker—involves inserting a cycle of ii V7s in front of the IV chord in a basic blues form. For a practical look at the various ways jazz musicians can elaborate and reharmonize a standard, see Levine, *Jazz Theory*, 257–380.

intentions in jazz improvisation either is a non-sequitur or relies on the openness of the composer to being a co-creator of the performed music.

Text and Theory

Recordings are the texts of jazz.[59] The recordings produced by jazz musicians serve a similar purpose to a text published by an author. Each is a means of communicating with an audience, but with a significant difference. As Kenneth E. Prouty writes, "The recording serves as a medium of transmission between the composer (i.e. the soloist) and the player/learner."[60] Note that Prouty talks about the player/learner as opposed to the audience; an author's audience may receive the text in a passive manner, but a jazz acolyte must actively receive the text. It is no coincidence that jazz is closely linked to the advent of recording technology; jazz musicians of the past and present consistently cite practicing along with recordings as a means of developing their abilities as improvisers.[61] The reception of the recording by the jazz musician involves going beyond listening to a recording to playing along with it. Listening to a recording multiple times and learning to play along with each note engrains habits of playing that can then be called upon in various circumstances. One can even go beyond "lifting" a solo[62] to an improvised engagement with the recording.[63] Robert Gelinas draws on this distinction in what he terms "jazzaneutics"—an active approach to hermeneutics—rightly pointing out that, "Jazz says we *don't know* until we *can do*."[64]

When jazz moved from its earliest forms to forms that became increasingly more harmonically and melodically complex, it became necessary for jazz musicians who were interested in playing later styles to understand what was going on theoretically in addition to absorbing the music through listening. As Howard McGhee said about bebop, "you had to *know*—not *feel*, you had to *know* what you were doing."[65] Jazz theory was constructed in order to meet this need, providing in the process systematic ways of practicing. Theoretical constructs derived from analysis of recordings provide ways

59. Monson, *Saying Something*, 126.

60. Prouty, "Orality," 327.

61. Prouty, "Orality," 326, describes the importance of recordings to the development of jazz.

62. Playing along with a recorded solo until it is memorized.

63. Levine, *Jazz Theory*, 254.

64. Gelinas, *Finding the Groove*, 125. Author's emphasis.

65. Howard McGhee, quoted in DeVeaux, *Birth of Bebop*, 227.

of conceptualizing and organizing information and a means of approach to new situations, often in the form of innovative compositions. In such cases, a composition may involve a chord progression that is very different in nature from what an improviser has encountered before, necessitating an approach that, while rooted in past approaches, must be adapted to meet the new need.

Yet theory can be a box that stifles freedom, placing musicians into the first type in Rinzler's taxonomy. As Ted Gioia points out, "The great mainstream jazz players never sounded like players following a rulebook."[66] Start Nicholson chimes in with his opinion that "[b]y framing jazz in tried-and-tested methods of articulation, American jazz has become steeped in certainties that fail to acknowledge uncertainty as a precondition for adventure."[67] While theory is a useful tool, it tends to marginalize whatever it cannot explain. Many important aspects of jazz simply cannot be fully communicated by written means; they must be heard and experienced. And while theory can be used to push boundaries, it seems more often employed in reinforcing them.[68]

In addition to recordings and theory, an aspiring jazz musician will benefit from a mentor. At times, a musician may not have access to such a person, and may even develop unique approaches to improvisation as a result, but in most cases, having access to a competent guide assists the neophyte in navigating a bewildering array of approaches to theory and a massive body of recorded work. Finding a mentor has the additional advantage of providing encouragement and incentive; otherwise, the work of developing the skills necessary to improvise competently in the jazz tradition can be lonely and discouraging.

The processes of internalizing jazz recordings, understanding jazz theory, and submitting to the wisdom of a mentor are ultimately freeing. Outside of this harrowing process, one is not free to improvise in the jazz tradition; if musical phrases have not been engrained, they will not be available to draw upon in a performance situation anymore than one can freely express one's self in a foreign language without absorbing its vocabulary, its grammar, and its idioms. Nor is it possible to listen passively to jazz and expect to play it. Even if one attains a solid grasp of jazz theory, having read and studied literature on jazz theory, it will still not be enough to play the music. The exhilarating freedom experienced by the seasoned improviser

66. Friedwald et al., *Future of Jazz*, 9.
67. Friedwald et al., *Future of Jazz*, 13.
68. See Ted Gioia's comments in Friedwald et al., *Future of Jazz*, 8–9.

only comes through actively working out the implications of theory physically, repeating exercises until they become second nature.

A History of Acceptance Tempered with Frustration

Matters of race have marked the history of jazz in all of its forms. In order to narrow the discussion, I look specifically at race relations at the dawn of the bebop era.[69] Most jazz scholars readily concede that jazz, and bebop by extension, originated with African Americans.[70] It was not, however, to remain a domain dominated solely by blacks. When white musicians were drawn into this music, both blacks and whites had to wrestle with the strong current of racism that permeated the American culture of the time. The swing era preceded bebop and served in some ways to break down barriers between black and white musicians and in other ways to reinforce them. During the 1930s, the music industry growing around big band swing was very lucrative, but the financial and social benefits were inequitably distributed across the race line. Eddie S. Meadows brings to light an example of a white musician and his relationship with black musicians and their music that exemplifies the complex feelings that ran between black and white musicians:

> [Benny] Goodman . . . was respected by some African American musicians because he was one of the first white bandleaders to hire African American musicians and he helped Billie Holiday obtain her first recording contract. However, not all African American musicians liked Goodman. He paid Teddy Wilson and Lionel Hampton less than he paid their white counterparts, and the media had anointed him "King of Swing," a title he achieved partially on the arrangements and compositions of Fletcher Henderson.[71]

In one sense, Benny Goodman advanced the cause of black musicians in America, but at the same time, he benefited to a far greater degree than they did through what was essentially an expropriation of their music. In contrast to the successes of their white counterparts, black big bands encountered appalling racial discrimination in the southern states and did not receive commensurate radio play, publicity, or even decent

69. For a broader look at the complex relationship between jazz and race relations, see Monson, *Freedom Sounds*.

70. See DeVeaux, *Birth of Bebop*, 18, and Porter, *What Is This Thing*, 2–3, among others.

71. Meadows, *Bebop to Cool*, 76.

accommodation.[72] The resulting tension must be kept in mind when considering the development of bebop.

This tension found its expression in painful ways. Red Rodney, a white trumpet player hired by Charlie Parker, has this to say about his experience in interacting with black musicians:

> But as far as the scene with the blacks and whites, when I first got in, there was hardly any ill will. . . . We lived together. Ate together. Thought together. Felt together. And it was really the only area in American life where this happened. And then the black revolution came in, and with the black revolution the same black musicians understandably gave vent to their feelings and became very hostile, and they included the white jazz musicians with every other part of American life. This was unfair. . . . most of us understood it, but we were hurt by it.[73]

Meadows suggests that Rodney did not understand the oppression felt by black musicians as a result of having their work appropriated by white musicians who profited from it without giving credit where credit was due. This feeling lay under the surface until the "social conscience evolved" at which point "the masks came off."[74] The incident points out the complex relationship that may exist between groups separated by race and oppression, even when they associate with one another in good faith.

On the other hand, even critics of jazz noticed the openness that its practitioners often had towards one another. Cameron's 1954 article on sociological aspects of the jam session (referred to above) states:

> The bond which unites jazzmen is so strong that differences in other things can be ignored. It is this which fosters the widely recognized tolerance of jazzmen toward race, religion, and class. Some do-gooders naively believe that a jazzman's tolerance is a high-minded fellow-feeling. It is fellow-feeling, but it does not stem from the kind of high-mindedness they seek. The jazzman tolerates these differences because they do not matter. It is easy to be tolerant in areas where one does not care, and the only thing he cares about seriously is jazz.[75]

---

72. See DeVeaux, *Birth of Bebop*, 146–57, for an extended discussion of the hardships faced by black big bands in the swing era.

73. Gitler, *Swing to Bop*, 307–8.

74. Meadows, *Bebop to Cool*, 87.

75. Cameron, "Sociological Notes," 181.

He makes an insightful observation: jazz mattered more to the musicians who played it than did their background or social position. It was not as though such things were irrelevant; contrary to Cameron's ignorant caricature ("the only thing he cares about seriously is jazz"), many jazz musicians of that era cared deeply about social issues.[76] The truly remarkable thing was that they exercised the freedom of coming together to make music in spite of the multitude of things that would otherwise have kept them apart. The mistakes and the pain of working through the deep cultural divides between white and black serve as a narratival testament to the fact that even antagonism of such depth can be transcended for a *constructive* cause.[77]

CONTINUAL CONSTRAINTS

Continual constraints differ from the types discussed above in terms of their ultimate immutability. Embodiment, for instance, cannot be escaped while one is alive; the sonic order is an inherent part of the physical laws of the universe; and time universally governs the course of life. Certainly, aspects of these constraints can be negotiated on a surface level—for instance, the body can be trained to transcend what it might be currently capable of, but there is a limit that one cannot ultimately transgress.

Embodiment

Embodiment is a universal aspect of the human experience as part of creation. It is also inescapable. For instance, Rinzler writes,

> Even if a free-jazz saxophonist plays the most outrageous honks and squawks (without even discrete pitches or rhythms in meter)—something in which a listener might find absolutely no rhyme nor reason [sic], and so may think is absolutely free— such music still rests, for instance, on the foundation of playing an instrument. It is, after all, still a saxophone making those sounds and therefore the improviser is limited at least by the physical nature of the instrument.[78]

76. See Kofsky, *John Coltrane*, for his view on the connection between jazz and politics in the 1960s. See also Heltzel, *Resurrection City*, for historical and contemporary connections between jazz and social justice.

77. As opposed to uniting in the face of a common enemy.

78. Rinzler, *Contradictions of Jazz*, 65.

In acoustic music, embodiment becomes particularly noticeable in the act of physically playing an instrument. Cymbals are struck, strings are plucked or strummed, wooden reeds vibrate, the piston moves up and down, while human bodies and wills accommodate themselves to these activities, striving to master instrument and body alike. It takes a great deal of time and energy to learn how to play an instrument well, but it is the only route to freely expressing one's intent through it. There is a sense of mastering or taking control of an instrument, much like Paul speaks of making his body a slave as he trains for the prize (1 Cor 9:24–27). The body can be oppressive when it is left untrained; without regular exertion, it will not develop the strength and coordination necessary to accomplish even the most basic of tasks. Similarly, a musician will not be able to execute musical phrases successfully without consistent practice. Yet the physical nature of an instrument can provide freeing restraint as well; melodic lines can emerge from the physical layout of an instrument. For instance, a musician playing a brass instrument will find that melodies related to the overtone series[79] emerge more naturally for her than a musician playing a keyboard instrument.[80] In a similar way, a trombonist faced with the limitations of a slide will naturally gravitate to more arpeggiated and diatonic musical phrases than a saxophonist, for whom chromatic lines can be played more naturally.[81]

On the one hand, it is essential to gain enough mastery over an instrument to engage effectively with the jazz tradition and with one's fellow improvisers. On the other, getting "caught up in the acquisition of technique" and the "mastery of the mechanical aspects of playing" can make one neglectful of interacting with others.[82] The instrument is paradoxically a barrier to surmount for the sake of the music and a form that offers ways of playing music. Great jazz musicians are not mastered by their instruments, yet they also work towards exploiting the physical aspects of their instruments for the purpose of the music. For instance, a trumpeter might use half valves to add effect to a note, or to slide between notes. In fact, jazz musicians have historically relied on ways of playing notes that are idiomatic to the instrument being played. Instead of approaching an instrument

79. For an explanation of the overtone series in the context of theological aesthetics, see Blackwell, *Sacred in Music*, 56–59.

80. The melodic use of phrases based on the overtone series is particularly evident in the improvised solos of J. J. Johnson.

81. For example, listen to the contrast in melodic phrases in the solos by J. J. Johnson (trombone) and Stan Getz (saxophone) in "Crazy Rhythm" on *At the Opera House*.

82. Patitucci, "Caught Up in the Present," 216.

like an enemy, learning to harness idiosyncrasies and apparent foibles can be liberating.

Sonic Order

All music, especially Western tonal music, is built from the overtone series.[83] Siegmund Levarie and Ernst Levy describe this phenomenon: "Nature . . . divides any vibrating body that produces a pure musical tone according to the whole-number series. As a result, the phenomenon that we recognize as one tone is in reality a complex of many partial tones. The partial tones above the fundamental are also called 'overtones.' Their existence is a manifestation of a natural law."[84] Without going into too much detail, music, like the physical world, is shaped by certain properties. A musical note is governed by this universal reality while simultaneously being a particular instantiation of it.[85] In the same way that gravitation is an inherent property of matter, music is caught up in inescapable properties whenever it is played—jazz is no exception.[86]

Time

Music is intimately tied to time.[87] No mistake, no compositional technique, no attempt to obliterate the traditional pulse of music can escape the fact that music is performed and heard in the context of time. Music could not exist without time; unlike a painting or a photograph, it depends on the cessation of one thing and the emergence of another. In traditional jazz, this passage through time is celebrated through the "groove"—a steady beat traditionally outlined by the drums and bass in the rhythm section.[88] If members of a jazz group, or even all save one, stop playing, the groove is

83. See Albert L. Blackwell's defense of this position in Blackwell, *Sacred in Music*, 71–76.

84. Levarie and Levy, *Tone*, 46.

85. In other words, musical tones do not follow the overtone series perfectly because none are completely pure.

86. For an extended assessment of the universal foundations of music and their implications for "anti-foundational thinkers," see Blackwell, *Sacred in Music*, 49–90.

87. See Begbie, *Theology, Music and Time*, for a well thought-out discussion of this relationship and the insights it provides for theology.

88. A "rhythm section" traditionally consists of drums, bass, and a piano and/or guitar. Together, these instruments provide a rhythmic and harmonic framework that supports a given soloist.

still present for the player or players that remain. This steady marking of time provides the foundation for a jazz melody to play with different aspects of the groove. For instance, in a time signature with four beats to a bar, the first beat in particular and then the third beat are felt most strongly; to begin a melodic phrase on the second or fourth beat creates tension and therefore excitement. Without the groove, this excitement would be impossible. Just as, in a painting, a figure of vivid red would stand out against a white background, and be lost against a background of the same color, the celebration of the passage of time in the groove provides a backdrop against which a given musical phrase finds meaning. The groove constrains and simultaneously liberates those who participate in it.

RISKS AND MISTAKES: "THE PROBLEM OF MILES DAVIS"

Risk taking is not a constraint but an approach to constraints. It intersects with all the constraints above because, as Begbie says, "[f]undamental to the improviser's attitude is patient trust";[89] trusting constraints allows them to prove their trustworthiness, and having "[t]his trust enables risk."[90] Musicians who compose solos ahead of time are actually refusing to engage with many of the constraints above; improvising with others and surrendering to the "*It*" factor necessarily require taking risks. Learning to trust these constraints enables one to take greater risks, knowing that one is in part sustained by the activities of others and the resources found in cultural constraints. According to Lee Brown, the risk inherent in jazz is an integral part of the music's appeal: "We find ourselves slipping back and forth between our hopes for the ultimate quality of the music and our fascination with the activity by which it is generated—even when those actions appear to threaten the quality of the resulting music. The strain contributes to the music's fascination, rather than detracting from it."[91] Perhaps this fascination is connected to the fact that "we are forced to improvise our way through life."[92]

Mistakes are a natural consequence of human risk-taking. In his article, "Out of Notes: Signification, Interpretation, and the Problem of Miles Davis," Robert Walser attempts to wrestle with a difficult question in the history of jazz:

89. Begbie, *Theology, Music and Time*, 243.
90. Begbie, *Theology, Music and Time*, 243.
91. Brown, "Feeling My Way," 121–22.
92. Rinzler, *Contradictions of Jazz*, 178.

Davis has long been infamous for missing more notes than any other major trumpet player. While nearly everyone acknowledges his historical importance as a band-leader and a musical innovator, and for decades, large audiences flocked to his concerts, critics have always been made uncomfortable by his "mistakes," the cracked and missed notes common in his performances. "The problem of Miles Davis" is the problem Davis presents to both critics and historians: How are we to account for such glaring defects in the performances of someone who is indisputably one of the most important musicians in the history of jazz?[93]

After surveying those who ignore this problem and the minority who deride Davis' ability based on conventional means (i.e., European-based musicological criteria) of evaluating jazz performances, Walser concludes that a different set of criteria is necessary to understand what Davis is doing. Walser's approach to answering this thorny question is not to deny that these were mistakes, but rather to give them the proper context. He asserts that Davis made mistakes because he was attempting to find sounds that were meant to project strain or other emotions as opposed to the clear, clean tones so cherished in a classical setting. Davis took risks, which sometimes succeeded and at times failed; it was his daring in taking such risks to which Walser attributes his appeal.

CONCLUSION

Jazz improvisation operates under a multitude of overt and subtle constraints. The apparently contradictory values at work within these constraints that a successful jazz performance embodies constitute much of its appeal. The beauty of jazz improvisation is not to be found in attempting to write something new on a blank slate. It is found, rather, in the way the constraints of song, tradition, space, and co-improvisers coalesce in time to produce not something of crystalline order and perfection, but an enactment of freedom that forms a link between the past, a transient present, and transcendence. The central argument of this book is that the analogy between the link between the past, present, and transcendence, and what happens in the enactment of Christian freedom is strong enough to use jazz improvisation as a descriptive and prescriptive model for it.

The strength of this analogy rests in part on uncovering corresponding analogues between the source domain of jazz and the target domain

93. Walser, "Out of Notes," 343.

of the Christian life.[94] In addition to plotting the basic analogues of "jazz musician" to "Christian" and "jam session" to "the local church," Begbie's types of constraints and the constraints that I discuss within these types provide further analogues and relationships between analogues that I map onto the target domain in chapter 5. Showing that the relations between the analogues and the relations between the relations between them resemble an isomorphism demonstrates the strength of my analogy according to the multiconstraint theory of analogy.

94. See the introduction for a description of how analogy works.

5

From Jazz Improvisation
to Christian Freedom

HAVING EXPLORED AND ORGANIZED the source domain of jazz improvisation, it is now time to turn it loose on the target domain of the Christian
life. I define the Christian life as the activities that a Christian engages in
to grow spiritually, to build up the church, and to further the Kingdom of
God. In this chapter, I limit this domain to biblical/theological concerns; in
chapter 6, I apply the conclusions of this one to the contemporary problem
of freedom that I describe in chapter 1. Broadly speaking, this chapter is
concerned with creating an isomorphism between jazz and the biblical/
theological area of Christian freedom. But beyond cataloguing corresponding analogues, I also aim to say something about how to navigate the constraints I deal with and to make connections and analogical arguments from
the source to the target domain. As in the preceding chapter, I follow Jeremy
Begbie's taxonomy of constraints and draw upon Paul Rinzler's insights in
showing how to navigate them.

OCCASIONAL CONSTRAINTS

In Begbie's taxonomy, occasional constraints are constraints that change
relative to the improviser. In the domain of the Christian life, the analogue
to the improviser is the individual Christian. The occasional constraints
of the previous chapter find corresponding analogues as they are mapped
onto the domain of the Christian life. The dynamic constraints of church
architecture, other Christians, and the direction of the Holy Spirit all change

relative to a practicing Christian.[1] Even architecture shifts relative to an individual Christian as she gathers in different places and even situates herself differently within a given space. She shapes the thought and actions of other Christians while being shaped by other Christians in her turn. Finally, being attuned to the direction of the Spirit demands the ongoing death of the constructed self. These constraints, especially the latter ones, help to liberate a Christian from constraints that impede the Christian life. They also demand creative improvisation with the resources they supply and renew.

Spaces and Audiences: Dividing the Church

The venues and audiences jazz musicians encounter find an analogue in church architecture. James F. White makes a forceful case that church buildings convey the theology held by their builders. He compares a certain Episcopal cathedral in which "the altar-Table and clergy seats are located in a distinct space, removed as a separate volume from the nave where the people and choir sit" with a certain Roman Catholic cathedral, that "thrusts the altar-Table into the midst of the congregation, and no one sits more than eight seats from it."[2] He argues that if he attempted to preach in the Episcopal cathedral building about the priesthood of all believers, "the building would shout [him] down" while the Catholic cathedral would be more conducive to his message.[3] While the way in which objects are placed and seats arranged may appear to be a superficial concern in relation to freedom, these factors do play a role in shaping how freedom is expressed (and who can express it) when the church gathers together. Just as jazz musicians are concerned with hearing one another when they play in a given venue, these factors shape the ability of the congregation to hear and interact with one another.

Early Christians used three different venues for worship and teaching: the temple, synagogues, and house churches. The temple was destroyed in AD 70 and the widening gap between Judaism and Christianity made synagogues an increasingly less viable option. The remaining option, the house church, was prevalent during the time of the New Testament and continued to be widely used for the first two centuries of Christian history.[4] The

---

1. When I write about the direction of the Holy Spirit changing relative to a Christian, I do so from a human point of view. See the introduction for my thoughts on Christian freedom in relation to Providence.

2. White, "How the Architectural Setting," 547.

3. White, "How the Architectural Setting," 547.

4. Block, *Glory of God*, 322.

constraint of space in a house church restricted the size of congregations to twenty or thirty persons—"the number that could comfortably gather in one room."[5] In other words, early churches were analogous to jazz combos rather than big bands in terms of size. House churches gave way to churches in basilicas after Constantine's rise to power.[6] This was a move from a private, intimate setting to a formalized, public one.[7]

This shift from the private to the public sphere marked changes for how individuals within the church participated in it. For instance, Edward Foley notes, "in the Greco-Roman world the home could be considered 'women's space,' and worship in that space would have been marked by the more equal participation of women and even their leadership. As Christian worship moves from domestic settings to more public buildings, however, the influence of women is going to diminish."[8] In describing the development of churches modeled on the basilicas, Foley also observes the distinction between clergy and laity being reflected in their architecture. The bishop's throne and the benches for presbyters are set apart from the congregation, and "in some churches in Rome, at least by the fifth century, the sanctuary and the pathway that led to it were open only to the clergy and to the choir."[9] The architecture of the church reflected and solidified the division in the church between those who pursued a vocation within the church and those who lived in the secular world outside of it. Instead of encouraging the active participation of all, architecture reinforced this division.

The increasing distinction between performers and their audience is magnified in larger spaces, especially when physical structures aimed at projecting a performance also create physical distance between them. As Edward Hall's work shows, this distance conveys something about their relationship.[10] In fact, the projection of performers on large screens is an attempt to overcome the distance between them and to suggest a more

---

5. Block, *Glory of God*, 322. Jerome Murphy-O'Connor suggests a slightly higher number based on an average of four Roman houses unearthed in excavations at Corinth, "the maximum number that the atrium could hold was 50, but this assumes that there were no decorative urns, etc. to take up space, and that everyone stayed in the one place; the true figure would probably be between 30 and 40." Murphy-O'Connor, *St. Paul's Corinth*, 164.

6. Foley, *From Age to Age*, 46.

7. Wiseman, "Bridging the Gap," 49.

8. Foley, *From Age to Age*, 51.

9. Foley, *From Age to Age*, 85.

10. Hall distinguishes between four distances—intimate, personal, social, and public—and explains the social significance of each. See Hall, *Hidden Dimension*, 113–29.

intimate connection.[11] A small club allows for a more personal connection between performer and audience and a concert hall does the reverse. A meeting in a home, like a jazz performance in a small club, will be more intimate and interactive, with all the benefits and difficulties that pertain to such a setting. In a larger, formal setting, the voices of the audience are safely muted; in a smaller, informal setting, the qualities of the audience (for good or for ill) will have an impact on how the word of God is delivered and received.

As the experience of jazz musicians and the history of church architecture indicate, moving from private to public space tends to place limits on the participation of all the individuals present. The larger the space and the more people who gather in it, the more difficult it is for quieter voices to be heard; without amplification they are lost altogether. In larger settings, actions must be formalized in order to avoid chaos; improvisation is minimized. The freedom of jazz musicians to improvise is inversely proportional to the size of the group; the larger the group, the more they will (typically) rely on notation rather than improvisation. In a big band, even when an individual has an opportunity to solo, they, and the rhythm section, are often constrained by the background figures of the larger ensemble. In the same way, the participation of all the members of the local church that Paul describes (1 Cor 14:26) is increasingly more difficult to maintain as the setting becomes larger and as rites are formalized. Just as jazz musicians must consider acoustics as they engage with one another musically, so local churches interested in the active participation of their members must consider the architecture of their buildings.

Community: Being Constrained by the Body of Christ

In jazz and in life there is perhaps nothing more challenging than trying to navigate the relationship between the self and the other. Paul wrote 1 Corinthians to a group of people that required a new way of envisioning themselves in relation to one another. Anthony Thiselton describes the Corinthians in Paul's time as "a thrusting, ambitious and *competitive* people" who enthusiastically engaged in self-promotion and were driven to climb the social ladder by any means necessary.[12] Many jazz jam sessions are affected by a similar malady as musicians strive to outdo one another on

11. Yet this intimation of intimacy is unidirectional; the performer is projected to the audience, but individual members of the audience are not projected to the performer.

12. Thiselton, *First Corinthians*, 9. Emphasis in original.

the bandstand. Paul's response is to redirect the energies of the Corinthians towards building up the church.[13] Analogously, the music takes precedence over the individual musician. The opportunity for each member in a jazz combo to solo is mirrored in 1 Cor 14, where Paul gives directives for speaking in tongues and prophesying in the church. He insists that in order for these gifts to be edifying to the church they must be exercised in sequence (27, 29–33). Tongues must be interpreted and prophesies must be weighed, indicating a posture of active listening and engagement with what is being said. The Corinthians have no difficulty with assertiveness; they need to learn to temper it with openness. But not everyone has the same difficulties; the Old Testament general Barak, for instance, lacks assertiveness (Judg 4). Some need to be liberated from a need to occupy the spotlight while others need to be liberated from a timid spirit. Only when one can graciously stand aside for the other *and* courageously step up to speak in the Spirit is one truly experiencing Christian freedom.

On August 23, 1963, Martin Luther King Jr. deftly demonstrated both assertiveness and openness in his speech, "I have a dream." He expended a great deal in preparing the text of his speech, writing and rewriting it and consulting with his advisors. Yet when he finally delivered the speech, as he neared his conclusion gospel singer Mahalia Jackson shouted, "Tell 'em about the dream, Martin."[14] King set aside his manuscript and spoke about a dream—developing an idea he had employed previously in a new way. The audience also contributed to the speech, applauding and interjecting, spurring King on. Open to others, King was propelled beyond the script into a momentous moment for the civil rights movement in America.[15] In finding the appropriate balance between assertion and openness, Christians can enjoy the freedom of transcending the self with and because of the other. If assertion is unaccompanied by openness, one is trapped by the limitations of the self. If openness lacks assertiveness then the self is trapped by the limitations of the other. Paul's analogy of the church as the body of Christ (1 Cor 12:12–31) contains the seeds of this balancing act; each member must be both alternately assertive and open in order for the body to act harmoniously.

A fine line exists between a battle of egos and spurring the other on to greater things. In so called "cutting sessions" in the formative days of bebop (a formative style within the jazz tradition), the two seemed to go hand

13. See 1 Cor 14.

14. The effectiveness of Jackson's interjection is disputed. Apparently, "King never subsequently confirmed that he had heard her." However, two witnesses insist that what Jackson said must have been audible to King. See Younge, *Speech*, 95–96.

15. Cf. Gelinas, *Finding the Groove*, 162–63.

in hand. Jazz historian Scott DeVeaux writes that "[i]ndividual reputations might be made or broken, but the ultimate purpose was to raise the quality of performance all around."[16] The difficulty in the domain of Christian freedom is to challenge for the right motives (i.e. not self-aggrandizement) and to accept a challenge without being discouraged or embittered. Being challenged by a fellow Christian is a lesson in humility and openness; it entails having one's eyes opened to something beyond and a stimulus to reach for it. Challenging someone else requires assertion governed by Christian love (Eph 4:15). In other words, the proper goal of challenging another is to spur them on "to love and good deeds" (Heb 10:24, NRSV).[17] The boundary is the limited scope of one's ambition in serving and loving God; it is transgressed by responding to the challenge of the other.

The Self, the "It" Factor, and the Holy Spirit

In order to properly balance assertion and openness, one must have a proper sense of self. Paul writes, "For by the grace given to me I say to everyone among you not to think of yourself more highly than you ought to think, but to think with sober judgment, each according to the measure of faith that God has assigned" (Rom 12:3). The human need for self-esteem makes this task next to impossible. Yet the religious consensus of humanity is that it is necessary. Kelly James Clark points out that the major religions share the common idea that "the ego must die because it impedes relating to something greater than the self."[18] In Christianity, unlike in Buddhism or Hinduism, the self does not dissolve, but dies to be resurrected (cf. Matt 16:25; 2 Cor 5:14–15, 17). Yet, unlike Christ's finished work, it must continually be dying (Luke 9:23). As Hal Crook and Bob Brookmeyer claimed on the basis of their own experiences in chapter 4, the ego ultimately gets in the way of experiencing music in its freest, most profound form.

Crook intuitively picks up on something that Clark distills from Ernest Becker: the need for human beings to construct a self as a shield against the world. From birth, "[i]nfants absorb the twin untruths that the world is safe and that it revolves around them. If infants and toddlers were not nurtured on these two untruths, though, they would grow insecure and anxious and become future candidates for psychosis or neurosis."[19] Their well-being and survival depend upon being carefully shielded from the world as it is.

16. DeVeaux, *Birth of Bebop*, 211.

17. Cf. Prov 27:17.

18. Clark, *When Faith Is Not Enough*, 168.

19. Clark, *When Faith Is Not Enough*, 139.

Perhaps the apostle Paul has this in mind when he writes, "When I was a child, I spoke like a child, I thought like a child, I reasoned like a child; when I became an adult, I put an end to childish ways" (1 Cor 13:11). Parents, by their words and actions, first convey these untruths to infants and toddlers, and then (hopefully) seek to gradually disabuse their children of them as they grow to maturity. Ideally, they shield the child from the full weight of the world while allowing them the freedom to explore reality. Yet the love, devotion, and valuation of the parents continue to shield the child from the indifference of the world. But as a child matures into adulthood, something is necessary to preserve his self-worth. According to Becker, "man lives by lying to himself about himself and about his world" and his character "is a vital lie."[20] In other words, even adults continue to lie to themselves about who they are in relation to the world. This is a deeply unsatisfying state of affairs.

The self—one's constructed character—is a barrier of self-preservation, but it is also a barrier of deceit. It masquerades "as a tyrannical king, which requires human victims for its magnification."[21] In order to know one's actual self, this king must be deposed and executed. Since one cannot face the world alone and unsupported, the only alternative aside from ending life is to turn to God; "[o]nce we recognize that we are creatures and not creators, we are relieved of the impossible task of creating a self."[22] When self-worth comes from God, it is no longer necessary to win it at the expense of others. Pride is extinguished in humility, humility being

> the ability, without prejudice to one's self-comfort, to admit one's inferiority, in this or that respect, to another. And it is the ability, without increment to one's self-comfort or prejudice to the quality of one's relationship with another, to remark one's superiority, in this or that respect, to another. As such, humility is a psychological principle of independence from others and a necessary ground of genuine fellowship with them, an emotional independence of one's judgments concerning how one ranks vis-à-vis other human beings.[23]

Freedom is found in humility when one's sense of self-worth is rooted in God. In fact, being rooted in God is the only way of practicing a livable humility. As Ellen T. Charry puts it, "Christian dignity comes from dwelling in the being of God, rather than from self-expression or the respect of

20. Becker, *Denial of Death*, 51.

21. Clark, *When Faith Is Not Enough*, 149.

22. Clark, *When Faith Is Not Enough*, 149.

23. Roberts, *Spiritual Emotions*, 83.

others."[24] In knowing God, "we turn into a self whose joy is now *from* and *for* God."[25]

Killing the constructed self is difficult. Søren Kierkegaard sees three stages in moving towards being rooted in God: 1) the aesthetic stage, 2) the ethical stage, and 3) the religious stage.[26] Each stage represents an attempt to answer the question, "What is the good life?"[27] The aesthetic stage bears a striking resemblance to the postmodern-self discussed in chapter 1; in this stage, the actor rejects moral constraints and pursues the satisfaction of her desires. One moves to the ethical stage by a free act of the will; one acknowledges an obligation to pursue what is good, to become what one ought to be. One learns to live for something beyond self. A jazz musician pursues technical proficiency and accuracy to escape from the aimless wandering and frustration of a musician who refuses to situate herself in relation to a tradition. In a similar manner, the self seeks to be liberated from the endless pursuit of novelty inherent in the aesthetic stage by pursuing moral excellence. And fails. As Kierkegaard says, the requirement of this stage "is so infinite that the individual always goes bankrupt."[28] Subject to frustration in the ethical stage, to escape one must make a leap of faith into the religious stage. In this stage, the constructed self dies in the face of its finitude and failure and the true self arises by appropriating God's forgives. The desires of the body and the desire to do what is right can be recovered when they are governed by the spirit, which is in turn guided by the Holy Spirit. In short, the things that drove the other two stages are recovered and put in their proper place.

The analogue corresponding to Kierkegaard's religious stage is the successful outworking of the "*It*" factor that Crook describes. The "*It*" factor is the thing that plays the music when a musician lets go of his ego.[29] When musicians are "in the zone," operated by the "*It*" factor, the ego drops away; instead of fighting to gratify the ego in relation to other musicians and then in relation to the infinite (the perfect solo) they let go and allow the music to play through them. This "zone" is lost as soon as the ego makes the caliber one's performance the goal rather than the music itself. In a similar way, Christian humility is not focused on one's performance (especially on trying to be humble) but acting within the will of God.

24. Charry, "Crisis of Modernity," 104.

25. Charry, "Crisis of Modernity," 105. My emphasis.

26. Kierkegaard, *Stages on Life's Way*, 476.

27. Westphal, *Becoming a Self*, 22.

28. Kierkegaard, *Stages on Life's Way*, 476.

29. See chapter 4 for a more detailed description of the "*It*" factor.

It is important to note that being in the zone is not achieved without mastering one's instrument and tradition; in the same way, the religious stage must take into account the content, and even the struggle, of the ethical stage. If we allow the analogue of the "*It*" factor to add to Kierkegaard's insights, it is possible to see the work of the Holy Spirit. In his study of the work of the Holy Spirit, Jack Levison suggests that in the case of the artisans Bezalel and Oholiab mentioned in Exod 31 and 35, their filling with the spirit "is not so much an endowment of the spirit as an enhancement of spirit."[30] Allowing the "*It*" factor to take over is analogous to allowing the Holy Spirit to work through one's life.

While Kierkegaard as an existentialist insists on the choice of the individual to progress from one stage to another,[31] Scripture teaches that the Holy Spirit convicts people in the aesthetic stage of their sin (John 16:8–9), and that the law that lies behind the ethical stage confronts those in that stage with the futility of escaping unaided from sin (Rom 7:7–13). The forgiveness God offers is predicated on the sacrifice of Jesus Christ and the life of the religious stage is made possible through the power of the Holy Spirit. If being "in the zone" is being in the religious stage, the "*It*" factor that makes it possible is the power of the Spirit. Just as a jazz musician is the one playing music and yet, in a sense, being played by the music, Paul can say to the Corinthians, "I worked harder than any of them—though it was not I, but the grace of God that is with me" (1 Cor 15:10).

CULTURAL CONSTRAINTS

The "frameworks and patterns brought to the improvisation" of the church are many-layered and complex.[32] Paul Rinzler's method of dealing with contradiction in jazz provides a way of navigating the head-on collision between tradition and creativity, while the very presence of tradition gives rise to the question of how its frameworks and patterns relate to a contemporary context. Employing and subverting roles, coming to terms with authorial intent, the place of theology, and navigating legacies of injustice are areas that provide formative patterns and contexts for the enactment of Christian freedom.

---

30. Levison, *Inspired*, 31. Note that Levison does not use capitalization to distinguish between "the human spirit" and "the divine spirit" because they are not distinguished in Hebrew or Greek (19).

31. According to Clark's reading of Kierkegaard, "[t]he ethical stage is entered into and sustained by self-conscious choice." Clark, *When Faith Is Not Enough*, 163.

32. Begbie, *Theology, Music and Time*, 201.

Creativity and Tradition in the Church

According to trumpeter Clark Terry, to be a jazz musician "[o]ne must imitate, then assimilate, and this will ultimately lead to being able to innovate."[33] In jazz, innovation is expected. In church tradition on the other hand, once church doctrine was standardized through the Ecumenical Councils,

> The established Christian doctrine had to be preserved without innovations (ἀκαινοτόμητα) and without any subtraction or addition (οὐδὲν ἀφαιροῦμεν, οὐδὲν προστίθεμεν). . . . It is thus not accidental that the terms νεωτεροποιῶ and καινοτομῶ (both meaning "to innovate") were mostly used in Patristic literature in connection with heretical innovations.[34]

In other words, the Church has historically been suspicious of theological innovation (often with good reason). When mapping tradition and innovation from the domain of jazz into the domain of Christian freedom, it is necessary to distinguish between tradition in terms of the historical life, death, and resurrection of Jesus Christ upon which the historic Christian faith rests that Paul writes about in 1 Cor 15:3–11 and tradition of the sort that Jesus criticizes in Matt 15:1–6 and Mark 7:1–13 and that Paul mentions in Gal 1:14. In this section and the one following, I deal with tradition in the latter sense—tradition that follows divine revelation as opposed to the revelation itself, unless otherwise stated.

Paul Rinzler's distinction between stimulus freedom and stimulus-bound freedom and his taxonomy of the intersection between creativity and tradition (discussed in chapter 4) provide a useful starting point for working out the relationship between freedom and tradition. In metaphysical terms, human beings can only operate with the things they are given; they are creatures, not the Creator. All aspects of human endeavor are necessarily dependent on God (Job 34:14–15; Col 1:17). In one sense, human beings are equally subject to what Rinzler calls stimulus-bound freedom; everyone must work from what is given. Tradition narrows this field, designating tools and materials for intended purposes. Yet human beings have the capacity to imagine things that do not (yet) have a corporeal reality; they can think outside of the box. This ability—which Rinzler calls stimulus freedom—allows human beings to combine apparently disparate things, to

---

33. Clark Terry, cited in Barnhart, *World of Jazz Trumpet*, 164.

34. Makrides, "Orthodox Christianity," 23. The irony is that tradition ultimately emerges from experience and innovation. As Steven M. Studebaker points out, "what we consider tradition was once experience." Studebaker, *From Pentecost*, 15–16.

re-imagine the structure of occasional and cultural constraints, and to find new ways of testing the limits of continual constraints.

Rinzler's taxonomy of the interaction between tradition and creativity provides a view of the possibilities. The first is to uphold tradition while minimizing creativity. In terms of the Christian life, this amounts to seeking to preserve and maintain a certain faith tradition with its accompanying rites and practices. In terms of the self and the other, individual assertion is mitigated by structure and ritual. The second is to explore the creative potential within the tradition; one works from the materials the tradition provides, but is reluctant to engage with resources outside of it. Wayne Grudem exemplifies such reluctance in his *Systematic Theology*, where he writes, "it is doubtful that liberal theologians have given us any significant insights into the doctrinal teaching of Scripture that are not already to be found in evangelical writers."[35] The third is willing to question tradition and to interact with non-traditional sources. One might, for instance, uphold the authority of Scripture while simultaneously calling into question the hermeneutical bias of a given tradition. Stanley Grenz and John Franke, for instance, attempt to move away from the foundationalist epistemology that has characterized much of evangelical theology while still upholding the authority of Scripture in their book, *Beyond Foundationalism*.[36] The fourth type freely calls into question the authority of Scripture and the content of the Ecumenical Creeds. External criteria govern the use of Scripture and determine what elements of tradition will remain intact. Mary Fulkerson, for instance, argues that "no part of the Christian tradition is exempt from scrutiny. The entire tradition is judged potentially complicit with definitions of gender that are oppressive for women."[37] Since the Christian tradition, including Scripture, must be subjected to this rubric of oppression, it follows that Scripture does not provide this rubric.

The extremities of Rinzler's taxonomy do not permit the expression of Christian freedom. The first type stifles freedom by an ossifying approach to tradition that crowds out any possibility of engagement with culture and any movement of the Holy Spirit that lies outside of the traditions in question. In the fourth type, other concerns stand over divine revelation and following traditions alike. Just as other genres of music borrow from jazz in many ways while staying clear of its improvisatory aspects, certain ideologies can also borrow from Christianity while denying, or at least holding

---

35. Grudem, *Systematic Theology*, 17.
36. See Grenz and Franke, *Beyond Foundationalism*.
37. Fulkerson, *Changing the Subject*, 38.

loosely, the core tenets of the Christian faith.[38] The remaining two types are characterized by elements that are more desirable: the second type allows tradition to be resourced in fresh ways and the third type allows tradition to be pruned back at the places where it stands in the way of fruitful growth. By itself, the second type is not in a position to see any problems with the tradition it works with. By itself, the third position risks neglecting tradition and drifting toward the fourth type. While much can be learned by paying attention to aspects of all four types, the optimal space for exercising responsible freedom is at the gap between the second and third types. Bringing the two together combines the strengths of a dynamic interaction with tradition and a willingness to critique that tradition in light of contemporary developments without compromising its core.

Improvising in the Gap Between Tradition and Contemporary Situations

As Kevin J. Vanhoozer writes, "The church is *always* having to improvise, and it does so not out of a desire to be original but out of a desire to minister the gospel in new contexts."[39] Improvisation is necessary to bridge the gap between tradition and contemporary life. This gap is similar to the one between the second and third types of Rinzler's taxonomy of the ways that tradition and creativity come together. The second type works within the bounds of tradition while the third is able to question the tradition and to consider using resources outside of it. Contemporary situations provide the impetus for creatively rethinking tradition, whether to set it aside or to re-appropriate it in a new context. In terms of tradition, the Scriptures and the Ecumenical Creeds do not exhaustively cover every aspect of life—especially life in the postmodern West. Revelation is not meant to be kept separate from reality; no matter how strong the bulwark, the contemporary world will leak in. The most traditional, sequestered communities in the West cannot avoid the theological and ethical questions raised by contact with a postmodern society addicted to technique.[40]

---

38. Whether a piece requires improvisation in the manner I lay out in chapter 4 in order to be considered as jazz music is a matter of debate (see Gridley, Maxham, and Hoff, "Three Approaches"), but for the purpose of my analogy, improvisation will be considered as a core aspect of jazz.

39. Vanhoozer, *Drama of Doctrine*, 128. Emphasis in original.

40. See chapter 1 for a fuller explication of the postmodern-self and Jacques Ellul's notion of technique.

Jeremy Begbie distinguishes between tradition as a process and tradition as the result of the process. Returning to David Ake's comparison of Wynton Marsalis and Bill Frisell from chapter 4, one can see how Marsalis exemplifies the latter while Frisell demonstrates the former. Marsalis engages with the deposits of the tradition, ignoring the process through which songs came into the jazz repertoire. Frisell sets aside the standard repertoire and engages with contemporary songs in a manner predicated on the way earlier jazz musicians drew upon the popular songs of their day. On the one hand, one can block the contemporary world by creating an alternative to it that draws upon the deposits of tradition. On the other, one can engage with this world through the patterns that tradition provides.

Each Christian community must improvise the relationship between the tradition it inherits and the context in which it finds itself. Communities endanger their freedom by swinging too hard to one side or the other. If they cling to the deposits of tradition, they lose the ability to communicate with the contemporary world and risk compromising the intentions that went into forming the tradition in the first place. If they let the contemporary world set the terms of the conversation, they risk losing anything meaningful to say as Christians. The apparent contradiction in jazz between tradition and innovation provides a model for improvising in the space between them; it allows tradition to give shape to how Christians come to terms with the contemporary world and its challenges.

Subverting Expectations: Hearing Quiet Voices

The activity of the New Testament church is predicated on the active participation of its members. Each brings something to the gatherings of local congregations (1 Cor 14:26), each is gifted by the Holy Spirit (1 Cor 12:7), and each plays a significant role within the body of Christ (1 Cor 12:14–25). Gifts and roles differ among members; just as all instruments in a jazz combo are not equally suited to all roles, not all Christians are equally suited to the same functions in the Church (1 Cor 12:29–30). Yet, as in the jazz combo, all Christians are expected to fulfill some role in the church; each voice ought to be heard.

Apostles and prophets occupy a role in the early church analogous to the trumpet in the jazz combo; they articulate the melody/theme of the church in a way that is clear, prominent, and easily heard. Teachers fill in the harmony, connecting the melody to the underlying forms found in Scripture and tradition. Serving (1 Pet 4:11) and assisting (1 Cor 12:28), exhorting and giving (Rom 12:8) are like the bass, grounding the harmony and keeping things together rhythmically. Those gifted in healing also maintain the pulse, while those who work miracles punctuate the proceedings like drum fills. Some voices are quiet while others are prominent, but all should be heard. Just as the trumpet does not typically play during a bass solo, so those with a public role within the church should at times be silent in order to listen to those who fill less conspicuous roles.

Moving from the transgression of roles in jazz into the domain of the church, perhaps certain roles could be switched to draw attention to certain issues. Those who quietly serve see things that those with public roles overlook. Hearing their voices on occasion can help the church as a whole be more attuned to their voices during the usual operation of the church, reminding everyone that "the members of the body that seem to be weaker are indispensable" (1 Cor 12:22). Witnessing leaders in a supportive role would also remind them of what Jesus said: "You know that among the Gentiles those whom they recognize as their rulers lord it over them, and their great ones are tyrants over them. But it is not so among you; but whoever wishes to become great among you must be your servant, and whoever wishes to be first among you must be slave of all" (Mark 10:42–44). The roles in the church provide useful and necessary constraints, but they need not be rigid. They certainly must not be used to silence and/or coerce others.

God's Intentions in Scripture

In one sense, Scripture is a record of improvisation; it records the dynamic interplay between God and his people over time. A significant portion of the Bible is narrative and the epistles bear the marks of occasional writing.[41] It bears the stamp of humanity. On the other hand, Scripture is God-breathed (θεόπνευστος, 2 Tim 3:16); he is the ultimate author. Moreover, God's words, including Scripture, are meant to have a perlocutionary effect on those who listen to it (Isa 55:10–11; Jas 1:22–25).[42] Viewed this way, Scripture is the corresponding analogue to a musical score and the Christian life is the corresponding analogue to its performance. Moreover, as Frances Young observes, like Scripture, "[m]usic is 'in two natures'" in that it is "incarnate in a medium of which 'physics' can give an account both explanatory and

41. By "occasional writing," I mean that each epistle is addressed to a certain group of people and that specific circumstances provide the impetus for writing.

42. See "God's Mighty Speech Acts" in Vanhoozer, *First Theology* (127–58), where he discusses how Scripture can be God's word without falling into bibliolatry by resourcing speech-act theory. He defends "identifying the Scriptures as the Word of God . . . so long as God's communicative acts are not mistaken for the divine being itself" (131).

necessarily reductive" while simultaneously being untranslatable "into any other medium, except by way of analogy: what music 'means' cannot be expressed in words without change and loss."[43] Like Scripture, "music has to be 'realised' through performance and interpretation."[44] If God intends Scripture to have a perlocutionary effect, how can this be realized?

Randall R. Dipert divides a composer's intent into three levels (see previous chapter). The low and middle-level intentions (instrumentation and intended sound respectively) find corresponding analogues with the text of Scripture *in relation to its historical context*. The prohibition of braided hair in 1 Tim 2:9 provides a convenient example. In an attempt to respect God's intentions in Scripture, it would be a simple matter to ban braided hair in contemporary Christian practice. Yet such a ban would do little to bring about God's high-level intentions ("the effects that the composer intends to produce in the listener").[45] The elaborate hairstyles of first-century Rome are no longer in vogue; to ban them would do nothing to achieve the goals behind the initial ban: modesty and humility. Some other action is necessary to fulfill God's high-level intentions. Yet making such divisions in the intent of Scripture is not always so simple. At times, a certain behavior is encouraged or prohibited universally; realizing low and middle-level intentions fulfills high-level intentions. For instance, Paul's injunction to married couples to fulfill one another's sexual needs is not limited by the particular circumstances of the Corinthian church (1 Cor 7:1–6). The challenge is discerning God's high-level intentions in Scripture.

N. T. Wright, writing on the authority of Scripture, suggests an analogy from dramatic improvisation. He imagines a Shakespeare play in which the final act was lost. Instead of writing a fifth act, trained Shakespearian actors work out this act themselves.[46] Samuel Wells amends Wright's analogy by insisting that the resolution of the final act lies with God; "[t]he church lies within the story, rather than at the end of it."[47] This fits nicely with the traditional jazz format of playing the "head" (the composed melody) before and after the solo section. Vanhoozer intentionally builds on both Wright's and Wells' work in the extended analogy he makes in *The Drama of Doctrine*, where he connects various analogues from drama to the church. For Vanhoozer, culture (the contemporary world) "sets the stage, arranges the

---

43. Young, *Art of Performance*, 22.

44. Young, *Art of Performance*, 22.

45. Dipert, "Composer's Intentions," 206–7.

46. Wright, "How Can the Bible," 18–19.

47. Wells, *Improvisation*, 52.

scenery, and provides props that supply the setting for theology's work."[48] On the side of tradition (i.e., Scripture), he argues that "[i]t is precisely by gaining canonical competence that one is enabled to be creative and faithful in new contexts."[49] The themes and threads of the previous acts guide the church by requiring a demonstration of continuity, but simultaneously require development and adaptation.

Once again, jazz improvisation provides a model for reconciling two apparently opposing objectives; this time it brings together continuity and development. While studying jazz improvisation in college, our instructor had us perform single-note improvisations[50] in a room by ourselves on a given song. A colleague was then to enter the room and to be able to identify where we were in the form of the song based on our improvisation. If one was successful, one's colleague would be able to discern in the improvisation the chord changes forming the harmonic backbone of the song and thereby be able to figure out where we were in the form of the song. We had freedom to select and arrange notes and rhythms, but were constrained by the need to signify the underlying harmony by various devices such as touching on certain key notes within a given chord (usually the third and/ or the seventh), marking a chord change by highlighting notes that changed between chords (e.g., if a major chord is followed by a minor chord, one can play the major third on the former and the minor third on the latter), and playing with expected resolutions (for instance, setting up the flat nine of a dominant chord and resolving it to the fifth of the following major chord). My point is that the exercise could only be successfully executed by thorough knowledge of the harmonic framework upon which the song was based and the jazz tradition with its devices and methods for navigating said framework.

Identifying high-level intentions with the harmonic structure of a song makes the challenge of "making the changes" in jazz analogous to living out the Christian life based on the high-level intentions of Scripture. Jesus says, "You will know them by their fruits" (Matt 7:16) when he warns his audience about false prophets. In other words, a genuine Christian life is discernible in what someone does. Christians have the freedom to select certain courses of action rather than others; to rest in contemplation and to

48. Vanhoozer, *Drama of Doctrine*, 129.

49. Vanhoozer, *Drama of Doctrine*, 129.

50. In such improvisations, all instruments—including chordal instruments such as piano and guitar—can play only one note at a time.

act. The gaps in low and mid-level instructions in Scripture compel Christians to cling to the deposits of tradition, to find an authority to follow, or
to improvise.

Text and Theory: Scripture and Theology

If Scripture is indeed a record of improvisation, it fits snuggly with the
analogue of a jazz recording. Robert Gelinas' concept of jazzaneutics—an
active engagement with the text of Scripture—is therefore a logical extension of the analogy. In addition to reading Scripture on different levels (e.g.,
critically and reflectively), Gelinas suggests that the forms of Scriptures can
serve as templates; Psalms provide examples of songs to write, the gospels
demonstrate how to write about encounters with God.[51] No system can
replace the need to engage directly with Scripture; by actively engaging with
the material one gains a sense of "what sounds right" or what is fitting (Prov
25:11). This engagement provides essential materials for improvisation; one
absorbs the phrases, patterns, and rhythms of the text. Yet at a certain point,
one begins to look for the laws that govern these materials.

Charles Hodge opens his *Systematic Theology* with an analogical argument for his methodology from science. Scripture is analogous to raw
scientific data; the task of the theologian is "to collect, authenticate, [and]
arrange" the truths contained in it and to exhibit them "in their internal
relations to each other."[52] His arguments in favor of such an approach are
compelling: humans "cannot help endeavoring to systematize and reconcile
the facts" that they accept; we cannot properly understand the whole until
we work out how "the separate truths" of Scripture are related; and teachers
must systematize in order to explain.[53] Like jazz theory, such an approach
has a legitimate place in developing the ability of a Christian to understand
and properly enact her faith. It also has similar limitations.

First, neither scientist, jazz theorist, nor theologian is capable of taking
in and explaining all of the facts. In fact, the stronger and more internally
consistent a system is, the more it is likely to marginalize any facts that
appear to disagree with it. Competing systems will inevitably emphasize
certain facts and deemphasize others in their efforts to make their systems
cohere. Second, jazz and theology differ in an important way from science.
Science relies on the assumption that the universe behaves in a predictable
way; if facts such as the speed of light, the gravitational constant, or the

51. Gelinas, *Finding the Groove*, 128–35.
52. Hodge, *Systematic Theology*, 1:1.
53. Hodge, *Systematic Theology*, 1:2.

relation of mass to energy was subject to random changes the science of physics would be doomed (not to mention the resulting destruction of the universe as we know it). Jazz, by contrast, is an art form; its rules are not rigid and immutable. Theology is the study of God and his relationship to his creation—and the narratives contained in Scripture do not suggest that this relationship is rigid or mathematically predictable. Although jazz relates to the sonic order inherent in the universe and God is bound by his character and his word, there is (at least from a human perspective) a place for the unexpected and unpredicted. In other words, while theology is in some respects a science, it must in others be an art form.

Theological systems may be necessary, but they are always in danger of being shattered by experience, or advances in biblical textual criticism, hermeneutics, or any number of related disciplines. Clinging to them entails being bound by them, unable to experience stimulus freedom. Worse, it may cause one to adopt a position that lies in stark contradiction to aspects of Scripture that the system marginalizes. On the other hand, working out systems provides a way to come to terms with new experiences and challenges that are not directly accounted for in the source material of Scripture. Inevitably, this requires trial *and error*.

In terms of freedom, theological systems can help to explain and maintain beliefs and practices that are fundamental to the Christian faith—the constraints that deliver Christians from slavery to the self, the world, and the Devil. When these systems calcify and become brittle, however, they impair the enactment of freedom by causing divisions between Christians, deemphasizing certain aspects of Scripture, and close off otherwise feasible courses of action. When they are seen for what they are—human attempts to come to terms with partially comprehended divine revelation—they provide a guide for navigating contemporary issues grounded in scriptural precedent. Theology itself is improvised as theologians endeavor "to make it possible for the gospel to be heard in our time."[54]

Of course, in order for theory of any kind to be at all useful it must be put into practice.[55] Here again, practice in jazz finds an analogue in the

54. McFague, *Speaking in Parables*, xiii. Nathan Crawford makes the argument that theology is inherently improvisational. While I agree with this thesis, I disagree with him on its implications for how we conceive of God. It seems to me that Crawford's project lacks the necessary constraints to say anything meaningful about God. See Crawford, *Theology as Improvisation*.

55. Vanhoozer observes "a new 'ugly ditch'" consisting of a dichotomy between theory and practice in the academy and the church. He argues, "Doctrines arise not from speculative theories but from the core practices—baptism, the Eucharist, prayer, worship—that constitute the ongoing life and identity of the church." Vanhoozer, *Drama of Doctrine*, 13. In a jazz context, theory must be worked out in practice in order to

liberating discipline required for the enactment of Christian freedom. Paul writes about subduing his body and running with the goal of winning the prize (1 Cor 9:24–27) and Jesus speaks about the daily need to deny oneself (Luke 9:23). The process of mastering an instrument requires a musician to develop fine motor skills through regular, careful, and consistent practicing. Anything less will hamper the musician's ability to execute music with the sound and rhythmic accuracy they desire. As good habits are developed and bad ones excised, the musician finds it physically more difficult to play poorly than to play well. The spiritual disciplines that Jesus demonstrates in his Incarnation, combined with his thorough knowledge of Scripture and his ability to expand the theological implications of the law and the prophets (in word and deed) provide the perfect model for employing the liberating resources of Scripture and theology in the Christian life.

Together for a Common Cause

The tension between black and white musicians in the birth and development of jazz finds a similar tension between Jews and Gentiles in the New Testament. Just as whites were in many ways the oppressors of blacks in America, so the Romans were the oppressors of the Jews. And just as European instrumentation, theory, and religion constrained the development of black music in America, so the development of Christianity was constrained by the Greek language as well as concepts, metaphors, and analogies drawn from Greco-Roman culture. Black musicians birthed jazz and played the central role in its development;[56] in the same way, Jews were the first Christians—they were the disciples of Jesus, the first apostles, and the ones to write the lion's share of the New Testament. Cooperation and resentment, acceptance and shunning mark both sets of relationships.

White American musicians and early Gentile Christians were drawn into a new paradigm filled with the promise of freedom. For white musicians it was the freedom of individual expression combined with a new set of improvisational devices; for Gentile Christians it was freedom in Christ from slavery to sin. Both were initially regarded to some extent as outsiders, demonstrated in the jazz domain by Red Rodney's experiences with black

---

be worthwhile; theory books often double as method books (see, for example, Levine, *Jazz Theory*). Yet even apparently esoteric works, provided they have practical implications, can result in practical innovations. John Coltrane's use of Slonimsky, *Thesaurus of Scales*, in his composition of "Giant Steps" is a celebrated case in point. See Porter, *John Coltrane*, 149–50.

56. See DeVeaux, *Birth of Bebop*, 18; and Porter, *What Is This Thing*, 2–3.

musicians (see chapter 4) and in the Christian domain by the insistence of some Jews that Gentiles conform themselves to the Jewish law (e.g., Gal 6:12–13). And both were on the whole accepted; the musicians on the basis of their musical ability and the Gentiles on the basis of their faith in Jesus Christ. The presence and evidence of the "*It*" factor and the Holy Spirit respectively brought together people divided by oppression and injustice.

A common strategy was employed by both African American musicians and by Jewish Christians in relation to those who oppressed them; in both cases, aspects of the culture of the oppressor, which were found to be useful, were incorporated into the expression of jazz and the birth of Christianity. For example, Charlie Parker, undeniably a key figure in the history of jazz, did not hesitate to make use of the European classical tradition in his improvisations.[57] Instead of insisting on a strictly African approach to music, black jazz musicians engaged with what they encountered and enriched their music in the process. In a similar way, Jewish Christians decided to write their letters and gospels in Greek instead of Hebrew or Aramaic because their focus was on proclaiming the message as opposed to preserving Jewish hegemony. In terms of the relationships between white and black, Jew and Gentile, the success of crossing the divide between groups was proportionate to the value placed upon the cause they now had in common. According to Sonny Rollins,

> Jazz has always been a music of integration. In other words, there were definitely lines where blacks would be and where whites would begin to mix a little bit. I mean, jazz was not just a music; it was a social force in this country, and it was talking about freedom and people enjoying things for what they are and not having to worry about whether they were supposed to be white, black and all this stuff.[58]

This practice of integration finds a corresponding (though far more reaching and radical) assertion in Gal 3:28 where Paul throws down any and all barriers to Christian unity in Christ.

In both domains, the bridge between sides quickly collapses when the concerns of a distinct cultural group or social and economic considerations begin to take precedence over the music or over the actual teachings of Scripture, especially when one side believes or acts as if they can do without the other. Such actions are, more often than not, rooted in a feeling or even a belief in one's superiority over others. Amos Jones Jr. illustrates this principle with a historical example:

57. Ibid., 75.
58. Sonny Rollins, quoted in Gitler, *Swing to Bop*, 303.

in 1845, or thereabout, virtually every major denomination in America split over the issue of slavery: whether black people in America should remain slaves or be set free. This was the white church's way, especially the white church of the South of saying to black people, "I have no need of you." The result of this devastating division was a Methodist Church of the North and a Methodist Church of the South, a Northern Baptist Convention and a Southern Baptist Convention and so forth.[59]

Peter Heltzel traces the notion of white supremacy to "replacement theology"—the problematic notion that Christianity replaces Judaism, making Christians superior to Jews.[60] From historic Spanish "purity of blood laws" to German anti-Semitism, European Christianity has a historical record of whitewashing the Jewish origins of Christianity in order to secure privilege over others.[61] Christian history bears deep scars from the sundering of ways between Jew and Gentile.

To avoid following white musicians such as Red Rodney in failing to take into account the full extent of societal injustices, white Christians in particular ought to inform themselves about the historical, sociological, and economic injustices that have existed and continue to exist in their particular contexts.[62] As Michael O. Emerson and Christian Smith show in an American context, "The fact that American's health, life, and death are racialized make gaping wounds. And the immense divisions between social networks, cultures, and religions not only contribute to the rawness of these wounds, but make their healing that much more difficult."[63] Enacting Christian freedom in this area, especially in a western context, will consist of informed, gracious, and determined acts to bridge the racial and socioeconomic gaps that continue to exist between God's people.

Three principles can be derived from these comparisons. The first is that, in order to cross between cultural groups, especially when they relate to each other on unequal terms, it is necessary to provide something that is genuine, sincere, and worthy of being pursued with might and main. In order for interaction between two sides to be worthwhile, to be worth being set free from societal, cultural, and economic restraints, they must share a strong common purpose. In other words, the Gospel must not be something

59. Jones, *Paul's Message*, 175–76.

60. Heltzel, *Resurrection City*, 10–11.

61. Heltzel, *Resurrection City*, 11–12.

62. For a good overview of relations between blacks and whites in the context of the church in America, see Emerson and Smith, *Divided by Faith*.

63. Emerson and Smith, *Divided by Faith*, 171.

only held in theory, but something deliberately exercised and enacted.[64] Second, boundaries can be crossed, but they must not be ignored, especially when they continue to be perpetuated and enforced outside of the church (there is no chance of success when the church does this herself). Just as Red Rodney found that playing with black musicians did not mean that all the rifts between blacks and whites were healed, the Church must be aware of the effects of injustice and oppression, take steps to address them, and allow time for healing. Thirdly, exchanging ideas and offering friendship across divisions often leads to transcending one's own limitations. African American musicians appropriated European instruments and music tradition in synthesizing jazz, which is arguably one of America's greatest cultural contributions to the world.[65] Such an act takes humility because it implies that one is lacking something of value that the other possesses. If the church were to take this seriously, its practices could be greatly enriched. Note that if this takes place only on a superficial level, then little will have been gained. Jazz musicians allowed European music to make a significant contribution to the music, not merely surface level modifications. On the other hand, interacting with the other in a truly productive way does not mean compromising the fundamental aspects of the faith. What it does mean is being open to making meaningful changes to the medium and manner through which the definitive aspects of the faith are expressed.

CONTINUAL CONSTRAINTS

The body, God's moral law, and time are unavoidable constraints in the realm of Christian freedom. The process of mastering an instrument in a jazz context provides an analogy for a Christian view of the body that avoids historical ascetic extremes on the one hand and slavery to the body on the other. The overtone series, as an expression of the physical laws of the universe that operate in music, provides an analogy for the moral order that God gives to the universe, which C. S. Lewis calls the *Tao*.[66] Finally, time

64. See the introduction for a survey of theologians who connect jazz with theology in order to emphasize the practical aspects of the Gospel.

65. Richard Palmer sees jazz as one of the "two aesthetic forms" that America has given the world. Palmer, "Jazz," 287. The growing consent behind such assertions is reflected in Burns, *Jazz*.

66. By the *Tao*, Lewis is referring to "the doctrine of objective value, the belief that certain attitudes are really true, and others really false, to the kind of thing the universe is and the kind of things we are." Lewis, "Abolition of Man," 701. He knowingly appropriates the term from Chinese thought, but uses it in a broader sense to refer to the shared values expressed in "Platonic, Aristotelian, Stoic, Christian, and Oriental

provides the movement necessary for Christians to improvise within other constraints; it creates the space necessary for the alternation and interplay of apparently contradictory values such as assertiveness and openness.

Embodiment: "Brother Ass" or Stallion?

The human body can be altered or mutilated in innumerable ways, but regardless of what one does to it, one cannot escape from it until one is dead. While I do not wish to become entangled in the particulars of the debate over whether human beings are bodies or souls inhabiting bodies (though I sympathize with the latter on the basis of 2 Cor 5:1–10), I am interested in the way the body constrains the enactment of Christian freedom.[67]

The history of Christianity is replete with examples of hermits and mystics who sought to master their bodies by subjecting them to all sorts of depredations. St. Francis of Assisi, while scourging himself to overcome temptation, addresses his body: "Ah, Brother Ass, thus must thou remain, thus shalt thou be scourged."[68] Similarly, St. Jerome writes:

> My limbs were roughly clad in sackcloth—an unlovely sight. My neglected skin had taken on the appearance of an Ethiopian's body. Daily I wept, daily I groaned, and whenever insistent slumber overcame my resistance, I bruised my awkward bones upon the bare earth. Of food and drink I say nothing, since even the sick drink only cold water, and to get any cooked food is a luxury. There was I, therefore, who from fear of hell had condemned myself to such a prison, with only scorpions and wild beasts as companions.[69]

And yet for all this he is still tormented by visions of dancing girls. The ascetic impulse in Christianity is matched by a desire for complete mastery over one's instrument in jazz. The heroic practice habits of luminaries such as Charlie Parker and John Coltrane are the stuff of legend. Unfortunately, so is their drug use and sexual excesses. Approaching complete mastery comes at a price. It easily becomes an end unto itself rather than a means to an end.

[Asian]" thought (701). His appendix (731–38) sets illustrations of underlying laws in the *Tao* from diverse sources side by side.

67. For a good interdisciplinary defense of dualism, see Turl, "Substance Dualism."

68. Assisi, *Works of the Seraphic Father*, 183.

69. Jerome, *Letters of St. Jerome*, 1:140.

Granted ascetic practices such as fasting do appear in Scripture; Jesus practices fasting, but he also "has come eating and drinking" (Luke 7:34). Paul writes on the one hand of making his body a slave (1 Cor 9:24–27) but on the other he shows a healthy respect for sexual drives when counseling singles and married couples (1 Cor 7:1–9). Scripture simultaneously affirms the goodness of the human body—it is, after all, created by God—and warns about the danger of being mastered by it. The body is finite, restricted, and comes with a set of basic impulses that are meant to ensure survival and re-production. Instruments contain various components designed to produce pitched sound. These things are not inherently evil, but in excess or when disordered or misplaced, they enslave.

To borrow from Rinzler's taxonomy of the ways in which apparent opposites can interact, perhaps the ascetic excesses of some of the church fathers can be explained by a dualism in which the body and the soul are mutually excluding or work in inverse proportion to one another. By way of contrast, jazz encourages musicians to both master their instruments *and* to exploit the foibles and quirks of their instruments in making music. In an age where synthesizers offer increasingly sophisticated simulacra of acoustic instruments, subtle manipulation of the mechanics of a physical in-strument allow jazz musicians to rebel against any absolutizing standard of perfection.[70] The physical nature of the instrument helps to set it apart from a disembodied ideal. It may never be possible to determine the relationship between body and soul empirically, but approaching their relationship as a gradation, two perspectives on a larger whole, or (stepping outside of con-tradiction) as sharing a symbiotic relationship may provide a constructive alternative that lies closer to what Scripture teaches.

Jesus once again provides the model of mastering the body and living fully through it. He fasts and prays (e.g., Matt 4:2; Mark 1:35; Luke 4:2); he touches people when he heals them (e.g., Matt 8:3; Mark 7:33; Luke 22:51) and when he prays for them (e.g., Matt 19:13–15); he weeps (John 11:35); he eats and drinks with others (e.g., Matt 9:10); and he washes feet (John 13:1–14). He suffers and dies. Even after the resurrection he still eats (Luke 24:41–43) and he allows Thomas to touch his scars (John 20:24–28). Jesus' body provides the constraint necessary to minister to his people, to suffer

---

70. Don Ihde observes, "the instrumentation within the jazz traditions . . . remains 'technologically' conservative." Ihde, *Listening and Voice*, 237. Considering the use of the saxophone in jazz, he notes, "[t]his expressive musical instrument enables the individual performer to express, interpret differently through a wide range of auditory possibilities. Rather than 'standardizing' an output, musical instruments may be said to 'destandardize'" (239). By "perfection," I mean a sterile and static ideal; not "perfection" in the sense of completeness and maturity that Jesus refers to in Matt 5:48.

in their place, and to mediate between them and God. By his actions, Jesus affirms the worth and dignity of the human body. As Mark Noll argues, "to confess the materiality of the incarnation is to perceive an unusual dignity in the material world itself."[71] Finitude is not evil; rather it constrains one to be dependent on God and interdependent within the body of Christ. The body allows persons to interact with one another and to enjoy being a part of God's creation.

In C. S. Lewis's *The Great Divorce*, a ghost wrestles with a lizard representing lust that sits perched on his shoulder. When the ghost finally gives permission to an angel to kill the lizard, the dead lizard is resurrected into a stallion while the ghost becomes a man.[72] This death and resurrection may only be completed after death, but through the process of working out salvation with fear and trembling—through the work of the Holy Spirit in sanctification—the desires and limitations of the body are turned from being masters into slaves to God's calling.

Sonic Order and C. S. Lewis's Tao

The universal nature of the overtone series finds its corresponding analogue in a universal moral sense that Lewis calls the *Tao* in *The Abolition of Man*.[73] In an appendix to this book, Lewis draws examples from a wide range of religious and philosophical sources across time to show their inherent similarities.[74] Paul sees something like Lewis's conception of Tao at work among the Gentiles:

> When Gentiles, who do not possess the law, do instinctively what the law requires, these, though not having the law, are a law to themselves. They show that what the law requires is written on their hearts, to which their own conscience also bears witness; and their conflicting thoughts will accuse or perhaps excuse them on the day when, according to my gospel, God, through Jesus Christ, will judge the secret thoughts of all (Rom 2:14–16).

The law written on the hearts of the Gentiles is not identical to the law of Moses that God gave to the Israelites, but it resonates with it in a

71. Noll, *Jesus Christ*, 35.

72. Lewis, "Great Divorce," 522–26.

73. See Blackwell, *Sacred in Music*, 56–59 for his discussion of the overtone series and 71–76 for his reflections on its (qualifiedly) universal influence on music.

74. See Lewis, "Abolition of Man," 731–38.

recognizable way. Perhaps it is more accurate to say that both laws are par-
ticularizations of God's intent for humanity (though the law of Moses, as
special revelation from God, is closer to the mark).[75] Jesus indicates that this
is the case when he describes the laws Moses gives concerning divorce as a
concession to the hard-heartedness of the Israelites (Mark 10:5; Matt19:8).
The author of Hebrews insists that the law of Moses itself "has only a shadow
of the good things to come and not the true form of these realities" (Heb
10:1). In other words, even the law of Moses is a particularization of God's
intention for humanity rather than the intention itself; it must be because
temporal human reality is always in a state of flux.

The law that God gave to Moses, then, is a reflection of God's intentions.
God's intentions as revealed in Scripture are a type of cultural constraint in
that they bear the marks of human authorship, including the setting and
circumstances under which they were written. God's intentions in Scripture
are simultaneously transcendent because they come from God, and they are
continual constraints because they reflect the morality inherent in God's
character and impressed into the hearts and minds of human beings.

The overtone series provides another way of understanding the relationship between God's intentions and Scripture in addition to the one described above. When the overtone series is embodied by instruments played
by human beings, the tones produced do not perfectly match the mathematics that lie behind the series. When two musicians play in tune, there is
a certain amount of deviation from the mean that still sounds pleasing to
the ear, that still works. Similarly, Christian freedom reflects God's perfect
law (the law that stands behind its particular instantiation in Scripture), but
instead of being flat and rigid, it is colored by the multiple constraints of the
Christian life. Albert Blackwell describes the overtone series as "manifold
in its structure, unlimited in its possibilities, and exceedingly hospitable
to creative human choices."[76] If one views God's intentions as revealed
in Scripture (interpreted through the life and teaching of Jesus Christ) in
such a manner, than they appear as what they are intended to be: liberating constraints that encourage diverse forms of creative improvisation. Life
is not meant to consist of an impossible reach for a Platonic form, but a
finite instantiation that reveals underlying principles while being beautiful
in its own right. Ignoring these underlying principles necessarily results in
aimless disorder, while being attuned to them provides a way of being consonant *and* a way to use dissonance constructively.

75. For a fuller discussion of the law in relation to Christian freedom, see chapter 3.

76. Blackwell, *Sacred in Music*, 76.

Time

Just as music requires time, so does the enactment of Christian freedom. Time allows for the movements of redemption and sanctification; unlike a static image or object, the Christian life interacts, intersects, and changes. It takes time to move from one set of constraints into another; it takes time to creatively improvise within these constraints—to move back and forth from different levels of assertiveness and openness, to work out music that reflects the intent of the composer, to transgress boundaries.

While time as a continual constraint intersects with all other constraints in jazz and the Christian life, it intersects with the occasional constraint of community in a particularly interesting way. Begbie observes that "part of our conferring particularity on each other is the conferring of time (I 'give time' to the other) such that the other person's distinctive temporality is allowed to engage with mine, and vice versa, to mutual benefit."[77] In jazz improvisation, one gives time to others through listening to them, allowing them to solo, and by dialing back one's assertiveness in order to be open to what they are saying. In the Christian life, listening also requires giving time. Giving time and sharing experiences in time allows Christians to grow to know one other, be accountable to one another, and perhaps to even change in relation to one another. Through listening to another, one's perception of them is enhanced. Through listening, one's own ideas and even identity is cast in a different light.

Just as improvised melodies in jazz play off a basic pulse, the birth, development, decline, and death of the body provides an underlying pulse to the physical life of Christians. So too their ongoing death to self, rebirth in Christ, ongoing sanctification, and the regular meeting of the church provides a complementary pulse to their spiritual lives.[78] Within this basic pulse, life is improvised in relation to the church and contemporary circumstances. The pulses of physical and spiritual life provide a way of coming to terms with unpredictable life events, including the work of the Holy Spirit. Part of enacting Christian freedom is doing one's part to keep the spiritual pulse going as part of the body of Christ. Otherwise, how will one hear what the Holy Spirit is doing in relation to it?

---

77. Begbie, *Theology, Music and Time*, 207.

78. Begbie develops the theological implications of repetition in music and the Eucharist in *Theology, Music and Time*, 155–75.

RISKS AND MISTAKES: MILES DAVIS AND THE
APOSTLE PETER

Miles Davis' music is beautiful in spite of his mistakes, perhaps because of his sincerity in attempting to convey emotion through his tone. His daring risks give his music a sense of immediacy lacking in overly-polished studio creations. The Apostle Peter's life is also marked by sincere risks and errors. He dared things that the other disciples did not and winds up being alternately praised and rebuked by Jesus. He provides a model for taking risks and recovering after errors. But before examining these aspects of Peter's life, I look at Jesus' *Parable of the Talents* as it is told in Matt 25:14–30 in order to make a solid case for risk-taking in the Christian life.

A master sets out on a journey, entrusting his three slaves with five, two, and one talent respectively (a laborer might hope to make one talent in half a lifetime).[79] Astonishingly, the first two slaves manage to double their money; Ulrich Luz suggests that Jesus' audience would assume that they were "dealing in commodities or speculating in land" or even resorting to "unscrupulous and cutthroat practices."[80] Meanwhile, the third slave buries his money. Upon the master's return, he settles accounts with his slaves. The first two are rewarded and the third is punished for his fear and trepidation. R. T. France concludes,

> In the circumstances, to bury money in the ground was proba-
> bly the better way to keep it safe; the course of action demanded
> by the master [i.e. depositing the money with the bankers] may
> have been no less risky than the commercial ventures attempted
> by the other two slaves. But risk is at the heart of discipleship
> ([Matt]10:39; 16:25–26); by playing safe the cautious slave has
> achieved nothing, and it is his timidity and lack of enterprise . . .
> which is condemned.[81]

At the heart of jazz and the enactment of Christian freedom is an element of risk. Yet one possible scenario is lacking in this parable: how would a master judge a servant who had risked and lost? Risk necessarily includes the possibility of failure.

Timothy Wiarda discerns a pattern that "appears to be repeated in many of the gospel narratives concerning Peter."[82] Peter tries to interact with Jesus based on his own presuppositions of what is right and fitting,

79. France, *Matthew*, 953.

80. Luz, *Matthew 21–28*, 3:252.

81. France, *Matthew*, 955–56.

82. Wiarda, *Peter in the Gospels*, 34.

only to have Jesus correct him. The important thing to note is that Peter has good intentions towards Jesus—he wants to be helpful and loyal. Wiarda compiles an extensive list of such occasions, ranging from Peter rebuking Jesus for speaking about his imminent death, and being strongly rebuked by Jesus in turn (Mark 8:31–33; Matt 16:22–23), to his "attempts to stay loyal to Jesus by following [him] into the high priest's courtyard," which falls apart when Peter denies Jesus three times (attested to in all four gospels).[83] Yet Peter's failures don't destroy his life or his connection to Jesus. Jesus reinstates Peter and affirms his role as a leader in the church (John 21:15–17). The beginning of Acts finds Peter, full of the Holy Spirit, leading the apostles in proclaiming the gospel.

In jazz, as in life, mistakes cannot be taken back. As Paul Berliner points out, "[i]mprovisers cannot retrieve their unintended phrases or unsuccessful 'accidents.'"[84] At times mistakes can be salvaged or even turned into part of the improvisation.[85] At other times, they simply happen. In both the cases of Miles Davis and Peter, boldness and sincerity are the key ingredients that prevent inevitable mistakes from becoming devastating. Mistakes are to be avoided—Davis shows a preference for studio takes with less mistakes.[86] When they happen one tries to learn from them, so as to avoid them. Yet living in fear of making mistakes prevents Christians from taking the risks that are essential to answer their calling. Mark Ellingsen, picking up on Martin Luther's notion of "brave sinning," argues that instead of focusing on avoiding sin, one should be liberated "to do God's 'thing' joyously and with reckless abandon."[87] Enacting Christian freedom means abandoning with Kierkegaard the impossibility of the ethical stage in favor of the religious stage—of risking everything in God's service while boldly claiming his forgiveness in the areas one falls short.

---

83. Wiarda, *Peter in the Gospels*, 36. See Mark 14:54, 66–72; Matt 26:58, 69–75; Luke 22:54–62; John 18:15–18, 25–27.

84. Berliner, *Thinking in Jazz*, 210.

85. Berliner provides several examples. In one a drummer loses control of his sticks. The sticks rebound on the drum "with a unique syncopated figure" that he turns into a musical motif. In another, a trumpet overshoots an intended note and then descends to the correct pitch. He proceeds to similarly "ornament each pitch of the chord . . . creating a new phrase from the maneuver." Berliner, *Thinking in Jazz*, 213.

86. Walser, "Out of Notes," 356.

87. Ellingsen, *Sin Bravely*, 64.

CONCLUSION

According to Begbie, improvisation entails particularizing cultural constraints "in relation to occasional constraints."[88] This, of course, takes place within the limitations of continual constraints. In the body, governed by time and in relation to the Tao, Christians take the constraints of tradition—including roles, God's intentions in Scripture, theology, and a checkered history of relating to others—and particularize it in relation to the places where they gather and to one another under the direction of the Holy Spirit. These resources, with all of their accompanying benefits and challenges, provide the constraints necessary to enact Christian freedom. The constant shifting of occasional constraints, the slower change of cultural constraints, and the fluctuations in continual constraints makes it necessary to improvise. The risk inherent in improvisation entails mistakes. But Christian freedom entails deliverance from the guilt of these mistakes along with the ability to continue in the service of God.

The following chapter takes this framework into the contemporary context of the West as described in chapter 1. The enactment of Christian freedom stands in stark contrast to authoritarian-fundamentalism *and* the postmodern-self. It also resists Marxist alienation and the dominance of technique.

88. Begbie, *Theology, Music and Time*, 215.

6

A Jazz-Shaped Approach
to the Problem of Freedom

IN HIS PREFACE TO the third edition of *The Pilgrim's Regress*, C. S. Lewis explicates the "equal and opposite evils" that reside in the North and South of the land in his allegory.[1] He notes that each side is "continually strengthened and made plausible by its critique of the other," much like the opposing forces of the postmodern-self and authoritarian-fundamentalism I describe in chapter 1.[2] To the North are those "of rigid systems" who are "signed and sealed members of highly organized parties," that is, the authoritarian fundamentalists.[3] To the South reside those who embrace the postmodern-self, who "are by their very nature less definable; boneless souls" that delight in "[t]he delicious tang of the forbidden and the unknown."[4] In the course of Lewis's tale, two of his characters journey to the North and the South in their pursuit of truth. After they find faith, they must journey back from whence they came, this time seeing things clearly. Similarly, after working through the preceding chapters, one is in a position to view the problem of freedom in a new light. Many of the concepts referred to in this chapter are defined and elaborated in the previous ones.

Lewis's characters are tasked with slaying dragons on their return journey. One must slay the dragon in the North and the other the dragon in the South. They find strength that they were previously lacking in the process of

1. Lewis, "Pilgrim's Regress," 10.
2. Lewis, "Pilgrim's Regress," 10.
3. Lewis, "Pilgrim's Regress," 10.
4. Lewis, "Pilgrim's Regress," 10.

slaying these dragons; their tendencies in opposite directions are corrected by an encounter with their opposites. In jazz, too, much can be learned from Ornette Coleman's legacy of setting aside boundaries and Wynton Marsalis' painstaking recreation of early forms of jazz. Coleman challenges those who listen to him to think outside of clichéd licks and Marsalis reminds those who listen to him of the wealth of resources that the jazz tradition has to offer. Yet, as I show in chapter 4, jazz is at its best and most rewarding when it embraces the apparent contradictions between tradition and innovation, assertion and openness. Within an interlocking web of constraints, an improviser is free to draw upon a certain tradition in one situation and to set it aside in another. One the one hand, she is liberated from the limits of her imagination and abilities in encountering the other. On the other, she is liberated from slavish obedience to a certain formulation of jazz theory. This web of occasional, cultural, and continual constraints finds corresponding analogues and relationships between analogues in Christian freedom (see chapter 5).

The task of the present chapter is to bring a jazz-shaped conception of Christian freedom to bear on the problem of freedom in the contemporary West set out in chapter 1. My object is not an exhaustive outworking of all the implications of this conception in relation to the problem, but rather to illustrate ways in which this conception can begin to address the problem's major features. Since I believe the church is the necessary vehicle for the expression of Christian freedom, I examine a number of the ways in which the Western church falls prey to the problem of freedom and outline how a jazz-shaped conception of freedom can aid in revitalizing it.

MOVING FROM A CULTURAL- TO A CANONICAL-LINGUISTIC TURN

Kevin Vanhoozer observes that:

> Many Evangelicals have unknowingly made the cultural-linguistic turn already, though the cultures they have appropriated have not been altogether holy. Practices that owe more to managerial, therapeutic, consumerist, and entertainment cultures increasingly characterize Evangelical churches, so much so they are in danger of becoming the de facto, if not the de jure, authority for the Evangelical way of life.[5]

5. Vanhoozer, *Drama of Doctrine*, 26. Vanhoozer uses "the capitalized term *Evangelical* in a sociohistorical sense to refer to those Protestants . . . who trace their Christian heritage back to the revival movements of the eighteenth and nineteenth centuries"

By the term "cultural-linguistic turn," he is referring to the approach to theology proposed by George Lindbeck in his influential book, *The Nature of Doctrine*. According to Lindbeck, "a religion can be viewed as a kind of cultural and/or linguistic framework or medium that shapes the entirety of life and thought."[6] This framework grounds "the description of realities, the formulation of beliefs and the experiencing of inner attitudes, feelings, and sentiments."[7] It is the *a priori* that shapes everything else. Vanhoozer's point is that Evangelicals, without being conscious of it, have absorbed aspects of surrounding cultures, which in turn shape their beliefs and practices. These surrounding cultures are permeated by the postmodern-self and authoritarian-fundamentalism, alienation and technique. The postmodern-self is largely responsible for the "therapeutic" and "entertainment" aspects of Evangelical churches that Vanhoozer is concerned with: therapy to affirm the self and entertainment to stave off boredom. Alienation and technique are in large part responsible for the "managerial" and "consumerist" aspects. Authoritarian-fundamentalism might appear to escape Vanhoozer's critique but, as I show below and in chapter 1, it too is shaped by *a priori* assumptions formed by a romanticized reconstruction of the past. The polarization between the postmodern-self and authoritarian-fundamentalism divides the church and burdens believers with beliefs and practices that are incongruous with the Christian faith.[8] Technique may appear to be a benign tool that the church can employ to good purpose, but, as I show in chapter 1 and below, it exacts a high cost. In short, the problem with the cultural-linguistic turn is that it makes the church vulnerable to forces that are necessarily opposed to Christian freedom.

Vanhoozer proposes a canonical-linguistic alternative to the cultural-linguistic turn. He wants to retain Lindbeck's postliberal perspective with respect to "communal practice" and yet replace Lindbeck's prioritization of culture with "an authoritative canonical script."[9] I concur with Vanhoozer that Scripture ought to take precedence over culture. Making theology dependent on culture renders theology incapable of offering a meaningful critique of it. In such a system, God's intentions blur into cultural norms.

(25n75).

6. Lindbeck, *Nature of Doctrine*, 33.

7. Lindbeck, *Nature of Doctrine*, 33.

8. This polarization is often expressed (broadly speaking) in the divide between left and right in politics. Jacques Ellul observes that while the fact that the church is divided is scandalous, "it is an even greater scandal, not that Christians belong to different political parties, but that they should hate and excommunicate one another for differing political choices." Ellul, *Ethics of Freedom*, 380.

9. Vanhoozer, *Drama of Doctrine*, 32.

Vanhoozer views Scripture as a primary means by which God makes his intentions known. He writes, "Scripture is not authoritative simply because the church needs a criterion but because it is part of the revelatory and re- demptive economies of the triune God. The canon is the locus for God's communicative action—past, present, and future—the divinely approved means by which God exercises his authority in, and over, the church."[10] Vanhoozer picks up Hans Urs von Balthasar's idea of a theo-drama, seeing in Scripture the record of the drama between God and his people and a foretelling of the eschaton. The present must be improvised in light of the past and the future. My project complements Vanhoozer's dramatic anal- ogy through a jazz-shaped conception of Christian freedom that offers a model for identifying and integrating the constraints that are proper to this improvisation.

THE POSTMODERN-SELF

The desire to be autonomous, liberated from authority is central to the postmodern-self. It takes the form of detaching oneself from any authority residing in community, tradition, Lewis's Tao, and (perhaps especially) in Scripture. In terms of a jazz-shaped conception of freedom, the postmod- ern-self exhibits an imbalance between assertion and openness. It exagger- ates the resources and wisdom of the self and denigrates the resources and wisdom of the past. Its search for significance and self worth are continually frustrated by the insatiable needs of the ego. The postmodern-self remains firmly entrenched in Kierkegaard's aesthetic stage; the ethical stage cannot be reached because the relativizing forces of pluralism appear to obscure the Tao. Observing the excesses and futility of the ethical stage as it is embodied in authoritarian-fundamentalism provides justification for staying away from any religious instantiation of it. But just as North and South smuggle in elements from one another in *The Pilgrim's Regress*, so a secular simulacra of the ethical stage emerges that insists on the universal validation of cer- tain lifestyles that transgress traditional norms. Without a solid foundation upon which to base accepting certain lifestyles and rejecting others, secular valuation is very vulnerable to groups with access to institutional power and mass media.

A jazz-shaped conception of Christian freedom offers a viable alterna- tive to the postmodern-self that is not reactionary and that has the space to affirm (albeit in a transformed form) elements of the aesthetic stage and the significance of the self in its differences and similarities to others.

10. Vanhoozer, *Drama of Doctrine*, 124.

I begin by contrasting God's intentions with the bid for autonomy of the postmodern-self and the work of the Holy Spirit with Kierkegaard's aesthetic stage. I conclude with the constraints of community and tradition. In what follows I allow these constraints to interface with each other and other constraints such as embodiment and time to address the different elements of the postmodern-self.

Acknowledging God's Intentions

Part of what makes jazz jam sessions possible is a common repertoire of standard tunes to improvise upon. The form, harmony, and to a lesser extent the melody of a given standard act as constraints upon improvised solos. The notes of improvised melodies are understood against the backdrop of the chord changes in the form. Scripture is in some ways analogous to this repertoire.[11] God's desired intent in giving Scripture finds an analogue in the constraints of playing jazz standards. It is precisely at this point that Christian freedom differs most sharply from the freedom of the postmodern-self. Just as Coleman did not wish to be constrained by form or given harmony, so the postmodern-self does not wish to acknowledge the revelation of a divine composer. But again, it is precisely the constraints of revelation that are liberating, that provide a firm place to push off from.[12]

Accepting the constraints of a jazz standard provides musicians with a form that can unify their efforts in relation to the sonic order. If the underlying harmonic structure of a song and the very form of the song itself do not remain constant, it becomes difficult, if not impossible, for improvisers to set up the melodic tension and release that this structure makes possible. Speaking of a b9 resolving to a 5th is meaningless outside of a chord progression.[13] In an analogous manner, Scripture provides an underlying structure that shapes the way the members of the church interact with one another in carrying out God's intentions. It clarifies the Tao (in C. S. Lewis's sense). Scripture provides resources to draw from and a structure upon which to build. It gives the church cohesion and coherence so that it does

11. One point of dissimilarity is the closed canon of Christian scripture compared to the ever-shifting set of tunes that are considered to be jazz standards. See chapter 5.

12. Igor Stravinsky writes, "In art as in everything else, one can build only upon a resisting foundation: whatever constantly gives way to pressure, constantly renders movement impossible." Stravinsky, *Poetics of Music*, 87.

13. For instance, the b9 of a G7 chord is Ab. It creates dissonance with the root of the G7 chord that can be resolved by moving to the 5th of a C chord: a G. The Ab only functions as a b9 in relation to a G7 chord and the G only functions as a 5th in relation to a C chord (major or minor).

not have to capitulate to the interest groups that surreptitiously govern the postmodern-self.[14]

The continual constraint of embodiment is also an aspect of God's intentions. Just as a composer notates music with the expectation that it will be in some way realized audibly by its performers, so God gives his word with the expectation that his people will realize it in their bodily actions (Jas 1:22–25). The body both makes possible and constrains human action. Its limitations and abilities are part of what gives individuals their unique characteristics. In the present life and in the resurrected life human beings are embodied. Bodies require care and maintenance and can be developed in different ways to increase things such as strength and mental dexterity.

The struggle of the postmodern-self to be free from authority extends to being free from nature. If the body is an accidental rather than given constraint, then altering it radically to fit a self-constructed identity becomes a possibility. One's self-identification allows one to override the accidental constraint of the body. Jacques Ellul's concept of technique comes into play here because it makes radical alterations possible. Slavoj Žižek, writing about the 2006 declaration by New York City authorities that choosing one's gender is an inalienable human right, notes "[t]he ultimate difference, the 'transcendental' difference that grounds human identity itself, thus turns into something open to manipulation: the ultimate plasticity of being human is asserted instead."[15] Problems emerge for the postmodern-self when the feelings tied to one's identity can themselves be constructed. Philip K. Dick's novel, *Do Androids Dream of Electric Sheep*, looks ahead to the possibility that persons in the future might dial "mood organs" to regulate what they feel. The problem with being liberated from nature, as C. S. Lewis points out in *The Abolition of Man*, is that one's humanity dissolves in the process.

Embodiment itself can only be liberating when one acknowledges that it is a gift rather than an accident. This is not to say that embodiment is a straightjacket; embodiment is quite malleable; the ways jazz musicians exploit the quirks of their particular instruments provide a useful analogue for the multiple ways the body can be employed. Half-valve effects, smears, and growls are all creative ways that a trumpeter can go beyond simply playing a note with good intonation. Yet it would be a perversion of the intended use of a trumpet to hit a snare with it. Repeated strikes would soon render it incapable of producing a note of any sort. Tearing apart an acoustic

14. In terms of enacting Christian freedom, this is what makes Vanhoozer's canonical-linguistic model liberating in contrast to the way Lindbeck's cultural-linguistic model fails to provide a way for the church to escape the problem of freedom.

15. Žižek, *Violence*, 33.

bass to build a guitar would destroy the nature of the bass and would not likely yield a high-quality instrument. Only acknowledging the intended purpose of the instrument (though again, this allows for considerable flexibility) allows one to use it in a way that is not destructive. So to, the human body has remarkable flexibility, but it also has intrinsic limits to how much it can be altered and to what purposes it can be employed. Transgressing these limits ultimately makes the body incapable of performing its intended tasks. Acknowledging the boundaries of God's intentions makes it possible to recognize when certain physical, mental, and spiritual states prevent a person from enjoying the freedoms that God intended. In short, it allows Christians to diagnose the maladies that affect the world and to follow Jesus in beginning to heal them (cf. Luke 4:16–21).

You Take Away and Give: The Holy Spirit and the Aesthetic Stage

The Holy Spirit proves "the world wrong about sin and righteousness and judgment" (John 16:8 NRSV). He shows that the determination of the postmodern-self to remain in Kierkegaard's aesthetic stage is wrong. Just as it is painfully obvious for informed listeners when a musician cannot improvise a line that reflects the underlying harmony of the song being played, the life of the postmodern-self refuses to hear and therefore cannot orient itself to God's intentions. A musician may passionately emote through their instrument in an attempt to satisfy their desire for self-expression, but without the constraints of tradition, harmony, and meaningful interaction with others, their efforts are ultimately banal and boring. Even playing deliberately outside of a chord requires knowing "what notes are 'wrong' with any given chord, using those notes in convincing *groups* of 'wrong' notes, as well as learning to use them singly in a mildly dissonant, but smooth manner. The experienced analyzer has very little difficulty distinguishing between errors and . . . outside playing."[16] In the same way, the never-ending, unconstrained pursuit of satisfying desire entailed by the aesthetic stage ends up being pathetic. Kierkegaard reasons that "[i]t is comic that a mentally disordered man picks up any piece of granite and carries it around because he believes it is money, and in the same way it is comic that Don Juan has 1,003 mistresses, for the number simply indicates that they have no value."[17] The unwillingness of the postmodern-self to adopt the constraints of the Christian life ultimately—and ironically—renders the satiation of its desires meaningless.

16. Coker, *Elements of the Jazz Language*, 83. Emphasis in original.
17. Kierkegaard, *Stages on Life's Way*, 293.

The freedom that Christianity offers in contrast to the freedom of the postmodern-self is not the endless striving of the ethical stage (though the path to Christian freedom might lead through this stage), but the surrender and forgiveness of the religious stage.[18] Instead of exchanging the pursuit of one's desires for the futile attempts of keeping the law (found in authoritarian-fundamentalism), one dies to self and is raised again in Christ. It is only through this transformation that one can "regress" like Lewis's pilgrim to the aesthetic stage and experience its delights fully—as they were meant to be enjoyed. In authoritarian-fundamentalism, one might indeed believe in one's death and resurrection in Christ, while remaining *de facto* in the ethical stage. In fact, the continual striving characterizing the ethical stage precludes the proper enjoyment of the aesthetic stage.[19] And the complete fulfillment of the desires of the aesthetic stage that the postmodern-self craves can never be attained by it. Desire must be surrendered before it can be grasped.

Even after one becomes a Christian, repenting from sin and receiving salvation as a gift from God, it is difficult to inhabit Kierkegaard's religious stage. Sanctification is an ongoing process, marked by the passage of time. It is an outworking of salvation with "fear and trembling." One must become aware of the constraints that supply and enable Christian freedom. One must, with patient practice, embrace these constraints and live by them— especially those constraints closest to God's intentions.[20] Part of this practicing is daily dying to self (Luke 9:23). Letting go of the "need to be revered by others because of our musical ability" in the jazz domain[21] corresponds to thinking of oneself with "sober judgment" in the domain of Christian freedom (Rom 12:3). In chapters 4 and 5, I show that the self-transcending moments experienced by jazz improviser are analogous to the religious stage. The thing that operates in the absence of the ego, Hal Crook's "*It*" factor, finds an analogue in the work of the Holy Spirit. Paul sets these ideas side by side in Gal 5:25–26: "If we live by the Spirit, let us also be guided by the Spirit. Let us not become conceited, competing against one another, envying one another." In short, the Christian alternative to the postmodern-self is death, resurrection, and life in step with the Holy Spirit.

---

18. See chapter 5 for an overview of Kierkegaard's three stages.

19. In authoritarian-fundamentalism, one might occasionally lapse into the hedonistic pursuits of the aesthetic stage, but this is a regression rather than a recovery.

20. See Wells, *Improvisation*, 73–85, for a discussion of "training in improvisation" (85).

21. Crook, *Ready, Aim, Improvise!*, 318.

Being Tied to Community

Investing in a community is risky. Churches can house abusers and church structures can be oppressive. Lives lie littered in the wake of church splits and scandals. Nor are churches immune to the economic forces that cause people to move from place to place, making it hard to put down roots. Capitalist models of consumption shape Christians who "church shop," hopping from place to place to see who best meets their desires. But for all of its problems, community holds out an opportunity to transcend the limits of self. Only through the rhythms of speaking and listening, through mutual submission, does one encounter the other in mutually transformative ways.

Jazz music provides an analogy for what it means to be in community. Playing jazz in an authentic way necessarily entails mutual submission.[22] Ingrid Monson writes that "the improvising artist is always making musical choices in relationship to what everyone else is doing."[23] In order to achieve "a satisfying musical journey—the feeling of wholeness and exhilaration, the pleasure that accompanies a performance well done," jazz musicians must listen and respond to one another.[24] In the domain of Christian freedom, mutual submission is clearly mandated in Scripture (e.g., Eph 5:21) as is being "quick to listen" and "slow to speak" (Jas 1:19, cf. Prov 18:13; 19:20; 25:12). Creating an analogy from jazz provides a way of fleshing out what this entails. Chapter 5 marks out the analogues between the various instruments in a jazz band and the members of a given church. There I suggest that roles can be occasionally swapped to attune the church to the perspective of each member. In addition, if the quiet roles of those who serve are not felt pulsing through the church, the church will have no depth; it will be only "a noisy gong or a clanging cymbal" (1 Cor 13:1). And if those who speak publicly are not attuned to quiet service, the world will hear it. As Cecil McBee comments about the bass, "He's the heartbeat. . . . What I mean is *all* are listening to him . . . all are listening to that pulse, that sound for guidance."[25] Freedom in jazz and in the Christian community is found in listening and responding to all participants.

Mutual submission and interaction affirms the value of each participant and elevates them above what they are capable of as isolated

---

22. In making this claim, I assert that improvisation is a necessary ingredient in performing in the jazz tradition. For a carefully considered look at the challenges of defining jazz (including finding consensus on its core elements), see Gridley, Maxham, and Hoff, "Three Approaches."

23. Monson, *Saying Something*, 27.

24. Monson, *Saying Something*, 27.

25. Cecil McBee, quoted in Monson, *Saying Something*, 30.

individuals. If the church can model a community that exhibits the same willingness to alternate between speaking and listening and to foster communication between quiet and prominent voices as a jazz combo it will show to the postmodern-self a way to be in community that does not view the self merely as a passive cog in a machine, but as a dynamic person with a voice in the direction that the community takes. The postmodern-self is concerned that it must surrender a degree of autonomy—a certain type of freedom—to be in community. While acknowledging that this is true, the church ought to demonstrate that the transformation and transcension of the self is a superior form of freedom, that the constraints of community open more vistas for creative improvisation than the detached, autonomous self. It must demonstrate that community is worth the risk.

Recovering Tradition

Few in the West argue for one course of action over another on the basis of tradition. If tradition is viewed as simply the way things have been done in the past, it falls over as soon as someone provides a pragmatic reason for doing things differently. The postmodern-self has no reason to be constrained by tradition and a technological society will discard practices based on tradition when more efficient alternatives are available. Except in the cases of happy coincidences, tradition is not especially valuable in technological or economic innovation. In contrast, tradition *is* valuable in law and the arts; in practicing the former one seeks to distribute justice consistently and practicing the latter entails drawing materials and method from it.

The Christian tradition operates as a liberating constraint in two ways: it provides continuity with the past—countering the tyranny of the present, and it provides a wealth of resources to draw from in enacting Christian freedom. G. K. Chesterton calls tradition "the democracy of the dead."[26] It resists "the small and arrogant oligarchy of those who merely happen to be walking about," combating those interest groups who, embracing Nietzsche's will to power (consciously or unconsciously), use mass media and political clout to their own ends.[27] Tradition provides an escape from the temptation of the postmodern-self to conform to the apparent consensus of the fashionable. It also calls into question "the assumption that whatever has gone out of date is on that account discredited," reopening old mines lost to neglect.[28] The resources of tradition free one "*from* the anxiety of

26. Chesterton, *Orthodoxy*, 74.
27. Chesterton, *Orthodoxy*, 74.
28. Here C. S. Lewis is describing what he calls "chronological snobbery." He credits

having to create structure from scratch, forms which will give meaning to improvisation—*we* don't have to 'make it happen' we can entrust ourselves to the given."[29] Instead of attempting to construct the self from the ground up, one can draw from the given: first from God's gifts and intentions and second from the experiences and reflections of those who have gone before.

Making tradition a secondary constraint helps to guard against its potential tyranny. Providing a viable alternative to the postmodern-self requires recovering tradition, but certain circumstances and prior constraints make it necessary to handle tradition with caution. The desire of the postmodern-self to escape the authority of tradition is at times warranted. Drawing from the analogy of jazz, it is possible for tradition to override acts of freedom, or even to calcify previous acts of freedom into rigid proscriptions. For example, according to trumpeter Benny Bailey, "If a band had an arrangement of 'String of Pearls' you almost had to play Bobby Hackett's solo. It's a beautifully constructed solo which fits the tune. It helps the tune somehow, and it's part of the whole picture. If you played any other solo, it would take away from the tune."[30] Yet, when bands play written solos instead of allowing instrumentalists to improvise, they preserve the past at the expense of the present. Without pruning, tradition crowds out freedom. As Jeremy Begbie points out, "there may be some traditions which are antagonistic to our freedom."[31] Happily, that does not necessarily mean "that past tradition is inevitably of this character."[32]

AUTHORITARIAN-FUNDAMENTALISM

Crossing from the South to the North, one encounters those who flee from the postmodern-self into the waiting arms of strict order and authority. If the postmodern-self seeks to escape from authority, authoritarian-fundamentalism seeks to escape from freedom. Constraints are amplified as choices are narrowed. Authoritarian-fundamentalism tries to escape the dynamic nature of community by making relations between members as unidirectional as possible. Instead of considering the broad mosaic of tradition, it claims to reach back to the pure form of the faith. It takes God's intent in Scripture and attempts to dictate certain particulars through certain theological systems as its only legitimate realization. Stuck in Kierkegaard's

this insight to Owen Barfield. Lewis, *Surprised by Joy*, 207.

29. Begbie, *Theology, Music and Time*, 244.

30. Benny Bailey, quoted in Berliner, *Thinking in Jazz*, 98–99.

31. Begbie, *Theology, Music and Time*, 219.

32. Begbie, *Theology, Music and Time*, 219.

ethical stage, authoritarian-fundamentalism reaches for the impossible. The broken lives of those who fail in some way to measure up are no less tragic than the ones wasted away in the pursuit of their desires.

A jazz-shaped conception of Christian freedom offers a reimagining of the constraints of authoritarian-fundamentalism. It affirms community but insists on mutual submission. It opens up the broad vista of tradition but refuses to allow it to trample on the present. It affirms the priority and authority of Scripture but shows that Scripture teaches freedom, not bondage. Finally, it uncovers the liberating power of the Holy Spirit. I work through these contrasts below, again bringing other constraints into play where needed.

Rethinking the Nature of Werktreue

Perhaps one of the strongest points of authoritarian-fundamentalism for believers is its (ideally) sincere desire to faithfully enact the will of God. Setting aside for the moment other motivations for adopting authoritarianism, I assume for the sake of argument that these believers are genuinely trying to please God. It is the *way* that authoritarianism seeks to be faithful to God's intent that is problematic, not the desire itself. It is simpler to slide into passive conformity than it is to exercise freedom through improvisation. Adopting and enforcing a uniform set of behavior, a trait of authoritarian-fundamentalism, naturally focuses on particulars, just as musicians aiming for an authentic performance of the composition of a past figure can go to great lengths to use period instruments, the correct number of instruments, instrumental techniques and the like. Ironically, focusing on these particulars (dress codes, regulating interaction between the sexes, etc.) misses "the weightier matters of the law" by straining out gnats and swallowing camels, so to speak (Matt 23:23–24). In musical terms, the lower level intentions of a composer are attempted, but the desired effect of the piece on its listeners is missed.[33]

In Rom 14, Paul allows the Christians in Rome to express different practices in the areas of diet and observing sacred days. Instead of passing judgment on one another, Christians are to remember that ultimately they are accountable to God. In other words, the mandated conformity of the Law with respect to these areas as it operated in ancient Israel need not be

---

33. For a more detailed look at *werktreue* and the different levels of a composer's intention, see chapter 1 under "Wynton Marsalis, *Werktreue*, and Authoritarian-Fundamentalism."

binding for Christians.[34] Being the people of God no longer requires cultural conformity in all externals (though Christians still ought to be marked
by their conduct); rather, it means being "transformed by the renewing
of your minds, so that you may discern what is the will of God—what is
good and acceptable and perfect" (Rom 12:2). This process of renewing and
transformation does not equate to ticking off a checklist; it entails engraining certain traits and habits—developing character.[35]

Developing character finds an analogue in the process of engraining
solos, phrases, and working out the implications of theory that is necessary
to become a successful improviser in the jazz tradition. To be a jazz musician, one must begin with the goal of becoming one; one must not only
play scales, but also play music with others. One must not only listen to
recordings, but play along with them. A jazz solo can follow all the rules of
a jazz theory text book and still sound uninspiring; a master musician goes
beyond the rules to the heart of the matter—creative engagement with all
of the constraints that make jazz possible. These simply cannot be reduced
to the reproduction of notated patterns and exercises. Furthermore, such an
approach tries to eliminate risk, a key ingredient not only in jazz improvisation, but also in Christian freedom.[36] Rules are only helpful as part of a
greater whole.

N. T. Wright proposes virtue ethics as a way of avoiding the either/or
of trying to be true to one's self on the one hand or strict rule keeping on
the other. For Wright, virtue ethics in a Christian framework are governed
by the *telos* of the Kingdom of God: "*God's future is arriving in the present,
in the person and work of Jesus, and you can practice, right now, the habits
of life which will find their goal in that coming future.*"[37] Wright goes on to
point out that sinful habits often masquerade as righteous ones.[38] In other
words, it is possible to appear as if one is keeping all the rules while actually
being full of wickedness. After all, one can devise techniques for keeping the

34. As Douglas Moo observes, the "weak" that Paul describes "are not able to accept for themselves the truth that their faith in Christ implies liberation from certain
OT/Jewish ritual requirements." Moo, *Romans*, 836.

35. According to Moo, "This 're-programming' of the mind [in Rom 12] does not
take place overnight but is a lifelong process by which our way of thinking is to resemble more and more the way God wants us to think." Moo, *Romans*, 757.

36. According to Jacques Ellul, "the freedom which we are given by God plunges us
into a risk which the non-Christian cannot even imagine. This risk is in the strict sense
the culminating expression of freedom in Christ." He describes this risk as "a wager on
the faithfulness of God." Ellul, *Ethics of Freedom*, 355, 356. See also chapter 5 under the
heading "Risks and Mistakes: Miles Davis and the Apostle Peter."

37. Wright, *After You Believe*, 103. Emphasis in original.

38. Wright, *After You Believe*, 118.

rules, and even insist on a best way of keeping them. But, as I show below, technique entails a narrow-minded focus on achieving a designated goal and has no use for anything else. But the rules are not ends in themselves; they point towards something else. Authoritarian-fundamentalism is about devising techniques to keep rules while missing the transformation of character that the rules in Scripture point to. This is why Jesus says in Mark 7:14–22 that it is not by eating certain foods that one becomes unclean, but by the evil that comes out of the heart. Only by the sanctifying work of the Holy Spirit can one replace evil habits with good ones, engrained ways of thinking and living that then spill out naturally in creative improvisation.[39]

The Ethical Stage and the Spirit

Kierkegaard's ethical stage overlaps with authoritarian-fundamentalism with respect to the desire of both to fulfill the law. They face the similar problem of being unable to do it. The problem is linked to an ongoing struggle with the self. If in authoritarian-fundamentalism "all individuals must belong to a religious collective, and their everyday lives must be governed by the normative traditions of such collectives," the element of risk is lost.[40] The self cannot step aside because it is too invested in maintaining these traditions, of conforming to a code of behavior. The self finds security and identity in relation to the code.

Picking up from the previous section, the Holy Spirit is necessary to transcend the grasping for perfection that characterizes the ethical stage. The religious stage is not just rule-abiding with occasional jumps to forgiveness when required. It means leaving behind the guilt and fears of the ethical stage; it is a renunciation of the self. A jazz musician opening herself up to the "*It*" factor must let go of the fear of playing wrong notes. She denies her ego's demand to be responsible for the solo with its corresponding ties between performance and feelings of superiority and inferiority. Instead, she is free to be in the zone; she experiences the music without the fear. Kelly Clark's reading of Kierkegaard sums up the analogous Christian experience well:

> As Aristotle argued, there is only one way to go right but an infinite number of ways to go wrong; the chance of hitting that narrow mark of goodness is precious thin. So the ethical person may be paralyzed by fear of wrongdoing. But the religious

39. See also Jack Levison's discussion of the link between the Holy Spirit and virtue in Levison, *Inspired*, 38–47.
40. Jahanbegloo, "Reading *Either/Or* in Tehran," 19.

person is liberated from the tyranny of fear and guilt. He is
motivated by the encouragement of the possible, not by fear of
doing something wrong. He moves boldly into his calling, accepting the risks that life presents.[41]

The liberating work of the Holy Spirit casts out the fear and guilt that
accompany the rule-keeping inherent in authoritarian-fundamentalism and
replaces them with boldness borne out of trust in God's faithfulness.

Reimagining Community

Belonging to the body of Christ entails surrendering a certain degree of
one's autonomy. It means accepting the right of fellow believers in the local
church to speak into one's way of life, even when what they say conflicts with
what one is doing. Switching again to jazz, musicians necessarily engage in
mutual submission in order to play together coherently. Yet when mutual
submission devolves into unilateral submission, when, in other words, one is
no longer willing to assert oneself, the possibility of collective improvisation
is lost. Christian freedom is lost. While it is true that improvisation cannot
be entirely effaced as long as human agents act, it can be hampered, bent,
and pent-in. After all, even slaves can exercise a certain degree of freedom.

The charismatic leader (explicit or implicit) in authoritarian-fundamentalism accepts the surrender of autonomy and assertion from their
followers. Authority flows primarily in one direction from the charismatic
leader to subordinates through them to their subordinates and so forth. The
problem does not lie in a prominent person leading a group of people—otherwise one would have to discount the numerous biblical characters who
do this—but rather in the limitations of a single self. If the leader of a jazz
combo were to write out the various parts in full, the result would be limited
to what this leader could produce apart from the group. Only the leader
could experience of improvising under the "*It*" factor (and only in the initial
stages of composing the music); the rest of the group would experience it
only as mediated by the leader.

Those who are subordinate clearly surrender their freedom. Their
voices only amplify; they do not contribute. The community demarcates
their roles in such a way that their voices are unheard and their actions
conform to the will of the charismatic leader. It is perhaps less obvious that
those who exercise unilateral authority in a community also lose freedom.
They cannot transcend themselves. Like the postmodern-self, they refuse to

41. Clark, *When Faith Is Not Enough*, 167–68.

submit to others; they are similarly isolated. They may claim authority from a sacred text, but it is their interpretation of it that is de facto authoritative.[42] These leaders become de facto intermediaries between God and the congregation, justifying the power they wield.

By way of contrast, a jazz-shaped conception of community affirms the worth and contribution of each member not in relation to the charismatic leader, but in relation to the mission of the community. Instead of passively implementing what is passed down from the charismatic leader, it insists on creating space for each member to be heard. In such a scenario, leaders (those with prominent voices in the community analogous to the horns in a jazz band) are not alienated from the rest of the group; they can respond to other voices in the community without worrying about how it might undermine their authority precisely because they are not obsessed with holding on to it. They can lead without having to control (cf. 1 Pet 5:3). Martin Luther argues that "there is no true, basic difference between laymen and priests, princes and bishops, between religious and secular, except for the sake of office and work, but not for the sake of status."[43] The instruments in a jazz band have different roles to play, but they are not continually bound by them. The bass can play the melody; a horn can accompany a solo.[44] Active participation by all, and a flexible attitude towards roles, undermines authoritarianism.

Just as turning from the postmodern-self to the Christian community requires surrendering one's (apparent) complete autonomy, so turning from authoritarian-fundamentalism requires surrendering power and influence on the part of the charismatic leader and surrendering a sense of comfort and security on the part of the subordinates. Being in the Christian community requires taking risks; it requires taking on the vulnerability required in opening oneself to others. In a jazz combo, taking a solo exposes one's knowledge of the jazz tradition, one's ability to "make the changes," and to interact thoughtfully with others. One cannot control the responses of the other instruments; an interjection may disrupt the vision one had for a solo. If one's ego is engaged, the response of the other musicians, audience, or

42. Jonathan Burnham chronicles a conflict between two charismatic leaders in the early Brethren movement that demonstrates how theology (closely linked with one's interpretation of Scripture) can be used as a mask for a personal power struggle. See Burnham, *Story of Conflict*.

43. Luther, "To the Christian Nobility," 129.

44. Listen to the melody of "So What" by Miles Davis on *Kind of Blue* for an example of a melody played in the bass and to trombonist Bob Brookmeyer's supporting role at the beginning of Jim Hall's solo in "I Hear a Rhapsody" on *Live at the North Sea*. A transcription of Brookmeyer's supporting lines can be found in Hudson, *Evolution*, 69 (errata sheet).

one's own taste can distort one's concept of self-worth. Analogously, actively participating in the Christian community exposes our knowledge and practices to others. It means being challenged, corrected, and ultimately liberated from the constraint of self.

Recovering the Broad Scope of Tradition

A spectrum of options exists in authoritarian-fundamentalism with respect to tradition. On one side of the spectrum, authoritarian-fundamentalism can reflect its modern origins by sidestepping traditional interpretations and practices in the faith in question in favor of the interpretation of the charismatic leader. On the other side of the spectrum, authoritarian-fundamentalism can refashion tradition in its own image. When tradition is used in authoritarian-fundamentalism, it functions in the same way as a sacred text; it is used selectively to support the agenda of the charismatic leader. In fact, tradition is much more malleable because it lacks the (relatively) fixed nature of the sacred text.

The charismatic leader shares much in common with the postmodern-self. By refusing to be "bound by the precedents set by traditional interpreters and commentators on the divine law or sacred texts, who faced fundamentally different challenges and political contexts," the charismatic leader acts on behalf of the community to fashion their identity.[45] Instead of drawing upon the full scope of tradition, authoritarian-fundamentalism constructs "a myth of the golden age when the norms of the [faith] tradition are presumed to have held sway."[46] This myth underlies the rigid division of roles according to gender that I discuss in chapter 1. Malise Ruthwen holds up the additional examples of an idealized version of the 1950s and the American revolution in the case of American fundamentalists.[47] Traditions that fall short of the standards of this golden age (or rather, its reconstruction) are simply of no use.

In the domain of jazz, the entire tradition lies open to examination. Saxophonist Red Hollaway can throw a quote from "Jeepers Creepers"

---

45. Almond et al., *Strong Religion*, 17.

46. Ruthven, *Fundamentalism*, 28. In the domain of jazz, this myth takes the form of a constructed history of jazz that divides jazz standards from their origins as show tunes. It even extends to reconstructing the unrecorded playing of the earliest figures in the history of the music. As Christopher Meeder observes, "Musicians as young as Wynton Marsalis are able to claim authority in describing [trumpeter Buddy] Bolden's style and contributions in alarming detail without ever having heard a note of his playing." Meeder, *Jazz*, 29.

47. Ruthven, *Fundamentalism*, 28.

(popularized by Louis Armstrong) into a solo on an album with Horace Silver decades after Armstrong's performance.[48] Saxophonists Coleman Hawkins and Sonny Rollins can play on the same songs while drawing on very different sources.[49] Uncovering the past and its motivations can undermine the myth of the golden age, allowing those who draw from tradition to see it for what it is and giving them the liberty to select what to resource and what to lay aside. Tradition challenges apparently de novo interpretations of a jazz standard or Scripture by reminding the present of the past; it offers a way of identifying old problems in new guises and uncovers forgotten but potentially useful solutions to apparently new problems. It undermines nostalgia for an imaginary golden age by bringing the reality of that age to light; it reminds one that God's dealings with humanity have always been complicated by human sin and frailty. In short, recovering tradition undermines the authoritarian narrative.

TECHNIQUE AND ALIENATION

Alienation, in Marx's use of the term, is a necessary outworking of capitalism. Capitalism reduces workers to commodities and consumers. Workers are alienated from one another as they compete for work; they are alienated from their employers because their goals are at odds with one another (both want more profit at the expense of the other). As consumers, they are trained to think in terms of applying a cost-benefit analysis to every situation, attempting to maximize the benefits they accrue while minimizing the cost. As soon as capital or other forms of benefit are stipulated, Ellul's conception of technique enters into the fray, employing the rational use of technical procedures to determine the most effective and efficient way of producing this benefit at a minimum cost. Anything or anyone that does not contribute to the stipulated benefit is devalued and discarded.

As I note above, these forces have already entered into the organization and practice of many churches in the West. Instead of attempting to describe this effect broadly and abstractly, I first trace the way a certain technique

---

48. Hollaway takes the first solo after the vocal in "The Hillbilly Bebopper" in 1993 on Silver, *It's Got to Be Funky*. The quotation occurs at the beginning of the bridge. "Jeepers Creepers" was premiered by Armstrong in 1938. Quoting songs from a wide variety of sources is a common practice in jazz improvisation.

49. Listen in particular to the interplay between the two in "Yesterdays" on *Sonny Meets Hawk!* Hawkins developed his playing in the swing era, but championed the younger players playing bebop. Rollins, at the time of the recording, was experimenting with the ideas of Ornette Coleman (though still keeping the form of the pieces he played).

was discovered and implemented with the goal of making the church grow, and then consider the parallels between megachurches and corporations. With these case studies in mind, I make preliminary suggestions on how a jazz-shaped conception of Christian freedom can operate in the church to mitigate the effect of alienation and technique in its operations.

The Technique of Growing a Church in America

The forerunner of the church growth movement in America was Donald McGavran's *The Bridges of God.*[50] McGavran's experience as a missionary in India provided him with the insight that the mission-station approach to evangelism was ineffective in comparison with the evangelistic efforts of churches made up of a single ethnic identity to their own people group.[51] C. Peter Wagner, following in McGavran's steps, applied McGavran's insights to the church in America. Like attracts like. In his aptly titled, *Our Kind of People*, he argues that, "[i]f the option of maintaining a homogeneous congregation is chosen, the direct benefit of close intercultural relationships will be sacrificed, but in all probability the evangelistic potential of the congregation will be higher. Other things being equal, a higher rate of conversion growth can be predicted for the homogeneous unit church."[52] Wagner's work goes beyond providing pragmatic reasons for advocating for homogeneous churches, but identifying a desired goal (growth) and a means (homogenous unit churches) inevitably results in someone employing technique.[53]

Bill Bishop and Robert Cushing's *The Big Sort* locates McGavran's "homogeneous unit principle" in the larger social trend in America for like-minded people to cluster together.[54] Contrary to Wagner's optimistic picture of churches that are homogeneous and nonetheless avoid sectarian-

50. For a good historical overview of the beginnings of the church growth movement, see Conn, "Looking for a Method."

51. McGavran suggests that "growing churches" are defined as "organized cells of the movement of a people. Folk join these cells by conversion without social dislocation, without entering a new marriage market, and without a sense that 'we are leaving and betraying our kindred.'" McGavran, *Bridges of God*, 109. See also McGavran, *Ethnic Realities.*

52. Wagner, *Our Kind of People*, 33.

53. For example, Wagner makes a compelling case for homogenous unit churches with reference to the problems of assimilation and loss of identity for minority groups. Wagner, *Our Kind of People*, 146–50.

54. Harvie M. Conn names this principle in his essay on the early history of the church growth movement. Conn, "Looking for a Method," 79.

ism and racism,[55] Bishop and Cushing forcefully argue that "like-minded, homogeneous groups squelch dissent, grow more extreme in their thinking, and ignore evidence that their positions are wrong."[56] They draw a line from McGavran and his disciples to contemporary megachurches such as Rick Warren's Saddleback Church, who extrapolate from the homogenous unit principle to create tailor-made services, Sunday School classes, and small groups for certain demographics. The principle/technique is undoubtedly effective in drawing people to the church, but Bishop and Cushing observe what is perhaps an unintended side effect. Political scientist James Gimbel tells Bishop, "I find very little evidence that churches are really transforming their congregations. . . . It's quite the reverse. Ministers depend on pleasing a particular congregation for their longevity. The last thing they want to do is offend those people or try to transform their viewpoint. . . . It's conformity all the way."[57]

As Paul Louis Metzger shows, the homogeneous principle also prevents believers from having meaningful interactions with those from different ethnic and socio-economic backgrounds. He writes,

> Homogeneous, small-group breeding grounds nurture small-minded and shortsighted attempts to address race and class divisions. While helping us become sensitive to one another's struggles with the individualism that is so prominent today, homogeneous small groups desensitize us to the plight of those individuals who are outside our social networks.[58]

Yet the difficulty of stepping outside these homogeneous groups should not be underestimated. When Miles Davis hired Bill Evans (a white pianist) to play in his band, Evans had to deal with the resentment of the black community.[59] Davis stood by his decision in spite of the criticism,

---

55. Wagner writes, "Christian interdependence must be promoted by all available means if church members belonging to different homogeneous units in the same geographical area are to bring this aspect of Christian experience to fruition." Wagner, *Our Kind of People*, 154. I concur with Wagner that churches *ought* to be interdependent, but in light of the "big sort" described by Bishop and Cushing, I am skeptical about the feasibility of his model of interdependence on a large scale, especially since communities themselves are often segregated along racial and political lines. The homogeneous unit principle is strong; the natural attraction of those who think alike works against interacting with those who are different.

56. Bishop and Cushing, *Big Sort*, 39.

57. James Gimbel, quoted in Bishop and Cushing, *Big Sort*, 180.

58. Metzger, *Consuming Jesus*, 62.

59. Davis and Troupe, *Miles*, 231.

but eventually Evans left to form his own, all white, band. Looking back on Evans' choice of bandmates, Davis observes,

> It's a strange thing about a lot of white players—not all, just most—that after they make it in a black group they always go and play with all white guys no matter how good the black guys treated them. Bill did that, and I'm not saying he could have gotten any black guys any better than Scott [Lefaro] and Paul [Motian], I'm just telling what I've seen happen over and over again.[60]

Davis does not call into question the competence of Lefaro or Motian; he sounds more disappointed that his own bridge building between whites and blacks was not reflected in Evans' group. In later groups, Evans did hire black musicians, but his initial choices after moving on from Davis' group evidently stuck in Davis' mind. An essential part of the beauty and appeal of jazz is its hybridizing tendencies, its ability to blend disparate elements from different cultures. An essential part of the gospel of Jesus Christ is breaking through barriers of class, race, and gender: "There is no longer Jew or Greek, there is no longer slave or free, there is no longer male and female; for all of you are one in Christ Jesus" (Gal 3:28).

Whatever the merits of McGavran's approach in India, it appears that a technical approach to church growth in America not only plays into the larger cultural trends towards polarization in America, but also prevents the church from liberating its members from these trends. Segregation according to race, age, and political inclination may make it easier to grow a church, but it bypasses the need to take those with different perspectives into consideration (cf. Rom 14:1; 1 Cor 8:9), cuts out meaningful interaction between young and old (cf. Titus 2:3–5; 1 Tim 5:1–2), and fails to answer Paul's rhetorical questions in 1 Cor 12:17 "If the whole body were an eye, where would the hearing be? If the whole body were hearing, where would the sense of smell be?" (NRSV). Technique militates against the messiness of the clash of diversity. Instead of pruning and tending foliage, it paves it over.

Technique sidelines all activities and bodies that do not assist in accomplishing the designated objective in the most efficient and productive way possible. Just as jazz cannot be reduced to instrumental technique or even mastery of jazz vocabulary, so the Christian life cannot be reduced to church growth. The gospel is multifaceted; attempting to reduce it to one or two factors makes it a caricature of itself. I am not suggesting that churches should not be concerned with managing their resources responsibly, or that

---

60. Davis and Troupe, *Miles*, 232.

growth is unimportant. I am suggesting that the church be very careful, when designating objectives, to see the whole picture.[61]

The church ought to consider the careful integration of multiple elements in jazz improvisation as a model for keeping goals such as growth balanced with needs such as intergenerational discipleship and the right of teachers within a local church to challenge the complacency of its members. If the church can do no better than to mirror contemporary techniques to the world, it will lose its ability to challenge it. Instead, it will once again act to stifle freedom.

Alienation and the Corporate Model of Ecclesiology

The corporate model is presently the dominant model for many of the more prominent churches in North America, especially in the case of megachurches. In 1995, even Catholics were considering adopting the Protestant trend of blending elements of business with the church. After detailing the troubling trend of youth abandoning their religious heritage, John Considine writes, "Such drastic attitudinal and behavioral shifts necessitate that churches, like other profit and nonprofit organizations, must become more marketing-oriented in order to survive."[62] Churches began to gear themselves towards attracting certain segments of the population, making these people analogous to consumers and viewing themselves as producers. Along with the successes of the church growth movement discussed above came a need to effectively manage the product and the brand of large churches. Dan Hotchkiss, along with others, advocated borrowing governance models from big business.[63] When critics expressed unease about the side effects of a business-shaped approach to doing church, Scott Thumma and Dave Travis responded with the often-cited *Beyond Megachurch Myths: What We can Learn from America's Largest Churches*. This book allegedly counters the critics with hard data. Sociologists, however, have no qualms about pointing out some of the more disturbing aspects of the close ties

61. It is encouraging to note that Bill Hybels, once a proponent of the "homogenous unit principle" has since repudiated it as an approach to church growth. See Gilbreath and Galli, "Harder Than Anyone Can Imagine," 38. In a conversation with J. D. Greear, Hybels says that, if he could do it again, he would not have used this approach, even if it meant reaching fewer people, arguing that "the corporate witness of the body of Christ . . . a witness magnified by cultural diversity, will have a larger evangelistic impact on our world than will a numbers surge at any one congregation." Greear, "Great Commission Multiplication," 341. Cf. Metzger, *Consuming Jesus*, 55–58.

62. Considine, *Marketing Your Church*, 15.

63. Hotchkiss, "Borrowing from Business." Cf. n66 below.

between megachurches and capitalism. Marion Maddox, in her article, "'In the Goofy Parking Lot': Growth Churches as a Novel Religious form for Late Capitalism," concludes with the statement, "Growth churches are capitalism's cathedrals."[64] Maddox shows clear connections between growth churches and corporations, noting that the line between them is almost effortlessly crossed as growth churches provide models for business and vice versa.[65]

Even a surface comparison of the way a corporation and a megachurch are structured reveal some startling similarities. The scope of the power wielded by the head pastor warrants a discussion in its own right. In a megachurch, the head pastor functions in a way analogous to the CEO of a corporation.[66] When the head pastor functions as CEO, he "must exert control, which is accomplished best when the church operates with efficiency, calculability, and predictability," but if he fails to "generate growth, either his methodology needs to be changed or [he] should be removed and replaced with a more effective leader."[67] While the head pastor wields a great deal of power, his ties to the church are reduced to his ability to draw a crowd. A pastor who can successfully accomplish this, however, is often granted immunity from criticism in the eyes of those who have invested in his brand. Glenn Starks, writing about the issue of sexual misconduct in megachurches, observes, "There is evidence that the members of megachurches support their church leaders even when there is overwhelming evidence of their guilt by virtue of the leaders' power and/or position, dismissing the acts of church leaders on the basis of forgiveness, or condemning a secular spotlight on what is deemed an internal church matter."[68] Furthermore, megachurches that are built around such a charismatic figure tend to lack strong denominational ties, leaving this figure without external accountability.[69]

64. Maddox, "'In the Goofy Parking Lot,'" 155.

65. Maddox catalogues the connections, including, for instance, the importance of Peter Drucker's writings on corporations for lead pastors Bill Hybel and Rick Warren. More surprising is the fact that Coca-Cola, Ford, and Walmart have adopted the forty days of purpose programme from Warren's best selling *The Purpose Driven Life*. Maddox, "'In the Goofy Parking Lot,'" 154.

66. Even Thumma and Travis concede, "There is no denying that megachurches are reflections of the leadership abilities of a senior pastor or directional leader. Nearly always, the megachurch pastor is the most prominent and high-profile position in the congregation. The pastor is the center of the staff and the energy bug around which the congregation revolves." Thumma and Travis, *Beyond Megachurch Myths*, 57.

67. White and Yeats, *Franchising McChurch*, 79.

68. Starks, *Sexual Misconduct*, ix.

69. Thomas White and John Yeats write, "In our post-denominational era, churches

The power that is necessary to accumulate capital in the capitalist system centralizes power in the hands of the head pastor when this system is implemented in the church. It also necessarily alienates the head pastor from the average person in the congregation.[70] As Thomas White and John Yeats argue, the "'pastor as CEO' is not the scriptural image presented of the pastor. Instead, Scripture offers the challenging image of the pastor of the church as a shepherd."[71] In other words, for the typical pastor of a megachurch, the alienation built into a capitalist approach to attracting consumers overrides the pattern set forth in Scripture.

The ministers or pastors who serve under the head pastor are his board of directors. Under the directors come the staff—the term is univocal between the domains of a corporation and a megachurch. His volunteers are de facto salespeople and the seekers are clients or customers.[72] Such a structure is open to the Marxist critique of alienation. Potential staff compete for positions; they are hired and fired. Instead of belonging to a body, they are commodities, valued for their expertise and experience. Instead of being put out of the church only as a disciplinary measure, they risk permanently losing their place in the church (who will attend a church they have been fired from?) for a perceived or real failure to meet the expectations of the management. A corporation can pretend to divide employment from personal relationships, but the church is hardly in the position to make the same claim.[73]

Growth, the goal that drives the formation of megachurches, is great when it entails non-Christians accepting Jesus as Lord and Savior. However, when the growth of one church comes at the expense of the other, the corporate model discloses a hidden mapping between competing companies in a capitalist system and churches that now must compete with one another for congregants.[74] I am not referring to people leaving a given local church

---

are more frequently associated with the name of the pastor over ties to a denomination." White and Yeats, *Franchising McChurch*, 81.

70. Thumma and Travis concede, "As a church grows larger, the pastor is much less likely to have direct personal contact with the average person in the pews." Thumma and Travis, *Beyond Megachurch Myths*, 57.

71. White and Yeats, *Franchising McChurch*, 78.

72. As Maddox observes, "'The liminal phase of the altar call marks the transition from customer to member of the sales force." Maddox, "'In the Goofy Parking Lot,'" 151.

73. The layers of separation between a head pastor in a megachurch and "the average person in the pews" create an alienating distance between them. The staff who create the buffer zone around the head pastor are also alienated from the average member of the congregation because they are bound by the need to promulgate the brand of the head pastor in order to keep their jobs.

74. See Chadwick, *Stealing Sheep*.

for reasons of doctrine or personal conflict, but rather people leaving a given church for another on the basis of what they can gain from the latter. There is no precedent for this in Scripture. The important question is whether the concept of a consumer can be properly mapped onto the concept of a disciple.

Finally, and tellingly, the corporate model lacks an analogue corresponding to Scripture. Nothing in a corporation resembles a canon because, for a corporation, the past has no intrinsic value. All of its energies are focused upon the present and the future because its primary goal is profit. Any technique or approach that does not serve this goal is promptly discarded. The temptation for churches that employ the corporate model is to emphasize and deemphasize certain portions of Scripture in order to achieve the objective of growth. At best, this aspect of the corporate model can be discarded—at worst it can lead to a distortion of the gospel.

Towards a Jazz-Shaped Alternative

Providing a formulaic alternative to the corporate model of ecclesiology would only be falling prey once again to technique. However, I am convinced certain approaches to ecclesiology foster more freedom than others. The constraints of Christian freedom that counter the postmodern-self and authoritarian-fundamentalism are also incompatible with churches permeated by technique and afflicted with alienation. Mutual submission is incompatible with efficiency as a primary principle and branding altogether.[75] Risk taking is anathema to the carefully choreographed performances and interactions within a megachurch; risk is incompatible with control. Tradition is rendered superfluous once one adopts technique. A jazz-shaped ecclesiology rests squarely on participation and listening to all voices; no one is anonymous on the bandstand. The point is not to blend in passively, but to be heard and known. The goal is not personal comfort or a sense of ease—quite the opposite—the goal is to be transformed by an encounter with God through his word and his people.

---

75. Having the pendulum swing the other way into a haphazard use of resources would be equally problematic for the local church. With respect to branding, the brand (if one must use the term) of the church cannot reside in anyone other than Jesus Christ. Paul, writing to Corinthians about divisions in the church, upbraids them for identifying with anyone other than Christ: "What I mean is that each of you says, 'I belong to Paul,' or 'I belong to Apollos,' or 'I belong to Cephas,' or 'I belong to Christ.' Has Christ been divided? Was Paul crucified for you? Or were you baptized in the name of Paul?" (1 Cor 12–13).

Three approaches to aspects of ecclesiology, once adopted, will aid the church in expressing Christian freedom. The first is limiting the size of the congregation. The goal of bringing all to actively participate cannot be achieved when it is prohibited by size.[76] Second, the church must resist, or at least mitigate, the tendency to silo its members on the basis of age, interests, and economic standing. As in a jam session, the objects of worshipping God and engaging in mission should override all divisions. Third, power must not be exercised unilaterally in the church. Prominent voices should lead with confidence, but not to the point of drowning out, suppressing, or neglecting quieter voices. Each church must find its own way of attempting this in relation to its own tradition. Beyond these approaches, the church must be wary of adopting the techniques of the contemporary world. All models, including a jazz-shaped ecclesiology, must be held up against the light of a biblical theology of Christian freedom.

CONCLUSION

Jacques Ellul rightly asserts that "[t]here is never freedom without transgression."[77] Christian freedom transgresses the constraints of the relationship between the postmodern-self and authoritarian-fundamentalism by refusing to identify with one side or the other. It agrees with authoritarian-fundamentalism that God's revelation is foundational, but it refuses to reduce God's revelation to rule-keeping. It agrees with the postmodern-self that the self ought to be expressed, but simultaneously insists that one must die to self. In order for the church to demonstrate what true freedom looks like, it must throw off the shackles of alienation and technique; it must adopt something like Vanhoozer's canonical-linguistic approach to counter the strong current running through the unconscious use of the cultural-linguistic approach. Finally, Christian freedom is not something to be pursued as individuals, but collectively as the body of Christ. When the church adopts the constraints of the Kingdom of God (seen through a jazz lens or otherwise), it will experience liberation from the oppressive forces at work in the world and stand not as another passive entity among others, but as a beacon of hope in the midst of despair and emptiness.

---

76. Some larger churches have responded to this difficulty by encouraging small groups. Problems arise when these groups are formed based on demographics, thereby negating (or at least mitigating) the benefits of a diverse body.

77. Ellul, *Ethics of Freedom*, 344.

7

Tying Up the Analogy

MY JAZZ-SHAPED CONCEPTION OF Christian freedom rests upon confessional assumptions. My analogy reflects this; it would undoubtedly look different in the hands of someone with a different agenda. This does not, however, reduce the role of jazz in my argument "to a mere proof-text for biblical doctrine."[1] Jazz serves as a reminder that biblical practices such as mutual submission have corresponding concrete examples in a contemporary art form. It holds out an alternative to the models that the Western church has chosen to adopt and to the troubled history of the church with respect to freedom. As an (imperfect) embodiment of freedom analogous to a biblical theology of freedom, it reminds the church of the place of freedom in Scripture, demonstrates what enacted freedom looks like, and suggests ways that the church can pursue liberation from the polarities and ruinous forces of the contemporary West. These functions make the analogy useful in a Western context.

But before evaluating the analogy, it is necessary to address a potential criticism arising from my use of Jacques Ellul's conception of technique that, at first glance, threatens to undermine my use of jazz as an analogy for Christian freedom: namely, that it is simply another technique the Western church can appropriate to achieve certain ends. Jazz is a relational art form, not a science, and an analogy based on it will be similarly oriented towards relational as opposed to strictly pragmatic objectives. True, blinding virtuosity can be achieved with technique, but virtuosity cannot replace the

1. Epstein, *Melting the Venusberg*, 84. This is Heidi Epstein's critique of Jeremy Begbie's use of music "to enable theology to do its job better." Begbie, *Theology, Music and Time*, 271.

emotional, expressive, and communal aspects of jazz. Working within the network of constraints this work describes is hardly an efficient way of getting things done. Jazz improvisation, by placing so much of music-making into the hands of performers, is inherently not nearly as efficient as allowing performers to focus their attention on a written score. Nor are the instruments most often used in jazz as efficient as digital programming. Furthermore, the risks it entails are simply incompatible with any attempts to find a single, best way of getting things done. Though aspects of my project are prescriptive, they cannot be reduced to a package of steps or procedures that will work in all contexts. Rather, much like learning to play jazz, working them out requires ongoing growth and development in multiple areas. In many respects, jazz improvisation (when considered holistically) is the antithesis of technique.

I turn now to the task of demonstrating that my analogy is coherent. To this end, I revisit below the criteria I laid out in the introduction from the multiconstraint and articulation models of analogy. Next, I provide an explicit system mapping of the analogy by outlining how the various constraints I map between the source domain of jazz and the target domain of the Christian life interact. I show how these constraints overlay the Western problem of freedom, giving the church the mandate to transgress the polarizing effects of the relationship between the postmodern-self and authoritarian-fundamentalism and to gleefully toss out of the church the culturally-dominant forces of technique and alienation.

LAYING OUT AND EVALUATING THE ANALOGY

Chapters 4 and 5 map the analogy from the source domain of jazz onto the domain of the Christian life. It is now time to step back from the process to examine the structure of the analogy in order to demonstrate the isomorphism between the domains and to formalize the analogical arguments I make in these chapters and in chapter 6. First, I look at the implicit analogues in the domains of jazz and Christian freedom. Second, I examine Jeremy Begbie's three categories of constraints—occasional, cultural, and continual—and my own category of transcendental constraints, which overlaps with Begbie's. Third, I look at the particular constraints within these categories. Fourth, I evaluate the analogy according to the first two points in the rubric of the multiconstraint theory. Fifth, I examine analogical arguments within the larger analogy according to the forms laid out in Paul Bartha's articulation model.

Mapping the Analogy

In the introduction, I describe the three levels of mapping (showing relationships between the source and target domains) in Keith Holyoak and Paul Thagard's *multiconstraint theory*. In my analogy, the simplest analogues include musicians and bands, along with the various constraints they interact with in the source domain of jazz. Attribute mapping is connecting these analogues with the corresponding simple analogues of Christians, the local church, and the various constraints Christians interact with respectively in the target domain of the Christian life. More specific instances of attribute mapping include mapping the various instruments in jazz to various gifts and roles in the Christian life. The relationships between the simple analogues are themselves then mapped in relational mapping. For instance, as I note below, the relationship between a jazz musician and jazz theory can be mapped onto the relationship between a Christian and theology. The final stage in mapping is system mapping, which maps the relations between these relations. In my analogy, this works in two stages. First, I map the collective improvisation of jazz musicians in relation to various constraints onto the activity of the church (which, as Kevin Vanhoozer points out, "is *always* having to improvise").[2] Second, granting the premise that improvisation is the enactment of freedom, I assert that freedom in the domain of jazz is analogous to Christian freedom.

In this work, chapter 4 lays out the source domain of jazz, chapter 5 maps the analogues and their relationships onto the target domain of the Christian life, and chapter 6 works out some of the ways these relationships interact in response to the problem of freedom. In the *multiconstraint theory* of analogy, the more relevant similarities one demonstrates between the domains—the closer it approaches becoming an isomorphism—the more plausible the analogy becomes. With this in mind, I briefly survey the mappings between the various analogues and relationships in these chapters below. Since I have already laid out the basics of the attribute mappings above, the mappings below are primarily relational mappings. They are organized according to categories of constraints.

Constructing a biblical theology of freedom leads me to the conclusion that freedom is about being liberated from one set of constraints into another. Focusing on constraints, therefore, provides a way of thinking about freedom. Begbie's categories of constraints provide a useful way of organizing the various analogous constraints across the domains. My additional category of transcendental constraints is an effort to preserve the

2. Vanhoozer, *Drama of Doctrine*, 128. Emphasis in original.

priority of God's actions and intentions while acknowledging the way they overlap with other constraints.

The occasional constraints, or the things that change in relation to the improviser, that I address are spaces, community, and the "*It*" factor. Space determines the acoustics that shape the way musicians interact with one another; this is analogous to the way church architecture shapes the way Christians interact with one another as a church. Space is also attached to certain cultural expectations that shape the mood (including how audiences respond) across both domains.

The jazz band and the church as communities act as constraints on jazz musicians and Christians. Here Paul Rinzler's insight into the contradictions between assertion and openness, individuality and interconnectedness in jazz, provide a way of organizing and understanding corresponding analogues in the Christian life. For example, the practice of alternating soloists, including the corresponding need for active listening, finds an analogous practice in Paul's instructions to the Corinthians to interpret tongues and to weigh prophesies (1 Cor 14:27–33) and illustrates a balance between assertion and openness. Individuality and interconnectedness are illustrated in the jazz domain by instances where interaction between musicians allows them to transcend the limitations of the individual. This interaction is mirrored in Paul's metaphor of the body of Christ. Finally, the competitive jam sessions in jazz find positive and negative analogues in the domain of Christian life. Positively, Christians can spur one another to good deeds when they confront one another in love. Negatively, Christians can foster competition between themselves that results in alienation.

The "*It*" factor overlaps between being an occasional constraint (because it changes from the perspective of the improviser) and a transcendental constraint (because it involves an "outside" factor). Hal Crook's understanding of the formative but ultimately distracting role of the ego in jazz finds an analogue with Paul's distinction between thinking and acting as a child versus thinking and acting as an adult (1 Cor 13:11). Crook's ego is analogous to the Christian self that must be denied and sacrificed. Once jazz improvisation is detached from self worth, an indescribable "*It*" factor takes over, corresponding to being filled with the Holy Spirit. Just as the "*It*" factor uses the musical abilities of a jazz musician, so the Holy Spirit uses the abilities of a Christian. Reaching the place where the "*It*" factor takes over is analogous with reaching Kierkegaard's religious stage, where one finds grace from God after giving up the impossible struggle in the ethical stage.

The cultural constraints I examine are: the relationship between creativity and tradition, traditional roles, a composer's intentions, the relationship between text and theory, and historical oppression. Rinzler once again provides a dynamic contradiction in pairing creativity and tradition. He employs a taxonomy of four levels of interaction between the pair that transfers well between the source and target domains. The first favors tradition: preserving a traditional form of jazz free of later influences corresponds to Christian practice that seeks to, as far as it is possible, to keep rites and practices unchanged. The second allows creativity to operate within the boundaries and resources of a given tradition: the young lions of the 90s correspond with approaches to theology and practice that ignore outside sources. The third allows creativity to challenge tradition without abandoning it: Miles Davis' band in the 60s corresponds with an approach to theology and practice that engages with outside sources and is free to transgress tradition where necessary. The fourth sets aside even the fundamentals of a tradition in favor of expression in the source domain, and concerns extraneous to Christianity in the target domain.

The traditional links between certain jazz instruments and the roles they play in a jazz band are analogous with the gifts and corresponding roles that Christians use and inhabit in the church. Apostles and prophets are analogous to the horns; teachers are analogous to chordal instruments; those who serve to the bass; and healing and miracles to the drums. The need to accommodate each instrument in certain ways when it solos is analogous to Paul's insistence that every member of the body of Christ is treated with respect.

The intentions of a composer are transcendental constraints in addition to being cultural constraints because they operate (in a sense) from outside the improvisation of a given group. The analogy at the root of this constraint is that a composition is to a jazz musician what Scripture is to a Christian. The lower levels of a composer's intention are analogous to the aspects of Scripture governed by its historical context while the upper levels of their intention—which I interpret as the melody and deep harmonic structure of a song in a jazz context—are analogous to the intended effect (Vanhoozer would say perlocutionary effect) of Scripture.

Closely related to the above constraint is the analogy that jazz recordings are to jazz theory what Scripture is to theology.[3] Just as improvisers play along with recordings, so (in Robert Gelinas' notion of jazzaneutics) Christians ought to use the forms of Scripture as templates in dialoguing with God and witnessing to what he has done in their lives. The positive aspects of jazz theory are analogous to theology in that both aid in thinking through new situations. The negative aspects of jazz theory, namely that it marginalizes what it cannot explain, are also true of theology in how it uses

---

3. I call this text and theory above.

Scripture. Jazz theory and theology alike are vulnerable to experience and fresh insights on recordings and Scripture respectively.

Historical oppression is written into the circumstances of jazz recordings and into the narrative of Scripture. The oppression of blacks by whites in America is analogous to the oppression of the Jews by the Romans. The black appropriation of European instruments and certain elements of European music is analogous to Jewish Christians appropriating the Greek language in writing the New Testament. Finally, the commitment to making jazz that allows whites and blacks to work together without denying the inequality in their environment corresponds to the commitment of Gentiles and Jews to faith in Jesus Christ and the corresponding work of the Holy Spirit.

In the last category, continual constraints, I consider embodiment, universal order, and time. In embodiment, the tension in jazz between achieving mastery over one's instrument and using the foibles and limitations of one's instrument as a constructive constraint are analogous to the tension in the Christian life between mastering one's body for righteousness and working through the body to do God's work. The universal order behind music is the overtone series and the universal moral order is found in God, indicated by his law and hinted at in Lewis's conception of the Tao. The finite instantiation of the overtone series in human performance is analogous to Christians attempting to live out the principles of the Kingdom of God in a fallen world. Finally, time provides the constraint necessary to resolve apparent contradictions by allowing tension and resolution to occur in music and the process of sanctification in the Christian life.

The multiconstraint theory provides a rubric of three means of evaluation to determine whether an analogy is coherent: structural consistency, semantic similarity, and pragmatic effectiveness.[4] In terms of structural consistency, the mappings above demonstrate a one-to-one correspondence between multiple analogues. Semantic similarity is shown in the way the various constraints line up in both domains with similar relationships with the simple analogues of musician/Christian and band/church. The ease with which taxonomies and concepts move between the domains also demonstrates similarity in meaning. I defer the final means of evaluation until I show how certain arguments satisfy Bartha's articulation model.

4. See introduction for more details.

Arguing from Analogy: Using the Articulation Model

Bartha's articulation model of analogy focuses on making analogical arguments. His model makes it possible to look at the analogical arguments being made within the larger analogy. Bartha's models of predictive and explanatory arguments cover the particular arguments I make within the larger analogy. Since I have already covered many of the analogues above, I provide three analogical arguments that I make in the body of this work as examples instead of cataloguing each argument.

The first is a predictive analogical argument.[5] The different sizes of jazz ensembles are facts that have the observed result that smaller ensembles tend to emphasize improvisation more than larger ones.[6] The analogous facts in the domain of the Christian life are the different sizes of churches. The analogous result is that smaller churches are better able to improvise than larger ones. Since I argue that improvisation is the enactment of freedom, it follows that Christian freedom is more likely to be found in smaller churches than larger ones. Naturally, this argument breaks down at its extremities; I am not arguing for churches of two or three members. Placed within the larger analogy, I can draw from the positive aspects of diversity to qualify this argument.

A recurring theme of mutual submission in jazz provides a good example of an explanatory analogical argument. In the domain of jazz, I provide the explanation of careful listening and balancing assertiveness and openness for the fact that good jazz musicians can follow one another without dominating each other. The analogous fact in the domain of the Christian life is Paul's instruction that members of the church are to submit to one another (Eph 5:21). Where mutual submission takes place, it is likely that something analogous to the careful listening and balancing of a good jazz ensemble is taking place.

I conclude with another predictive analogical argument. The fact of competition between jazz musicians yields the observed result of an increase in their ability. The analogical fact in the domain of Christian freedom is Christians challenging each other to do better by how they live. The analogical result ought to be the "love and good deeds" mentioned in Heb 10:24. Again, this argument must be qualified by the need for humility in giving and accepting a challenge. Looking at the analogical arguments embedded

---

5. See introduction for an overview of Bartha's explanatory and predictive types of analogical arguments.

6. In working through these arguments, I endeavor to use Bartha's terminology. See the Introduction.

in the larger analogy reinforces the value of the larger analogy as a way of qualifying and directing these arguments.

Improvising in Church: System Mapping the Analogy

In addition to Begbie's assertion that "[i]n improvisation, *cultural constraints are particularized in relation to occasional constraints,*" it is also true that this process is achieved in relation to continual constraints and, ideally, grounded especially in transcendental constraints.[7] For instance, the discipline of theology (a cultural constraint) is particularized in relation to the local church (an occasional constraint), which is comprised of embodied people (embodiment is a continual constraint). Additionally, Scripture, which is simultaneously a cultural and a transcendent constraint, informs theology. The way a jazz musician interacts with these categories of constraints in a musical context is analogous to the way a Christian participates in the local church. Jazz musicians are expected to have a repertoire of memorized songs, a vocabulary of musical phrases, and the ability to play their instruments competently when they come together to play music. In the same way, in order to participate effectively in the local church, Christians need to familiarize themselves with Scripture, have worked through a personal theology (formally or informally), and be living lives that demonstrate the fruits of the Spirit. In other words, jazz musicians and Christians alike must absorb and be shaped by cultural and transcendental constraints so that they have a framework for improvisation and content with which to fill it. They also go through a similar process of learning, practicing, and doing to get there. Being shaped by these constraints gives a jazz musician the ability to creatively draw upon them when faced with the occasional constraints of space, other musicians, and the direction of the "*It*" factor. In fact, the occasional constraints trigger connections in the content of the cultural constraints that the improviser then acts upon. In the domain of the Christian life, it is interesting to read how Paul's letters particularize his knowledge of the Old Testament and his experience of the risen Christ in relation to the challenges different churches presented him with under the inspiration of the Holy Spirit. In this case, improvisation became Scripture.

The act of improvisation—the spontaneous choice of how to employ cultural constraints in relation to occasional constraints—is an expression of freedom. The nature of the constraints, especially the ones that are also transcendent, is what makes these choices an expression of Christian freedom in particular. They liberate Christians from bondage to sin and self

---

7. Begbie, *Theology, Music and Time*, 215. Emphasis in original.

into creative improvisation as the church within the will of God. Every act, even a commonplace act, that is performed in relation to the constraints in the domain of the Christian life, is an act of freedom. For an act performed in relation to these constraints necessarily transgresses the constraints that govern a life lived contrary to God's will.

REAL TRANSGRESSION IN THE WEST

Authoritarian fundamentalists and those with a postmodern-self alike, when considering the word "transgression," will likely think of some further assault on cultural norms or scruples. Slavoj Žižek notes that "in today's era of permissiveness . . . performance and other artists [sic] are under pressure to stage the most intimate private fantasies in all their desublimated naked-ness. Such 'transgressive' art confronts us directly with *jouissance* precisely at its most solipsistic."[8] The compulsive pursuit of pleasure by the self indeed transgresses God's design for human flourishing, but it is hardly an earth-shattering act of breaching oppressive/sacred boundaries. Rather, as Žižek goes on to point out, this narcissistic, solipsistic *jouissance* "is precisely *not* a distinct communal network but a *conglomerate of solipsistic individuals*—as the saying goes, one is by definition lonely in a crowd."[9] Such "transgression" only lumps together people with the same insatiable, self-consuming desire for pleasure; it does nothing to break down barriers between people or even to transcend the self.

Embracing Christian freedom is a way of being meaningfully trans-gressive, because it refuses to be caught up in the cultural polarization between authoritarian-fundamentalism and the postmodern-self and, like Jesus, it refuses to employ the powers of the world. And the powers of tech-nique and capitalism are dominant powers in the West. As Jacques Ellul observes, "To serve Satan, who is himself bound, is lack of freedom *par excellence*. To renounce the means of power, to serve by willing to obey God, and thus worship God alone, is a mark of the freedom that Jesus Christ gives."[10] Yet one can desire to serve God and be completely mistaken con-cerning God's intentions, as the Apostle Paul was when he was persecuting the early church. Understanding that "[for] freedom Christ has set us free" (Gal 5:1 NRSV) means understanding that the Christian life ought to be a joyful, obedient, improvisation on the principles of the Kingdom of God, not a fearful obedience to an authoritarian intermediary.

8. Žižek, *Parallax View*, 311.
9. Žižek, *Parallax View*, 311. Emphasis in original.
10. Ellul, *Ethics of Freedom*, 57. Emphasis in original.

The constraints of Christian freedom vie with the constraints of the contemporary West, just as Jesus' Sermon on the Mount vies with sinful human nature and the way the world appears to work. A life improvised within the constraints of Christian freedom should be noticeably different. This difference is not found merely in a rigid dress code or a list of activities and substances to abstain from (though a person expressing Christian freedom will naturally dress in ways reflecting its constraints and will abstain from destructive activities and substances), but rather a disregard for the temptation to indulge in *jouissance*, fearful rule-keeping, and the impulse to employ technique in accomplishing every designated goal.

It is well past time that the church repudiated its reputation as an oppressive institution. Isolated acts of Christian freedom are insufficient; the pattern established in Scripture is that God liberates his people. I for one am convinced that, if Western churches discover and enact Christian freedom in a meaningfully transgressive way, the songs they improvise will be as siren calls to peoples in chains.

Conclusion

THE BURDEN OF THIS work has been to demonstrate the effectiveness of a jazz analogy in illustrating and prescribing the enactment of Christian freedom in a postmodern context. I began in chapter 1 by illuminating the enslaving forces that operate in this context, including the opposing poles of authoritarian-fundamentalism and the postmodern-self and the forces of technique and alienation. I then endeavored to describe Christian freedom, listening to a broad spectrum of recent scholarship and to construct a biblical theology of freedom. With a context and an understanding of Christian freedom in place, I brought jazz into the discussion, building an analogy that revolves around improvising with and within a set of constraints. I showed how this analogy describes the apparently contradictory attitudes necessary for Christian freedom and suggests ways they might be enacted creatively and in opposition to the enslaving forces described in chapter 1.

God initiates Christian freedom by liberating Christians from the constraints of the self and the world into the constraints of the Kingdom of God. Christians enact this freedom by improvising with these constraints, which inevitably entails transgressing the self and the forces at work in the world, including (but not limited to) the polarity and alienation rampant in the postmodern west. Christian freedom, though not synonymous with political freedom, has political implications in that it opposes oppressive political structures and undermines and subverts illegitimate authority by acknowledging the priority of God's rule.

Living out Christian freedom means, paradoxically, taking up the yoke of Christ (Matt 11:30). Jesus' yoke is easy when one habitually inhabits the constraints of the Christian life, seeking out and enacting the Father's will in the process of improvisation. If one rejects these constraints, or denies the need for improvisation in the Christian life, the yoke appears to be unbearable. By taking up Christ's yoke (including surrendering one's self to the work of the Holy Spirit) and enacting their freedom, Christians will impress upon an unbelieving world the reality of the liberating power of the Gospel.

"FURTHER EXPLORATIONS" IN JAZZ, THEOLOGY, AND CHRISTIAN FREEDOM[1]

My work is just one way of approaching the topic of Christian freedom. One alternative approach would be to use a different analogy. For instance, if my expansion and application of the basic contours of Begbie's jazz analogy proves useful, surely the dramatic analogies employed by Hans Urs von Balthasar, N. T. Wright, Samuel Wells, and Kevin J. Vanhoozer could also be productively employed in describing Christian freedom.[2] Another approach would be to write a full monograph constructing a biblical theology of freedom. If Peter Richardson and Wayne Coppins can write books addressing Paul's thought on freedom alone, surely a biblical theology of freedom is more than warranted.[3] Looking at Christian freedom (or the lack thereof) in Church history would be a fascinating endeavor. And although I, like Jacques Ellul, am skeptical of approaches to Christian freedom that entail exercising political power,[4] it would be interesting to discuss Christian freedom in the context of liberation theology.[5] If my assessment of the problem of freedom in the contemporary West is even partially correct, the church is in need of such endeavors.

In terms of using jazz as a way of aiding the task of theology, my analogy demonstrates that its multifaceted character resonates in many ways with the Christian life. Leadership is closely related to freedom, but requires a discussion of its own. The analogy is already in play from an unlikely source; the corporate world is using jazz as a way of conceptualizing leadership.[6]

1. My subject heading references the jazz album, *Further Explorations*, by the Horace Silver Quintet.

2. See Balthasar, *Theo-Drama*; Wright, "How Can the Bible"; Wells, *Improvisation*; Vanhoozer, *Drama of Doctrine*.

3. Richardson, *Paul's Ethic*; Coppins, *Interpretation of Freedom*.

4. Ellul writes, "To say that the Christian must take part in politics to save the world seems to me theologically untrue. What is at issue is the freedom which serves God in the world. Service of the world, even of the world God has so much loved, is never enjoined in the Bible. To say that the establishment of terrestrial justice is a concrete way of expressing love and that power is a way to achieve it seems to me historically and politically untrue." Ellul, *Ethics of Freedom*, 369n1.

5. Boff and Boff, *Introducing Liberation Theology*, provides a basic overview of the tenets of the movement from a couple of its foremost practitioners.

6. See, for example, Pree, *Leadership Jazz*.

Perhaps those who employ the corporate model in the church will take notice. In addition to being a seminal analogy, jazz has an intriguing history, including several major figures strongly influenced by the Christian faith, which has the potential to inspire theological reflection, as Jamie Howison has ably demonstrated.[7] Work at the intersection between jazz and theology has just begun.

7. Howison, *God's Mind in That Music*.

Appendix

THE NUMBER OF BOOKS specifically devoted to the intersection of jazz and theology has significantly increased since the turn of the millennium, along with a growing number of articles and book chapters. This material can be roughly divided into two categories: writing that uses jazz as an analogy for how to do theology (including hermeneutics) and writing that uses jazz as an analogy for given theological issues. In the discussion below, I focus especially on what resonates with my own thesis, that jazz is an effective analogy for a Christian theology of freedom, but I also analyze the methodological approach each author uses to bring jazz and theology into conversation with one another.

JAZZ-SHAPED WAYS OF DOING THEOLOGY

The authors below use jazz as a resource to refocus the purpose and shape of theology. Most of them are directly concerned with matters of social justice, calling on theology to look beyond theological propositions to pragmatic and/or contextual concerns. Hermeneutics also features prominently; many of these authors see in the diversity of jazz a way to approach the problem of the plurality of interpretations of Scripture.

Bruce Ellis Benson has written five chapters that resource aspects of jazz for theological reflection.[1] He has also published a musicological monograph, a book chapter, and a couple articles on improvisation.[2] The recurring themes in Benson's work at the intersection of jazz and theology include thinking of God as an improviser, God's call and our response, and

---

1. Benson, "Improvisation of Hermeneutics"; "Improvising Texts"; "Call Forwarding"; and the chapters "Call and the Response" (33–48) and "Improvising like Jazz" (71–98) in Benson, *Liturgy as a Way of Life*.

2. Benson, *Improvisation of Musical Dialogue*; "Stealing Licks"; "Ingarden"; and "Fundamental Heteronomy."

an analogy between jazz improvisation and interpreting Scripture.[3] Highlighting God's improvisatory work provides impetus to a view of the Christian life as an improvisation governed by the constraints of God's revelation,
tradition, and interpretive communities. Two of Benson's chapters, "Call
Forwarding: Improvising the Response to the Call of Beauty" and "The Call
and the Response," concern the "occasional" and "continuous" constraints
of God's providence.[4] Benson argues that, as in jazz improvisation (in which
musicians respond to one another), the Christian life is always a response
to God's previous call. When we respond to it, we simultaneously repeat
and improvise it back to him "and forward out to all of creation."[5] In "The
Improvisation of Hermeneutics" and "Improvising Texts, Improvising
Communities," Benson compares the process of interpreting jazz standards
to interpreting Scripture, noting the role of improvisation (in the sense of
being simultaneously repetitive and transformative) in both. He strives for
"hermeneutical justice" in acknowledging the significant (though not necessarily equal) roles of authorial intent, the response of individual readers, the
interpretive community, and its traditions. By highlighting the improvisational role of readers, he provides an opening for my concern with enacting
Christian freedom in relation to the constraints he describes. Benson also
contemplates the conflict that often results from differing interpretations
and distinguishes the heteronomy of perspectives that can operate inside of
Christian orthodoxy from the heterodoxy that stands outside of it. Methodologically, Benson acknowledges that his argument is analogical, but
stops short of working it out formally.[6] Benson's views on the nature of improvisation and the challenge of working through the constraints of God's

3. W. David Buschart and Kent D. Eilers draw upon Benson's work to discuss "constraint and freedom in jazz improvisation" (233) as it relates to "those who seek to appropriate the Christian tradition" for the purpose of performing it in a transformative
manner "without destroying its identity" (236). See Buschart and Eilers, *Theology as
Retrieval*, 233–37.

4. God's providence, viewed under the taxonomy Begbie provides for improvisation
(see chapters 4–5), can be thought of as an occasional constraint insofar as God engages
with us temporally and also as a continuous constraint insofar as Christ upholds and
sustains the world (Col 1:17).

5. Benson, "Call Forwarding," 83.

6. Benson begins outlining his approach by arguing "that jazz improvisation provides a model of something at least *approximating* a 'hermeneutical justice,'" and goes
on to say, "I think there are some essential features of jazz interpretation that are sufficiently analogous to interpretation of literary, legal, biblical, theatrical, and other sorts
of musical texts." Benson, "Improvisation of Hermeneutics," 194. Emphasis in original.
It is not surprising that Benson would refrain from explicating his view of analogy in a
single chapter focusing on hermeneutics, but the scope of my project warrants a close
look at the theories on analogy that underlie my approach.

intentions, Scripture, and fellow Christians provide valuable resources for my own project.

Like Benson, Anthony G. Reddie makes a connection between jazz improvisation and hermeneutics.[7] Like Ellis and Gelinas, he has an interest in how to move theology beyond past formulations and sees in appropriating jazz as an analogy a way to do hermeneutics that has the potential to reinvigorate biblical interpretation. His particular focus is black theology and, coupled with the notion of improvisation that he finds in jazz, he offers a way beyond the liberal versus conservative debates that Western theology finds itself embroiled in, especially with respect to interpreting Scripture. Reddie is concerned that black theology has traded its tradition of interpreting Scripture in the light of African American experience for "arcane arguments around doctrine and metaphysical postulations."[8] Seeking to avoid "the sterility of perennial arguments around evangelical and liberal approaches to Christian theology"[9] Reddie sees in jazz improvisation a model for balancing the old and the new that can enable Black worshipers to be "faithful to the spirit inherent within the Word of God."[10] This last observation is especially pertinent to my project. On the one hand, I see two extremes on the spectrum of jazz performance: one attempts to construct a "pure" notion of jazz by painstakingly reconstructing the performance practices of past styles while the other attempts to throw off all constraints in a way that mirrors postmodern relativity. On the other hand, I (too) see hope in a middle way that eschews the excesses of both stances.

Peter Heltzel's book, *Resurrection City: A Theology of Improvisation*, is primarily concerned with the experience of blacks and other oppressed

7. See Reddie, "Dramatic Improvisation"; and "Dialectical Spirituality."

8. Reddie, "Dramatic Improvisation," 61. Reddie cites Vincent L. Wimbush's study, *The Bible and African Americans*, which in turn lays the blame for a rift in the black community at the feet of those who join with white fundamentalists (63–70). Wimbush argues, "Those African Americans who actually join white fundamentalist communities have found themselves for the most part having to relativize race and culture as factors in religious faith and piety, and having to argue for the universal nature of the fundamentalist perspective." Wimbush, *Bible and African Americans*, 66–67. See chapter 1 for a description and critique of "authoritarian fundamentalism" and chapter 6 for a jazz-shaped response to it as well as a challenge to cultural homogeneity in the church.

9. Reddie, "Dialectical Spirituality," 161.

10. Reddie, "Dialectical Spirituality," 163. Reddie goes on to criticize the position "that the WORD [Scripture] has to be taken literally and is inerrant," arguing that "many of us worship a living God and not a dead, fixed book!" (163). Unfortunately, he does not flesh out what he means by this; if he is a Barthian he does not say so. If he is denying the historicity of Scripture, then I disagree with him (cf. 1 Cor 15:14). For my own view of Scripture, see chapter 5.

groups. His narrative is not focused on jazz; rather, jazz is used as an explanatory analogy that aids Heltzel in telling the narratives that frame his agenda. These narratives are built primarily around the civil rights movement in America, but certainly have wider implications. For Heltzel, jazz improvisation is a model for deconstructing entrenched hegemonies and building a better city, useful not only for the church, but for those outside of it.[11]

William Harmless creatively combines Henri Marrou's work on Augustine[12] and his comments that link improvisation in ancient oratory with jazz improvisation[13] in his article, "A Love Supreme: Augustine's 'Jazz' of Theology." He argues that examining Augustine's work through the lens of jazz is "illuminative of his theological method."[14] Bringing classic recordings into conversation with Augustine's sermons, Harmless does an exceptional job of treating both jazz and Augustine seriously. The result is fascinating insights into the interaction between performer and audience, and the way old themes can be reworked in new ways. He lauds Augustine's "live theology" that is "inherently dialogical, [and] inherently audience-centered," suggesting that academic theologians do (or ought to do) the same thing in their classrooms.[15]

Nathan Crawford, like those considered above, is concerned with how to do theology, but in a decidedly academic vein. In *Theology as Improvisation: A Study in the Nature of Theological Thinking*, he asserts that, "theology is improvisation."[16] His object is to avoid all totalizing accounts of "thinking God," keeping the discussion open to multiple interpretations of Scripture, and informed by human knowledge of creation in all its forms. To this end he uses Heidegger and Derrida to deconstruct totalizing approaches to theology, or thinking God, and sets the stage for an improvisational solution to the problem. Crawford's rigorous engagement with jazz improvisation is worthy of emulation. However, unlike his celebration of the vagueness of (some of) his terminology, I hope to provide a functional definition of the terms that I use, even if they "cannot be definitively described."[17]

11. See Heltzel, *Resurrection City*. For a related chapter coauthored by Heltzel, see Benson, Berry, and Heltzel, "Improvising."

12. See especially Marrou, *Saint Augustin*.

13. Marrou writes, "Improvisation in both literature and music is always greatly helped by a well-stocked memory—as anyone will soon find out if he wants to develop a 'hot' technique in playing jazz." Marrou, *History of Education*, 200.

14. Harmless, "Love Supreme," 150.

15. Harmless, "Love Supreme," 177.

16. Crawford, *Theology as Improvisation*, 4.

17. According to Crawford, "The goal of my use of these terms—attunement,

Although she is the last author considered here in my survey of those who use jazz as a model for how to do theology, Sharon D. Welch precedes many of the authors above chronologically. I give her the last word in how jazz offers a model for doing theology because she departs from the authors above in significant ways, in spite of the concern for social justice that she shares with many of them. In *Sweet Dreams in America: Making Ethics and Spirituality Work* and her chapter, "'Lush Life': Foucault's Analytics of Power and a Jazz Aesthetic," she plays a sober Qoheleth to the calls to end oppression and marginalization. She observes that "[o]ne of the most disorienting things that can happen to a radical critic of patriarchal, authoritarian, racist, and elitist power structures is to win."[18] As a voice decidedly outside of an evangelical perspective, she highlights and then deconstructs any notions of a theoretical utopia emerging from placing the right people in power or ending the oppression of certain groups. For her, jazz improvisation is a useful analogy for life in the postmodern West because it does not strive for perfection and takes up within itself the unavoidable errors and transgressions human beings make. Hers is an important voice to attend to, but, from a Christian perspective, it must be listened to with caution because she also rebuffs the eschatological hopes that are central to the Christian faith.[19]

JAZZ PLAYING A GIG FOR THEOLOGY

The authors below are more concerned with what jazz can contribute to theology. In other words, jazz becomes an analogy that illuminates certain theological subjects. Most scholars begin with a theological subject or subjects, but, as can be seen below, one can also use the reverse strategy. The object is to cast these subjects in a different light and to expand and expound upon their implications.

Ann Pederson's book, *God, Creation, and All That Jazz*, is the first devoted entirely to linking jazz to theology.[20] Openly acknowledging the influ-

---

improvisation, and form—is to maintain their slippery nature, the fact that they cannot be definitively described." Crawford, *Theology as Improvisation*, 38. Perhaps no term can be "definitively described," but one still ought to strive for the best description possible. Definitions are necessary for any sort of meaningful dialogue.

18. Welch, *Sweet Dreams*, 27.

19. For another perspective on Welch, see Haardt, "'It Don't Mean a Thing,'" 36–37.

20. Pederson has also coauthored a book with Arthur Peacocke, a biologist and minister, in which the idea of God as an improviser is explored in the context of creation. This book, *The Music of Creation*, includes a discussion of jazz as a model for Christian action but interacts very little with the literature on jazz or with significant musicians in the tradition, giving it the impression of being a more popular as opposed

ence of feminist and process theologies, she suggests that jazz can be used as a way of critiquing "classical" theology.[21] In this respect her project resonates with Ellis's, though Pederson is drawing from different sources. She is not suggesting that Christians "simply jettison the themes of past generations," yet maintains that "the traditional models of God and the world, while still helpful as themes on which to build do not adequately convey the creative presence of God's action in the world. Neither do they provide a helpful strategy for helping Christians address the issues in our complex, messy world."[22] Her work, including the *Music of Creation* with Arthur Peacocke, is primarily concerned with the theological topics of creation, providence, and ecclesiology. My presuppositions with respect to special revelation preclude my use of the aspects of her model that are grounded in process thought, yet Pederson's work with jazz touches on many of the areas that are significant to my own work, such as drawing parallels between the jam session and the church.[23]

Thomas E. Reynolds' article, "Improvising Together: Christian Solidarity and Hospitality as Jazz Performance," builds on the work of both Begbie and Pederson by applying it to how the church balances solidarity with hospitality. After stating his thesis, "Christian community is a praxis of 'solidarity' opened outward in 'hospitality' toward the stranger, the different, the other, who is in fact my neighbor and loved by God," Reynolds points out parallels between jazz and the church:

> As jazz performance depends upon a musical heritage, the presence of other musicians, and a song structure, yet opens up to new and different interpretations in the play between musicians, so, too, Christian community trades upon a heritage, the presence of other Christians, and the good news of God's redemptive

---

to academic work.

21. Although she does not mention Ellis, her argument is sympathetic to his notion of theology as something that needs to engage with the realities of the contemporary world. Yet Pederson goes beyond Ellis by suggesting that classic models of theology need to be altered in significant ways as opposed to his complementary model.

22. Pederson, *God, Creation, and All That Jazz*, viii–ix.

23. My presuppositions in this dissertation include a view of Scripture as a reliable and authoritative special revelation from God. Pederson's most recent work with Arthur Peacocke makes it clear that her view of Scripture differs from my own. They advocate following "the sciences" at points where the sciences appear to conflict "with much of the Christian tradition as generally received." Peacocke and Pederson, *Music of Creation*, 36. With Alvin Plantinga, I am not convinced that such a conflict exists; see Plantinga, *Where the Conflict Really Lies*. See Peacocke and Pederson, *Music of Creation*, 49–63, for a discussion of the implications of a jazz model for the church.

work; yet, it opens outward toward differences in anticipating the innovative and transformative continuation of this work.[24]

Reynolds uses the word "metaphor" to describe the way in which he is linking jazz to the church, but he sets up his argument like an analogy. Following in the steps of Begbie, most of the emphasis in the article is placed on aspects of jazz improvisation, but this is done in a way that also considers the world behind the cultural text of jazz. He references a couple of jazz musicians as well as certain aspects of African religious practices to support his argument.[25] Although I find certain aspects of his conclusions frustratingly vague,[26] his article brings up aspects of the analogy between jazz and Christian community, such as balancing tradition and creativity, that I explore in further detail in chapters 4–7.[27]

J. D. Buhl's brief article, "Free Jazz and the Freedom of a Christian," takes on my subject area directly, but uses an approach very different from the one I outline below.[28] Buhl draws upon the rupture that free jazz represents in the jazz tradition. He connects this rupture to Jesus' statements in the Sermon on the Mount ("you have heard it said . . . but I say"), emphasizing the newness of Jesus message. Yet Buhl's emphasis on the radical misses out on the continuity of what God is doing from the Old Testament into the New. He rightly observes that Christians ought to be free with respect to the culture around them, but he is ambiguous regarding the constraints that govern Christian freedom. I find the disjunction of free jazz more useful as a model of postmodern relativism.

Another short article, "Negotiating Tension toward a Hipper Groove: Jazz Improvisation as a Metaphor within Christian Ethics," by Ross Kane, uses the way jazz musicians work out tension and resolution in relation to

24. Reynolds, "Improvising Together," 46.

25. Reynolds, "Improvising Together," 48–49.

26. Reynolds acknowledges that "too much flexibility can compromise the integrity of Christian tradition, yielding not the living preservation of its foundational story but a fragmenting chaos in which nothing is remembered and 'anything goes.'" Reynolds, "Improvising Together," 63. Yet he also criticizes the notion of "timeless truths" (62) and the "alleged possession of 'the' truth" on the part of certain churches (63). If by this he means that churches should exercise humility with respect to certain secondary doctrines, well and good. If, however, core aspects of Christian doctrine, such as the resurrection, are negotiable, then the core of the Christian faith is in jeopardy. My concern is that Reynolds declines to provide concrete examples to illustrate what he means. Judging whether or not "a viewpoint or position" is "inadequate or even pernicious" requires some criteria (54).

27. Reynolds also discusses discovering "identity in difference," the need for humility, and especially hospitality. Reynolds, "Improvising Together," 51–56.

28. Buhl, "Free Jazz."

chord progressions as a model for how the Church deals with tension and conflict. For Kane, Christian communities will deal best with tension when they are shaped by "formative practices," trust each other, and especially trust the Holy Spirit.[29] Like a jazz band, each member is given the opportunity to speak and to play a part in looking for resolution. Kane rightly points out that "tension is not occasional but a regular part of the Church's life, just as tension and resolution are regular features of jazz improvisation. To avoid such tension is to distance ourselves from the Church's own practices of truth-telling, confession, forgiveness, reconciliation and mutuality."[30] Methodologically, he treats jazz seriously, discussing theoretical aspects of the music and quoting from prominent jazz musicians.

Jamie Howison, in *God's Mind in that Music*, looks at the intersection between jazz and theology from a different angle than the authors addressed above; he begins not with theological constructs, but the life and music of John Coltrane. His work walks a fine line between a hard-nosed and penetrating look at the events in Coltrane's life on the one hand, and a necessarily subjective interpretation of Coltrane's music on the other. Although his keen ears and scholarly engagement with jazz criticism are successful in providing a thoughtful and engaging analysis of his subject, the theological content he derives from it is at times (but not always) tenuous and even arbitrary.[31] Howison stands with Buhl as one of the few theologians thus far to brave the murky waters of free jazz. He takes exception to Begbie's short shrift of this genre, deliberately engaging with it himself for a substantial part of his book, *God's Mind in That Music: Theological Explorations through the Music of John Coltrane*. His work stands as an example of engaging with the theological implications of the works of a jazz musician to an extent usually reserved for musicians such as J. S. Bach.[32]

29. Kane, "Negotiating Tension," 39.

30. Kane, "Negotiating Tension," 39.

31. For instance, Howison's hearing of Coltrane's piece, "Ascension," as "an acoustical icon of the ascended and enthroned Christ," is not grounded in any conclusive evidence that this was in fact Coltrane's intention. Howison, *God's Mind in That Music*, 167. Nor does he provide any criteria for demonstrating how "Ascension" in particular functions in this way while another composition/improvisation does not.

32. For example, see Barth, *Mozart*, and Pelikan, *Bach among the Theologians*. Sam Laurent's book chapter, "Improvisation and Divine Creation: A Riff on John Coltrane's *A Love Supreme*," also connects Coltrane with theology. The creativity, freedom, and risk-taking inherent in Coltrane's work find analogues in the process view of human experience in relation to the possibilities that God offers. Laurent draws from Alfred North Whitehead and John Cobb to describe this experience. Strangely, given their common interest in jazz and process thought, Laurent refrains from interacting with Pederson's work. His choice to ignore Howison is similarly puzzling. Unlike the works above, Laurent side-steps any mention of ecclesiology or Scripture; he mentions the

Finally, a couple chapters in *It Was Good: Making Music to the Glory of God* need to be mentioned.[33] William Edgar's chapter, "It Don't Mean a Thing if It Ain't Got 'Le Swingue,'" uses the history of French jazz, focusing especially on critic Hugues Panassié, as a springboard for reflections on the subversive nature of both jazz and the Gospel and on authenticity in jazz and the Christian faith.[34] While he does provide glimpses of the theological implications of the history of jazz, Edgar is closest in his approach to Hans R. Rookmaaker (whom he discusses at some length in his chapter) and James McClendon Jr. Secondly, "Caught Up in the Present" presents the intersection of jazz and theology from the perspective of an accomplished jazz musician: John Patitucci.[35] Writing in a conversational style, Patitucci weaves his own experiences of community in playing with jazz ensembles with Scripture and the Church, creating a valuable primary source.[36]

---

constraints of tradition, but fails to describe them. When he does refer to Christ's body, he is not referring to the church, but, as per Roland Faber, the whole world. In his conclusion, Laurent refers to a "deeper engagement of our own creativity" and "meaningful relationships with our fellow creatures, the creation itself, and with God," but what these sentiments actually entail is unclear. Laurent, "Improvisation," 65.

33. I limit myself at present to discussing the two chapters that specifically focused on jazz. However, jazz comes up several times in other chapters and a number of them have relevance to jazz even though the authors have a broader scope in mind. In particular, see "Making Music Soli Deo Gloria"; "The Best Thing in Life Is Free"; and "The Kingdom of God and Belly Buttons," in Bustard, *It Was Good*.

34. Edgar, "It Don't Mean a Thing." See also the recording of Edgar's performance lecture, *Heaven in a Nightclub*.

35. Patitucci, "Caught Up in the Present."

36. Patitucci writes about the need for risk-taking, authenticity, and true humility in improvised music and in the church. He also simultaneously affirms the need to be in the moment and the need to stand in a tradition. The apparent contradiction between jettisoning prefabricated ideas and being attuned to tradition doesn't seem to register when he writes, "Just as on the bandstand, when the musicians dare to let go of predetermined ideas and inward focus and interact based on the spirit they share with each other, they also have the opportunity to feel more connected to the elders that came before them and paved the way for them." Patitucci, "Caught Up in the Present," chapter 20, para. 9, location 4785. Taken at face value, Patitucci's comments are simply mistaken: after considering Thomas Owen's massive study of saxophonist Charlie Parker's improvised solos (Owens, "Charlie Parker"), Henry Martin acknowledges "[t]hat Parker indeed constructs his solos from a group of motivic formulas is incontestable." Martin, *Charlie Parker*, 3. Given Parker's stature in the jazz tradition, it would be absurd to denigrate his playing on the basis of his use of devices in his improvisations (cf. Patitucci's negative view of "'licks' and device-laden playing." Patitucci, "Caught Up in the Present," chapter 20, para. 4, location 4756). But if what Patitucci means can include the possibility that musical formulae can be recombined spontaneously in response to the playing of others, a resolution of sorts can be found between tradition (i.e., the use of formulae) and creativity. I explore the tension between tradition and creativity, assertion and openness that Patitucci implicitly raises in his chapter in chapter 4 with

ASSESSMENT

The works I examine above do not cohere around a set issue; jazz can be used as an analogy in diverse ways with respect to diverse theological methods and topics. Yet a number of themes emerge in each section. One particularly strong theme among authors writing about a jazz-shaped approach to theological method is social justice. From Ellis's and Reddie's desire for theology to be engaged with contemporary situations to Gelinas's and Heltzel's comments on the civil rights movement, theologians see in the history of jazz and its improvisatory nature a way of breaking through stifling theological systems into contemporary issues. While the scope of my interest in Christian freedom does not here focus primarily on social justice or liberation theology, I see in the history of jazz a resource for overcoming barriers that prevent those from oppressive or oppressed groups in society from constructively engaging with one another.

Moving between theological method and theological topics, I observe that Gelinas, Benson, Reddie, and Begbie (see introduction) are interested in the way jazz serves as a model of navigating or bringing balance to various constraints. Jazz improvisation provides a model for the interaction between the individual and the group; tradition and the present; recording/text, theory, and practice. Much of my project is concerned with working out the analogy between the way these constraints operate in the domain of jazz and the way they (ought to) operate in the Christian life.

Certain elements in the works discussed above and in my introduction are worthy of emulation. For instance: Crawford provides in-depth engagement with the philosophy of improvisation; Howison engages seriously with social and historical aspects of jazz; Begbie effectively employs jazz theory; and both Gelinas and Pederson orient their analogies from jazz to practical matters. Yet Benson's work in particular stands out as perhaps the most thorough and well-rounded use of the different aspects of jazz in theology. I have endeavored to follow his lead in considering the entire spectrum of jazz, from notes and chords to its social history, in building my analogy. In terms of content, Begbie's conception of freedom in relation to constraint provides an invaluable starting point for my own work. This book builds on his work and situates it in relation to the problem of freedom in the West that I described in chapter 1. None of the above, however, provides a systematic way of transferring insights from the realm of jazz to the realm of theology. My approach seeks to rectify this through a systematic use of analogy.

---

the aid of Paul Rinzler's *The Contradictions of Jazz.*

Discography

Ayler, Albert. *Bells/Prophecy.* ESP Disk ESP 4006, 2005 [1964/1965], CD.

Coleman, Ornette. *Free Jazz.* Atlantic 8122-75208-2, 1998 [1961], CD.

Davis, Miles. *Kind of Blue.* Columbia CK 64935, 1997 [1959], CD.

Edgar, William. *Heaven in a Nightclub: An Evening of Jazz Music and History.* Chesterton House [no publisher's number], 2007, CD.

Getz, Stan, and J. J. Johnson. *Stan Getz and J. J. Johnson at the Opera House.* Verve 831 272-2, 1986 [1957], CD.

Hall, Jim, and Bob Brookmeyer. *Live at the North Sea Jazz Festival.* Challenge Records CHR 70063, 1999, CD.

Harrell, Tom. *Live at the Village Vanguard.* Bluebird 09026-63910 2, 2002, CD.

Horn, Paul. *Inside the Taj Mahal and Inside II.* Kuckuck 11062-2, 1989 [1968/1972], CD.

Rollins, Sonny, and Coleman Hawkins. *Sonny Meets Hawk!* RCA Victor 09026 63479-2, 2000 [1963], CD.

Silver, Horace. *It's Got to Be Funky.* Columbia CK 53812, 1993, CD.

Bibliography

Adamson, James B. *The Epistle of James*. NICNT. Grand Rapids: Eerdmans, 1976.

Adderley, Julian. "Cannonball Looks at Ornette Coleman." *Down Beat*, May 26, 1960, 20–21.

Adeyemi, Femi. "The New Covenant Law and the Law of Christ." *Bibliotheca sacra* 163.652 (2006) 438–52.

————. *The New Covenant Torah in Jeremiah and the Law of Christ in Paul*. Studies in Biblical Literature. New York: Peter Lang, 2006.

Adler, Mortimer J. *The Idea of Freedom: A Dialectical Examination of the Conceptions of Freedom*. Garden City, NY: Doubleday, 1958.

Adorno, Theodor W. "Perennial Fashion—Jazz." In *Critical Theory and Society: A Reader*, edited by Stephen Eric Bronner and Douglas MacKay Kellner, 199–212. New York: Routledge, 1989.

Ake, David. *Jazz Cultures*. Berkeley: University of California Press, 2002.

Almond, Gabriel A. et al. *Strong Religion: The Rise of Fundamentalisms around the World*. Chicago: University of Chicago Press, 2003.

Anderson, Walter Truett. *The Future Self: Inventing the Postmodern Person*. New York: Jeremy P. Tarcher/Putnam, 1997.

Ayers, David. "Jazz: Music and Background." *Journal of American Studies* 27.3 (1993) 409–15.

Bailey, Derek. *Improvisation: Its Nature and Practice in Music*. Englewood Cliffs, NJ: Prentice-Hall, 1980. Reprint, New York: Da Capo, 1993.

Balla, Peter. "Challenges to Biblical Theology." In *New Dictionary of Biblical Theology*, edited by T. Desmond Alexander et al., 20–27. Downers Grove, IL: InterVarsity, 2000.

Balmer, Randall. "American Fundamentalism: The Ideal of Femininity." In *Fundamentalism and Gender*, edited by John Stratton Hawley, 47–62. New York: Oxford University Press, 1994.

Balthasar, Hans Urs von. *Theo-Drama: Theological Dramatic Theory*. Translated by Graham Harrison. 5 vols. San Francisco: Ignatius, 1988.

Barber, Benjamin R. *Jihad Vs. McWorld: Terrorism's Challenge to Democracy*. New York: Ballantine, 2001.

Barnhart, Scotty. *The World of Jazz Trumpet: A Comprehensive History and Practical Philosophy*. Milwaukee, WI: Hal Leonard, 2005.

Barr, James. *The Semantics of Biblical Language*. Oxford: Oxford University Press, 1961. Reprint, London: SCM, 1983.

Barrett, C. K. *Freedom and Obligation: A Study of the Epistle to the Galatians.* Philadelphia: Westminster, 1985.

Barth, Karl. *Wolfgang Amadeus Mozart.* Grand Rapids: Eerdmans, 1986.

Bartha, Paul F. A. *By Parallel Reasoning: The Construction and Evaluation of Analogical Arguments.* New York: Oxford University Press, 2010.

Bauckham, Richard. *God and the Crisis of Freedom: Biblical and Contemporary Perspectives.* Louisville: Westminster John Knox, 2002.

Bauman, Zygmunt. *Freedom.* Concepts in Social Thought. Minneapolis, MN: University of Minnesota Press, 1988.

―――. *Postmodernity and Its Discontents.* New York: New York University Press, 1997.

Beck, James R., ed. *Two Views on Women in Ministry.* Rev. ed. Grand Rapids: Zondervan, 2005.

Becker, Ernest. *The Denial of Death.* New York: Free Press, 1973.

Begbie, Jeremy S. *Music, Modernity, and God: Essays in Listening.* Oxford: Oxford University Press, 2013.

―――. *Resounding Truth: Christian Wisdom in the World of Music.* Engaging Culture. Grand Rapids: Baker Academic, 2007.

―――. *Theology, Music and Time.* Cambridge Studies in Christian Doctrine. Cambridge: Cambridge University Press, 2000.

Bellah, Robert N., et al. *Habits of the Heart: Individualism and Commitment in American Life.* Berkeley: University of California Press, 1985.

Benson, Bruce Ellis. "Call Forwarding: Improvising the Response to the Call of Beauty." In *Beauty of God: Theology and the Arts,* edited by Daniel J. Treier et al., 70–83. Downers Grove, IL: IVP Academic, 2007.

―――. "The Fundamental Heteronomy of Jazz Improvisation." *Revue Internationale de Philosophie* 60.238 (4) (2006) 453–67.

―――. "The Improvisation of Hermeneutics: Jazz Lessons for Interpreters." In *Hermeneutics at the Crossroads,* edited by Kevin J. Vanhoozer et al., 193–210. Bloomington: Indiana University Press, 2006.

―――. *The Improvisation of Musical Dialogue: A Phenomenology of Music.* Cambridge: Cambridge University Press, 2003.

―――. "Improvising Texts, Improvising Communities: Jazz, Interpretation, Heterophony, and the Ekklesia." In *Resonant Witness: Conversations between Music and Theology,* edited by Jeremy Begbie and Steven R. Guthrie, 295–319. The Calvin Institute of Christian Worship Liturgical Studies. Grand Rapids: Eerdmans, 2011.

―――. "Ingarden and the Problem of Jazz." *Tijdschrift voor Filosofie* 55.4 (1993) 677–93.

―――. *Liturgy as a Way of Life: Embodying the Arts in Christian Worship.* The Church and Postmodern Culture. Grand Rapids: Baker Academic, 2013.

―――. "Stealing Licks: Recording and Identity in Jazz." In *Recorded Music: Philosophical and Critical Reflections,* edited by Mine Dogantan-Dack, 137–52. London: Middlesex University Press, 2008.

Benson, Bruce Ellis, Malinda Elizabeth Berry, and Peter Goodwin Heltzel. "Improvising for the Just and Peaceable Kingdom." In *Prophetic Evangelicals: Envisioning a Just and Peaceable Kingdom,* edited by Bruce Ellis Benson et al., 31–48. Grand Rapids: Eerdmans, 2012.

Berger, Peter L. "Introduction: Between Relativism and Fundamentalism." In *Between Relativism and Fundamentalism*, edited by Peter L. Berger, 1–16. Grand Rapids: Eerdmans, 2010.

———. "Western Individuality: Liberation and Loneliness." *Partisan Review* 52.4 (1985) 323–36.

Berlin, Isaiah. *Four Essays on Liberty*. New York: Oxford University Press, 1970.

Berliner, Paul. *Thinking in Jazz: The Infinite Art of Improvisation*. Chicago Studies in Ethnomusicology. Chicago: University of Chicago Press, 1994.

Betz, Hans Dieter. *Galatians: A Commentary on Paul's Letter to the Churches in Galatia*. Hermeneia. Philadelphia: Fortress, 1979.

Bishop, Bill, and Robert G. Cushing. *The Big Sort: Why the Clustering of Like-Minded America Is Tearing Us Apart*. Boston: Mariner, 2009.

Blackwell, Albert L. *The Sacred in Music*. Louisville: Westminster John Knox, 1999.

Bloch, Ernst. *The Principle of Hope*. Translated by Neville Plaice et al. 3 vols. Blackwell: Oxford, 1986.

Block, Daniel I. *Deuteronomy*. The NIV Application Commentary. Grand Rapids: Zondervan, 2012.

———. *For the Glory of God: Recovering a Biblical Theology of Worship*. Grand Rapids: Baker Academic, 2014.

Bock, Darrell L. *Luke*. 2 vols. Baker Exegetical Commentary on the New Testament. Grand Rapids: Baker Academic, 1994.

Boff, Leonardo, and Clodovis Boff. *Introducing Liberation Theology*. Translated by Paul Burns. Maryknoll, NY: Orbis, 1987.

Bovon, François. *Luke*. 3 vols. Hermeneia. Minneapolis: Fortress, 2013.

Broadhead, Bradley K. "An Overview and Analysis of the Present Discussion between Theology and Music." *MJTM* 14 (2012–2013) 148–70.

Bromiley, Geoffrey W. "Editor's Preface." In *The Ethics of Freedom*. Grand Rapids: Eerdmans, 1976.

Brown, Delwin. *To Set at Liberty: Christian Faith and Human Freedom*. Maryknoll, NY: Orbis, 1981.

Brown, Lee B. "'Feeling My Way': Jazz Improvisation and Its Vicissitudes—A Plea for Imperfection." *The Journal of Aesthetics and Art Criticism* 58.2 (2000) 113–23.

Bruce, F. F. *The Epistle to the Galatians: A Commentary on the Greek Text*. The New International Greek Testament Commentary. Grand Rapids: Eerdmans, 1982.

Brueggemann, Walter. *Theology of the Old Testament: Testimony, Dispute, Advocacy*. Minneapolis: Fortress, 1997.

Buhl, J. D. "Free Jazz and the Freedom of a Christian." *The Cresset* 73.2 (2008) 12–16.

Burk, Denny. "Discerning Corinthian Slogans through Paul's Use of the Diatribe in 1 Corinthians 6:12–20." *Bulletin for Biblical Research* 18.1 (2008) 99–121.

Burnham, Jonathan D. *A Story of Conflict: The Controversial Relationship between Benjamin Wills Newton and John Nelson Darby*. Milton Keynes, UK: Paternoster, 2004.

Burns, Ken. *Jazz: A Film by Ken Burns*. DVD. PBS Home Video, 2001.

Buschart, W. David, and Kent D. Eilers. *Theology as Retrieval: Receiving the Past, Renewing the Church*. Downers Grove, IL: InterVarsity, 2015.

Bustard, Ned, ed. *It Was Good: Making Music to the Glory of God*. Baltimore: Square Halo, 2013. Kindle edition.

Cameron, William Bruce. "Sociological Notes on the Jam Session." *Social Forces* 33.2 (1954) 177–82.

Camus, Albert. *The Myth of Sisyphus and Other Essays*. Translated by Justin O'Brien. New York: Alfred A. Knopf, 1955. Reprint, New York: Vintage, 1991.

Carter, Warren. *John and Empire: Initial Explorations*. New York: T&T Clark, 2008.

Carter, William G. "Singing a New Song: The Gospel and Jazz." *Princeton Seminary Bulletin* 19.1 (1998) 40–51.

Cavanaugh, William T. "'What Do I Want?': Theological Anthropology and Consumerism." *Concilium* 4 (2014) 25–33.

Chadwick, William. *Stealing Sheep: The Church's Hidden Problems with Transfer Growth*. Downers Grove, IL: InterVarsity, 2001.

Charry, Ellen T. "The Crisis of Modernity and the Christian Self." In *A Passion for God's Reign: Theology, Christian Learning, and the Christian Self*, edited by Miroslav Volf, 89–112. Grand Rapids: Eerdmans, 1998.

Chesterton, Gilbert K. *Orthodoxy*. 1908. Reprint, Chicago: Moody, 2009.

Ciampa, Roy E. "Freedom." In *New Dictionary of Biblical Theology*, edited by T. Desmond Alexander et al., 503–6. Downers Grove, IL: InterVarsity, 2000.

Clack, Beverley. *Misogyny in the Western Philosophical Tradition: A Reader*. New York: Routledge, 1999.

Clark, Kelly James. *When Faith Is Not Enough*. Grand Rapids: Eerdmans, 1997.

Coker, Jerry. *Elements of the Jazz Language for the Developing Improvisor*. n.p.: Alfred, 1991.

Conn, Harvie M. "Looking for a Method: Backgrounds and Suggestions." In *Exploring Church Growth*, edited by Wilbert R. Shenk, 79–94. Grand Rapids: Eerdmans, 1983.

Considine, John J. *Marketing Your Church: Concepts and Strategies*. Kansas City: Sheed & Ward, 1995.

Coppins, Wayne. *The Interpretation of Freedom in the Letters of Paul: With Special Reference to the "German" Tradition*. Wissenschaftliche Untersuchungen Zum Neuen Testament 2 Reihe. Tübingen, Germany: Mohr Siebeck, 2009.

Craigie, Peter C. *The Book of Deuteronomy*. NICOT. Grand Rapids: Eerdmans, 1976.

Crawford, Nathan. *Theology as Improvisation: A Study in the Musical Nature of Theological Thinking*. Studies in Systematic Theology. Leiden: Brill, 2013.

Crook, Hal. *Ready, Aim, Improvise!* Mainz, Germany: Advance Music, 1999.

Crow, Bill. *Jazz Anecdotes: Second Time Around*. New York: Oxford University Press, 2005.

Cuvillier, Elian. "Torah Observance and Radicalization in the First Gospel: Matthew and First-Century Judaism: A Contribution to the Debate." *New Testament Studies* 55.2 (2009) 144–59.

Davids, Peter H. *The First Epistle of Peter*. NICNT. Grand Rapids: Eerdmans, 1990.

Davis, Miles, and Quincy Troupe. *Miles: The Autobiography*. New York: Simon & Schuster, 2005.

De Pree, Max. *Leadership Jazz*. New York: Dell, 1993.

Descartes, René. *A Discourse on the Method of Correctly Conducting One's Reason and Seeking Truth in the Sciences*. Translated by Ian Maclean. Oxford: Oxford University Press, 2006.

DeVeaux, Scott. *The Birth of Bebop: A Social and Musical History*. Berkeley: University of California Press, 1997.

————. "Constructing the Jazz Tradition: Jazz Historiography." *Black American Literature Forum* 25.3 (1991) 525–60.

Dipert, Randall R. "The Composer's Intentions: An Examination of Their Relevance for Performance." *The Musical Quarterly* 66.2 (1980) 205–18.

Dostoevsky, Fyodor. *The Karamazov Brothers*. Translated by Ignat Avsey. Oxford: Oxford University Press, 1995.

Dumbrell, William J. *Covenant and Creation: An Old Testament Covenantal Theology*. Exeter, Devon: Paternoster, 1984.

Dunn, James D. G. *Christian Liberty: A New Testament Perspective*. Grand Rapids: Eerdmans, 1994.

Durham, John I. *Exodus*. WCB 3. Waco, TX: Word, 1987.

Edgar, William. "It Don't Mean a Thing If It Ain't Got 'Le Swingue.'" In *It Was Good: Making Music to the Glory of God*, edited by Ned Bustard, chapter 19. Baltimore: Square Halo, 2013. Kindle edition.

Ellingsen, Mark. *Sin Bravely: A Joyful Alternative to a Purpose-Driven Life*. New York: Continuum, 2009.

Ellis, Carl F. *Free at Last?: The Gospel in the African-American Experience*. 2nd ed. Downers Grove, IL: InterVarsity, 1996.

Ellison, Ralph. *Living with Music: Ralph Ellison's Jazz Writings*. New York: Modern Library, 2002.

Ellul, Jacques. *The Ethics of Freedom*. Translated by Geoffrey W. Bromiley. Grand Rapids: Eerdmans, 1976.

————. *Sources and Trajectories: Eight Early Articles by Jacques Ellul that Set the Stage*. Translated by Marva J. Dawn. Grand Rapids: Eerdmans, 1997.

————. *The Technological Society*. New York: Alfred A. Knopf, 1965.

Emerson, Michael O., and Christian Smith. *Divided by Faith: Evangelical Religion and the Problem of Race in America*. Oxford: Oxford University Press, 2000.

Epstein, Heidi. *Melting the Venusberg: A Feminist Theology of Music*. New York: Continuum, 2004.

Feather, Leonard. "Another View of Coleman." *Down Beat*, May 26, 1960, 21.

Ferkiss, Victor C. *Technological Man: The Myth and the Reality*. New York: George Braziller, 1969.

Foley, Edward. *From Age to Age: How Christians Have Celebrated the Eucharist*. Rev. ed. Collegeville, MI: Liturgical, 2008.

France, R. T. *The Gospel of Matthew*. NICNT. Grand Rapids: Eerdmans, 2007.

Francis of Assisi, Saint. *Works of the Seraphic Father, St. Francis of Assisi*. Translated by A Religious of the Order. Paternoster Row, London: R. Washbourne, 1882.

Friedwald, Will, et al. *The Future of Jazz*. Chicago: A Cappella, 2002.

Fukuyama, Francis. *The End of History and the Last Man*. New York: Free Press, 1992.

Fulkerson, Mary McClintock. *Changing the Subject: Women's Discourses and Feminist Theology*. Minneapolis: Fortress, 1994. Reprint, Eugene, OR: Wipf and Stock, 2001.

The Fundamentals: A Testimony of the Truth. 12 vols. Chicago: Testimony, 1910–15.

Fung, Ronald Y. K. *The Epistle to the Galatians*. Grand Rapids: Eerdmans, 1988.

Gabriel A. Almond, et al. *Strong Religion: The Rise of Fundamentalisms around the World*. Chicago: University of Chicago Press, 2003.

Gebhardt, Nicholas. *Going for Jazz: Musical Practices and American Ideology*. Chicago: University of Chicago Press, 2001.

Gelinas, Robert. *Finding the Groove: Composing a Jazz-Shaped Faith.* Grand Rapids: Zondervan, 2009.

Gentner, Dedre. "Structure-Mapping: A Theoretical Framework for Analogy." *Cognitive Science* 7.3 (1983) 155–70.

Gentner, Dedre, Keith James Holyoak, and Boicho N. Kokinov, eds. *The Analogical Mind: Perspectives from Cognitive Science.* Cambridge, MA: MIT, 2001.

Gilbreath, Edward, and Mark Galli. "Harder Than Anyone Can Imagine: Four Working Pastors—Latino, Asian, Black and White—Respond to the Bracing Thesis of United by Faith." *Christianity Today* 49.4 (2005) 36–43.

Gioia, Ted. *The History of Jazz.* 2nd ed. New York: Oxford University Press, 2011.

Gitler, Ira. *Swing to Bop: An Oral History of the Transition in Jazz in the 1940s.* New York: Oxford University Press, 1985.

Goppelt, Leonhard. *A Commentary on I Peter.* Translated by John E. Alsup. Grand Rapids: Eerdmans, 1993.

Greear, J. D. "Great Commission Multiplication: Church Planting and Community." In *The Great Commission Resurgence: Fulfilling God's Mandate in Our Time,* edited by Chuck Lawless and Adam W. Greenway, 325–44. Nashville: B&H Academic, 2010.

Green, Gene L. *Jude and 2 Peter.* Baker Exegetical Commentary on the New Testament. Grand Rapids: Baker Academic, 2008.

Green, Sidney L. *Beating the Bounds: A Symphonic Approach to Orthodoxy in the Anglican Communion.* Eugene, OR: Wipf & Stock, 2013.

Grenz, Stanley J., and John R. Franke. *Beyond Foundationalism: Shaping Theology in a Postmodern Context.* Louisville, KY: Westminster John Knox, 2001.

Gridley, Mark, Robert Maxham, and Robert Hoff. "Three Approaches to Defining Jazz." *The Musical Quarterly* 73.4 (1989) 513–31.

Groothuis, Douglas R. *On Jesus.* Wadsworth Philosophers Series. South Melbourne: Thomson/Wadsworth, 2003.

Grudem, Wayne A. *Systematic Theology: An Introduction to Biblical Doctrine.* Grand Rapids: Zondervan, 1994.

Guinness, Os. "Pilgrim at the Spaghetti Junction: An Evangelical Perspective on Relativism and Fundamentalism." In *Between Relativism and Fundamentalism: Religious Resources for a Middle Position,* edited by Peter L. Berger, 164–79. Grand Rapids: Eerdmans, 2010.

Haardt, Maaike de. "'It Don't Mean a Thing If It Ain't Got That Swing': Desire and the City." In *City of Desires—A Place for God?: Practical Theological Perspectives,* edited by R. Ruard Ganzevoort, Rein Brouwer, and Bonnie Miller-McLemore, 29–38. Zürich: Lit Verlag, 2013.

Hajdu. "Wynton's Blues." *The Atlantic,* March 2003. www.theatlantic.com/doc/200303/hajdu.

Hall, Bill. "Jazz—Lewd or Ludens?" In *Creative Chords: Studies in Music, Theology and Christian Formation,* edited by Jeff Astley et al., 194–209. Leominster, Herefordshire, UK: Gracewing, 2000.

Hall, Edward T. *The Hidden Dimension.* Garden City, NY: Anchor, 1969.

Hamilton, Victor P. *The Book of Genesis.* 3 vols. NICOT. Grand Rapids: Eerdmans, 1990.

Harmless, William, S. J. "A Love Supreme: Augustine's 'Jazz' of Theology." *Augustinian Studies* 43:1/2 (2012) 149–77.

Harris, Harriet A. *Fundamentalism and Evangelicals.* Oxford: Oxford University Press, 2008.

Hauerwas, Stanley. "On Being a Church Capable of Addressing a World at War: A Pacifist Response to the United Methodist Bishop's Pastoral *In Defense of Creation*." In *The Hauerwas Reader*, edited by John Berkman and Michael Cartwright, 426–58. Durham: Duke University Press, 2001.

———. "Should War Be Eliminated? A Thought Experiment." In *The Hauerwas Reader*, edited by John Berkman and Michael Cartwright, 392–425. Durham: Duke University Press, 2001.

Hays, Richard B. *The Moral Vision of the New Testament: Community, Cross, New Creation; a Contemporary Introduction to New Testament Ethics*. New York: HarperSanFrancisco, 1996.

Heltzel, Peter. *Resurrection City: A Theology of Improvisation*. Prophetic Christianity. Grand Rapids: Eerdmans, 2012.

Hengel, Martin. *Was Jesus a Revolutionist?* Philadelphia: Fortress, 1971.

Hesse, Mary B. *Models and Analogies in Science*. Notre Dame: University of Notre Dame Press, 1966.

Hodge, Charles. *Systematic Theology*. 3 vols. New York: Scribner and Armstrong, 1873.

Hodson, Robert. *Interaction, Improvisation, and Interplay in Jazz*. New York: Routledge, 2007.

Holyoak, Keith James, and Paul Thagard. *Mental Leaps: Analogy in Creative Thought*. Cambridge, MA: MIT, 1995.

Hong, In-gyu. *The Law in Galatians*. Journal for the Study of the New Testament Supplement Series. Sheffield: JSOT, 1993.

Hotchkiss, Dan. "Borrowing from Business: How Church Boards Can Benefit from Secular Practices." *Congregations* 31.2 (2005) 28–33.

Howison, Jamie. *God's Mind in That Music: Theological Explorations through the Music of John Coltrane*. Eugene, OR: Cascade, 2012.

Hudson, Rob. *Evolution: The Improvisational Style of Bob Brookmeyer*. Vienna: Universal Edition, 2002.

Hunter, James Davison. "Fundamentalism and Relativism Together: Reflections on Genealogy." In *Between Relativism and Fundamentalism: Religious Resources for a Middle Position*, edited by Peter L. Berger, 17–34. Grand Rapids: Eerdmans, 2010.

Ihde, Don. *Listening and Voice: Phenomenologies of Sound*. 2nd ed. Albany: State University of New York Press, 2007.

Jahanbegloo, Ramin. "Reading *Either/Or* in Tehran: Either Kierkegaard or Fundamentalism." In *Kierkegaard Studies: Yearbook 2008*, edited by Niels Jørgen Cappelørn et al., 14–23. Berlin: Walter de Gruyter, 2008.

Janzen, J. Gerald. *Exodus*. Westminster Bible Companion. Louisville, KY: Westminster John Knox, 1997.

Jedlicki, Jerzy. "Heritage and Collective Responsibility." In *The Political Responsibility of Intellectuals*, edited by Ian Maclean et al., 53–76. Cambridge: Cambridge University Press, 1990.

Jenkins, Philip. *The Lost History of Christianity: The Thousand-Year Golden Age of the Church in the Middle East, Africa, and Asia—and How It Died*. New York: HarperOne, 2009.

Jerome, Saint. *The Letters of St. Jerome: Letters 1–22*. Translated by Charles Christopher Mierow. New York: Newman, 1963.

Jerónimo, Helena M., José Luís Garcia, and Carl Mitcham, eds. "Introduction: Ellul Returns." In *Jacques Ellul and the Technological Society in the 21st Century*,

Philosophy of Engineering and Technology, edited by Helena M. Jerónimo et al.,
    35–48. Dordrecht: Springer, 2013.

————. *Jacques Ellul and the Technological Society in the 21st Century*. Philosophy of
    Engineering and Technology 13. Dordrecht: Springer, 2013.

Johnson, Elizabeth A. *She Who Is: The Mystery of God in Feminist Theological Discourse*.
    New York: Crossroad, 1992.

Jones, Amos. *Paul's Message of Freedom: What Does It Mean to the Black Church?* Valley
    Forge, PA: Judson, 1984.

Joseph, Charles M. *Stravinsky Inside Out*. New Haven: Yale University Press, 2001.

Jüngel, Eberhard. *The Freedom of a Christian: Luther's Significance for Contemporary
    Theology*. Translated by Roy A. Harrisville. Minneapolis: Augsburg, 1988.

Kane, Ross. "Negotiating Tension toward a Hipper Groove: Jazz Improvisation as a
    Metaphor within Christian Ethics." *Theology* 115.1 (2012) 36–43.

Kant, Immanuel. *Groundwork of the Metaphysics of Morals*. Translated by Mary Gregor.
    Cambridge Texts in the History of Philosophy. Cambridge: Cambridge University
    Press, 1998.

Käsemann, Ernst. *Jesus Means Freedom*. Translated by Frank Clarke. Philadelphia:
    Fortress, 1970.

Keener, Craig S. *A Commentary on the Gospel of Matthew*. Grand Rapids: Eerdmans,
    1999.

Ker, Leander. *Slavery Consistent with Christianity*. 3rd ed. Weston, MO: Finch &
    O'Gormon, 1853.

Kierkegaard, Søren. *Stages on Life's Way: Studies by Various Persons*. Edited and
    translated by Howard V. Hong and Edna H. Hong. Kierkegaard's Writings XI.
    Princeton: Princeton University Press, 1988.

Kofsky, Frank. *John Coltrane and the Jazz Revolution of the 1960s*. 2nd ed. New York:
    Pathfinder, 1998.

Koperski, Veronica. *What Are They Saying about Paul and the Law?* WATSA. New York:
    Paulist, 2001.

Kuehne, Dale S. *Sex and the iWorld: Rethinking Relationship Beyond an Age of
    Individualism*. Grand Rapids: Baker Academic, 2009.

Larsson, Göran. *Bound for Freedom: The Book of Exodus in Jewish and Christian
    Traditions*. Peabody, MA: Hendrickson, 1999.

Laurent, Sam. "Improvisation and Divine Creation: A Riff on John Coltrane's *A Love
    Supreme*." In *The Counter-Narratives of Radical Theology and Popular Music*, edited
    by Mike Grimshaw, 51–65. New York: Palgrave Macmillan, 2014.

Levant, Oscar. *A Smattering of Ignorance*. Garden City, NY: Doubleday, 1942.

Levarie, Siegmund, and Ernst Levy. *Tone: A Study in Musical Acoustics*. 2nd ed. Kent,
    OH: Kent State University Press, 1980.

Levine, Mark. *The Jazz Theory Book*. Petaluma, CA: Sher Music, 1995.

Levison, Jack. *Inspired: The Holy Spirit and the Mind of Faith*. Grand Rapids: Eerdmans,
    2013.

Lewis, C. S. "The Abolition of Man." In *The Complete C. S. Lewis Signature Classics*,
    689–738. San Francisco: HarperSanFrancisco, 2007.

————. "The Great Divorce." In *The Complete C. S. Lewis Signature Classics*, 463–541.
    San Francisco: HarperSanFrancisco, 2007.

————. *Out of the Silent Planet*. New York: Macmillan, 1990.

————. *Perelandra: (Voyage to Venus)*. London: Pan, 1983.

———. "The Pilgrim's Regress." In *C. S. Lewis: Selected Books*, 1–221. London: HarperCollins, 2002.

———. *Surprised by Joy: The Shape of My Early Life*. Orlando: Houghton Mifflin Harcourt, 1966.

Lindbeck, George A. *The Nature of Doctrine: Religion and Theology in a Postliberal Age*. Louisville, KY: Westminster John Knox, 1984.

Litweiler, John. *The Freedom Principle: Jazz after 1958*. New York: William Morrow, 1984.

———. *Ornette Coleman: A Harmolodic Life*. New York: William Morrow, 1992.

Luther, Martin. "The Bondage of the Will." Translated by Philip S. Watson and Benjamin Drewery. In *Luther's Works: American Edition*, edited by Jaroslav Pelikan and Helmut T. Lehmann, 33:1–307. Philadelphia: Fortress, 1972.

———. "The Freedom of a Christian." Translated by W. A. Lambert. In *Luther's Works: American Edition*, edited by Jaroslav Pelikan and Helmut T. Lehmann, 31:327–77. Philadelphia: Muhlenberg, 1957.

———. "To the Christian Nobility of the German Nation Concerning the Reform of the Christian Estate, 1520." Translated by Charles M. Jacobs. In *Luther's Works: American Edition*, edited by Jaroslav Pelikan and Helmut T. Lehmann, 44:115–21. Philadelphia: Fortress, 1966.

Luz, Ulrich. *Matthew*. Translated by James E. Crouch. 3 vols. Hermeneia. Minneapolis: Fortress, 2005.

Lyotard, Jean François. *The Postmodern Condition: A Report on Knowledge*. Theory and History of Literature. Minneapolis: University of Minnesota Press, 1984.

Macagno, Fabrizio. "Analogy and Redefinition." In *Systematic Approaches to Argument by Analogy*, edited by Henrique Jales Ribeiro, 73–90. Cham, CH: Springer, 2014.

Maddox, Marion. "'In the Goofy Parking Lot': Growth Churches as a Novel Religious Form for Late Capitalism." *Social Compass* 59.2 (2012) 146–58.

Makrides, Vasilios N. "Orthodox Christianity, Change, Innovation: Contradictions in Terms?" In *Innovation in the Orthodox Christian Tradition?: The Question of Change in Greek Orthodox Thought and Practice*, edited by Trine Stauning Willert and Lina Molokotos-Liederman, 19–50. Farnham, Surrey: Ashgate, 2012.

Marrou, Henri-Iréné. *History of Education in Antiquity*. Translated by George Lamb, 1956. Reprint, Madison: University of Wisconsin Press, 1982.

———. *Saint Augustin et la Fin de la Culture Antique*. 2nd ed. Paris: de Boccard, 1949.

Marsden, George M. "Defining American Fundamentalism." In *The Fundamentalist Phenomenon: A View from Within; A Response from Without*, edited by Norman J. Cohen, 22–37. Grand Rapids: Eerdmans, 1990.

———. *Fundamentalism and American Culture*. 2nd ed. Cary, NC: Oxford University Press, 2006.

Martin, Henry. *Charlie Parker and Thematic Improvisation*. Lanham, MD: Scarecrow, 2001.

Marx, Karl. *Economic and Philosophic Manuscripts of 1844*. Translated by Martin Milligan. New York: International, 1964.

Maslow, A. H. "A Theory of Human Motivation." *Psychological Review* 50.4 (1943) 370–96.

Matera, Frank J. *Galatians*. Sacra Pagina Series. Collegeville, MN: Liturgical, 1992.

McClendon, James William, and Nancey C. Murphy. *Witness: Systematic Theology*. Nashville: Abingdon, 1986.

McFague, Sallie. *Models of God*. Philadelphia: Fortress, 1987.

———. *Speaking in Parables: A Study in Metaphor and Theology*. London: SCM, 2002.

McGavran, Donald A. *The Bridges of God: A Study in the Strategy of Missions*. London: World Dominion, 1955.

———. *Ethnic Realities and the Church: Lessons from India*. South Pasadena, CA: William Carey Library, 1979.

McKnight, Scot. *The Letter of James*. NICNT. Grand Rapids: Eerdmans, 2011.

———. *Sermon on the Mount*. The Story of God Commentary. Grand Rapids: Zondervan, 2013.

Meadows, Eddie S. *Bebop to Cool: Context, Ideology, and Musical Identity*. Jazz Companions. Westport, CT: Greenwood, 2003.

Meeder, Christopher. *Jazz: The Basics*. New York: Routledge, 2008.

Menninger, David. "Politics or Technique? A Defense of Jacques Ellul." *Polity* 14.1 (1981) 110–27.

Merton, Robert K. "Foreword." In *The Technological Society*, v–viii. New York: Alfred A. Knopf, 1965.

Metzger, Paul Louis. *Consuming Jesus: Beyond Race and Class Divisions in a Consumer Church*. Grand Rapids: Eerdmans, 2007.

Michaels, J. Ramsey. *The Gospel of John*. NICNT. Grand Rapids: Eerdmans, 2010.

Middleton, J. Richard. *The Liberating Image: The Imago Dei in Genesis 1*. Grand Rapids: Brazos, 2005.

Mill, John Stuart. *On Liberty and the Subjection of Women*. London: Penguin, 2006.

Miller, Michael St. A. *Freedom in Resistance and Creative Transformation*. Lanham, MD: Lexington, 2013.

Moe, Kenneth Alan. *The Pastor's Survival Manual: 10 Perils in Parish Ministry and How to Handle Them*. Bethesda, MD: Alban Institute, 1995.

Monson, Ingrid. *Freedom Sounds: Civil Rights Call Out to Jazz and Africa*. Oxford: Oxford University Press, 2007.

———. *Saying Something: Jazz Improvisation and Interaction*. Chicago: University of Chicago Press, 1996.

Moo, Douglas J. *The Epistle to the Romans*. NICNT. Grand Rapids: Eerdmans, 1996.

Moore, R. I. *The War on Heresy: Faith and Power in Medieval Europe*. London: Profile, 2012.

Morozov, Evgeny. *To Save Everything Click Here: The Folly of Technological Solutionism*. New York: PublicAffairs, 2014.

Murphy-O'Connor, Jerome. *St. Paul's Corinth: Texts and Archaeology*. Good News Studies. Wilmington, DE: Michael Glazier, 1983. Reprint, Collegeville, MI: Liturgical, 1990.

Nicholson, Stuart. *Is Jazz Dead?: (Or Has It Moved to a New Address)*. New York: Routledge, 2005.

Nietzsche, Friedrich. *Beyond Good and Evil: Prelude to a Philosophy of the Future*. Cambridge Texts in the History of Philosophy. Cambridge: Cambridge University Press, 2002.

———. *On the Genealogy of Morality*. Translated by Carol Diethe. Cambridge Texts in the History of Political Thought. Cambridge: Cambridge University Press, 1994.

Nisenson, Eric. *Blue: The Murder of Jazz*. New York: St. Martin's, 1997.

Njoh, Ambe J. *Tradition, Culture and Development in Africa: Historical Lessons for Modern Development Planning*. Aldershot, UK: Ashgate, 2006.

Noll, Mark A. *Jesus Christ and the Life of the Mind*. Grand Rapids: Eerdmans, 2013.

Nolland, John. *Luke 9:21–18:34*. WCB 35b. Dallas, TX: Word, 1993.

Ostransky, Leroy. *The Anatomy of Jazz*. Seattle: University of Washington Press, 1960.

Owens, Thomas. "Charlie Parker: Techniques of Improvisation." PhD diss., University of California, 1974.

Palmer, Richard. "Jazz: The Betrayed Art." *Journal of American Studies* 23.2 (1989) 287–94.

Patitucci, John. "Caught Up in the Present." In *It Was Good: Making Music to the Glory of God*, edited by Ned Bustard, chapter 20. Baltimore: Square Halo, 2013. Kindle edition.

Patterson, Orlando. *Freedom*. Vol. 1, *Freedom in the Making of Western Culture*. New York: Basic Books, 1991.

Peacocke, Arthur, and Ann Pederson. *The Music of Creation*. Theology and the Sciences. Minneapolis: Fortress, 2006.

Pederson, Ann. *God, Creation, and All That Jazz: A Process of Composition and Improvisation*. St. Louis, MO: Chalice, 2001.

Pelikan, Jaroslav. *Bach among the Theologians*. Philadelphia: Fortress, 1986.

Pinnock, Clark H. "Defining American Fundamentalism: A Response." In *The Fundamentalist Phenomenon: A View from Within; A Response from Without*, edited by Norman J. Cohen, 38–55. Grand Rapids: Eerdmans, 1990.

Piper, John. *Bloodlines: Race, Cross, and the Christian*. Wheaton, IL: Crossway, 2011.

Plantinga, Alvin. *Where the Conflict Really Lies: Science, Religion, and Naturalism*. Oxford: Oxford University Press, 2011.

Plastaras, James. *The God of Exodus: The Theology of the Exodus Narratives*. Impact Books. Milwaukee: Bruce, 1966.

Porter, Eric. *What Is This Thing Called Jazz?: African American Musicians as Artists, Critics, and Activists*. Music of the African Diaspora. Berkeley, CA: University of California Press, 2002.

Porter, Lewis. *John Coltrane: His Life and Music*. Ann Arbor, MI: University of Michigan Press, 1998.

Prouty, Kenneth E. "Orality, Literacy, and Mediating Musical Experience: Rethinking Oral Tradition in the Learning of Jazz Improvisation." *Popular Music and Society* 29.3 (2006) 317–34.

Räisänen, Heikki. *Jesus, Paul and Torah: Collected Essays*. Journal for the Study of the New Testament Supplement Series 43. Sheffield: JSOT, 1992.

Rasula, Jed. "Jazz and American Modernism." In *The Cambridge Companion to American Modernism*, edited by Walter Kalaidjian, 157–76. Cambridge: Cambridge University Press, 2005.

Reason, Dana. "Navigable Structures and Transforming Mirrors." In *The Other Side of Nowhere: Jazz, Improvisation, and Communities in Dialogue*, edited by Daniel Fischlin and Ajay Heble, 71–83. Middletown, CT: Wesleyan University Press, 2004.

Reddie, Anthony G. "A Dialectical Spirituality of Improvisation: The Ambiguity of Black Engagements with Sacred Texts." In *Black Religion and Aesthetics: Religious Thought and Life in Africa and the African Diaspora*, edited by Anthony B. Pinn, 153–71. New York: Palgrave Macmillan, 2009.

———. "Dramatic Improvisation: A Jazz Inspired Approach to Undertaking Theology with the Marginalized." In *Reading Spiritualities: Constructing and Representing the Sacred*, edited by Dawn Llewellyn and Deborah F. Sawyer, 51–64. Aldershot, UK: Ashgate, 2008.

Reno, R. R. *Genesis*. Brazos Theological Commentary on the Bible. Grand Rapids: Brazos, 2010.

Reynolds, Thomas E. "Improvising Together: Christian Solidarity and Hospitality as Jazz Performance." *Journal of Ecumenical Studies* 43.1 (2008) 45–66.

Richardson, Peter. *Paul's Ethic of Freedom*. Philadelphia: Westminster, 1979.

Rinzler, Paul. *The Contradictions of Jazz*. Studies in Jazz. Lanham, MD: Scarecrow, 2008.

Ritzer, George. "The Technological Society: Social Theory, Mcdonaldization and the Prosumer." In *Jacques Ellul and the Technological Society in the 21st Century*, Philosophy of Engineering and Technology, edited by Helena M. Jerónimo et al., 35–48. Dordrecht: Springer, 2013.

Roberts, Robert C. *Spiritual Emotions: A Psychology of Christian Virtues*. Grand Rapids: Eerdmans, 2007.

Rookmaaker, Hans R. *Modern Art and the Death of a Culture*. London: InterVarsity, 1973.

———. *New Orleans Jazz, Mahalia Jackson and the Philosophy of Art*. Vol. 2 of *The Complete Works of Hans Rookmaaker*. Carlisle, UK: Piquant, 2002.

Rosner, B.S. "Biblical Theology." In *New Dictionary of Biblical Theology*, edited by T. Desmond Alexander et al., 3–11. Downers Grove, IL: InterVarsity, 2000.

Ruthven, Malise. *Fundamentalism: A Very Short Introduction*. Oxford: Oxford University Press, 2007.

Sartre, Jean-Paul. *Being and Nothingness: A Phenomenological Essay on Ontology*. Translated by Hazel E. Barnes. New York: Washington Square, 1992.

———. *Existentialism Is a Humanism, Including a Commentary on the Stranger*. Translated by Carol Macomber. New Haven: Yale University Press, 2007.

Schnackenburg, Rudolf. *The Gospel according to St. John*. Translated by Cecily Hastings et al. 3 vols. New York: Seabury, 1980.

Schouls, Peter A. "Descartes and the Autonomy of Reason." *Journal of the History of Philosophy* 10.3 (1972) 307–22.

Shelley, Cameron. "Analogy Counterarguments: A Taxonomy for Critical Thinking." *Argumentation* 18.2 (2004) 223–38.

Skillen, James W. *The Good of Politics: A Biblical, Historical, and Contemporary Introduction*. Engaging Culture. Grand Rapids: Baker Academic, 2014.

Slonimsky, Nicholas. *Thesaurus of Scales and Melodic Patterns*. New York: Coleman-Ross, 1947. Reprint, New York: Amsco, 1975.

Smith, Tara. *Moral Rights and Political Freedom*. Studies in Social and Political Philosophy. Lanham, MD: Rowman & Littlefield, 1995.

Southgate, Beverley. *Postmodernism in History: Fear or Freedom?* London: Routledge, 2003.

Stanton, Graham N. "What Is the Law of Christ?" *Ex auditu* 17 (2001) 47–59.

Starks, Glenn L. *Sexual Misconduct and the Future of Mega-Churches: How Large Religious Organizations Go Astray*. Santa Barbara, CA: ABC-CLIO, LLC, 2013.

Stoltzfus, Philip E. *Theology as Performance: Music, Aesthetics, and God in Western Thought*. New York: T. & T. Clark, 2006.

Storkey, Alan. *Jesus and Politics: Confronting the Powers*. Grand Rapids: Baker Academic, 2005.

Stravinsky, Igor. *Poetics of Music in the Form of Six Lessons.* Translated by Arthur Knodel and Ingolf Dahl. Bilingual ed. Charles Eliot Norton Lectures. Cambridge: Harvard University Press, 1970.

Studebaker, Steven M. *From Pentecost to the Triune God: A Pentecostal Trinitarian Theology.* Grand Rapids: Eerdmans 2012.

————. "Servants of Christ, Servants of Caesar: A Theology for Life in Post-Christian America." In *The Globalization of Christianity: Implications for Christian Ministry and Theology,* edited by Gordon L. Heath and Steven M. Studebaker, 52–68. McMaster Theological Studies Series. Eugene, OR: Pickwick, 2014.

Sudnow, David. *Ways of the Hand: The Organization of Improvised Conduct.* Cambridge: Harvard University Press, 1978. Reprint, Cambridge, MA: MIT, 1993.

Swain, Dan. *Alienation: An Introduction to Marx's Theory.* London: Bookmarks, 2012.

Swartley, Willard M. *Slavery, Sabbath, War, and Women: Case Issues in Biblical Interpretation.* Scottdale, PA: Herald, 1983.

Thielicke, Helmut. *The Freedom of the Christian Man.* Translated by John W. Doberstein. 1963. Reprint, Grand Rapids: Baker, 1975.

Thiselton, Anthony C. *First Corinthians: A Shorter Exegetical and Pastoral Commentary.* Grand Rapids: Eerdmans, 2006.

Thumma, Scott, and Dave Travis. *Beyond Megachurch Myths: What We Can Learn from America's Largest Churches.* San Francisco, CA: Jossey-Bass, 2007.

Tigay, Jeffrey H. *Deuteronomy.* The JPS Torah Commentary. Philadelphia: Jewish Publication Society, 1996.

Tirro, Frank. "The Silent Theme Tradition in Jazz." *The Musical Quarterly* 53.3 (1967) 313–34.

Tocqueville, Alexis de. *Democracy in America.* Translated and edited by Harvey C. Mansfield and Delba Winthrop. Chicago: University of Chicago Press, 2002.

Traina, Cristina. "Commodifying Sex: A View from the Margins." *Concilium* 4 (2014) 44–52.

Tuell, Steven. *Ezekiel.* New International Biblical Commentary. Peabody, MA: Hendrickson, 2009.

Turl, John. "Substance Dualism or Body-Soul Duality?" *Science and Christian Belief* 22.1 (2010) 57–80.

Vanhoozer, Kevin J. *The Drama of Doctrine: A Canonical Linguistic Approach to Christian Theology.* Louisville, KY: Westminster John Knox, 2005.

————. *First Theology: God, Scripture & Hermeneutics.* Downers Grove, IL: IVP Academic, 2002.

————. *Is There a Meaning in This Text?* Grand Rapids: Zondervan, 1998.

Wagner, C. Peter. *Our Kind of People: The Ethical Dimensions of Church Growth in America.* Atlanta: John Knox, 1979.

Walser, Robert. "Out of Notes: Signification, Interpretation, and the Problem of Miles Davis." *The Musical Quarterly* 77.2 (1993) 343–65.

Walsh, David. *After Ideology: Recovering the Spiritual Foundations of Freedom.* San Francisco: Harper & Row, 1990.

Walton, John H. *Genesis.* The NIV Application Commentary. Grand Rapids: Zondervan, 2001.

Ward, Graham. *Cities of God.* Radical Orthodoxy. London: Routledge, 2000.

————. *The Politics of Discipleship: Becoming Postmaterial Citizens.* The Church and Postmodern Culture. Grand Rapids: Baker Academic, 2009.

————. "A Postmodern Version of Paradise." *Journal for the Study of the Old Testament* 65 (1995) 3–12.

Warren, Jeff R. *Music and Ethical Responsibility.* Cambridge: Cambridge University Press, 2014.

Watson, Duane F. "1 Corinthians 10:23–11:1 in the Light of Greco-Roman Rhetoric: The Role of Rhetorical Questions." *Journal of Biblical Literature* 108.2 (1989) 301–18.

Weber, Max. *Economy and Society: An Outline of Interpretive Sociology.* 2 vols. Berkeley: University of California Press, 1978.

Welch, Sharon D. *Sweet Dreams in America: Making Ethics and Spirituality Work.* New York: Routledge, 1999.

Wells, Charles. *The Subject of Liberation: Žižek, Politics, Psychoanalysis.* New York: Bloomsbury, 2014.

Wells, Samuel. *Improvisation: The Drama of Christian Ethics.* Grand Rapids: Brazos, 2004.

West, Angela. "Sex and Salvation: A Christian Feminist Study of I Corinthians 6:12–7:39." *Modern Churchman* 29.3 (1987) 17–24.

Westermann, Claus. *Genesis 1–11: A Commentary.* Translated by John J. Scullion S.J. Minneapolis: Augsburg, 1984.

Westphal, Merold. *Becoming a Self: A Reading of Kierkegaard's Concluding Unscientific Postscript.* Purdue Univeristy Press Series in the History of Philosphy. West Lafayette, IN: Purdue University Press, 1996.

White, James F. "How the Architectural Setting for Worship Forms Our Faith." In *Music and the Arts in Christian Worship*, edited by Robert E. Webber, 546–48. Book Two, The Complete Library of Christian Worship 4. Nashville, TN: Star Song, 1994.

White, Roger M. *Talking about God: The Concept of Analogy and the Problem of Religious Language.* Transcending Boundaries in Philosophy and Theology. Farnham, Surrey, UK: Ashgate, 2010.

White, Thomas, and John M. Yeats. *Franchising McChurch: Feeding Our Obsession with Easy Christianity.* Colorado Springs: David C. Cook, 2009.

Wiarda, Timothy. *Peter in the Gospels: Pattern, Personality and Relationship.* Wissenschaftliche Untersuchungen zum Neuen Tastament. Tübingen: Mohr Siebeck, 2000.

Wierzbicka, Anna. *What Did Jesus Mean?: Explaining the Sermon on the Mount and the Parables in Simple and Universal Human Concepts.* New York: Oxford University Press, 2001.

Williams, Richard. "Ornette and the Pipes of Joujouka." *Melody Maker*, March 17, 1973, n.p.

Wilmer, Valerie. *As Serious as Your Life: The Story of the New Jazz.* London: Allison & Busby, 1977.

Wimbush, Vincent L. *The Bible and African Americans: A Brief History.* Minneapolis: Fortress, 2003.

Wiseman, Karyn L. "Bridging the Gap: Creating Intimate Preaching Encounters in Spaces that Separate Us." *Encounter* 72.3 (2012) 43–59.

Wolffe, John. *The Expansion of Evangelicalism: The Age of Wilberforce, More, Chalmers and Finney.* A History of Evangelicalism: People, Movements and Ideas in the English-Speaking World 2. Downers Grove, IL: InterVarsity, 2007.

Wright, Christopher. *Deuteronomy*. New International Biblical Commentary. Peabody, MA: Hendrickson, 1996.

Wright, N. T. *After You Believe: Why Christian Character Matters*. New York: HarperOne, 2010.

———. "How Can the Bible Be Authoritative?" *Vox Evangelica* 21 (1991) 7–32.

———. *Jesus and the Victory of God*. Minneapolis: Fortress, 1996.

Young, Frances. *The Art of Performance: Towards a Theology of Holy Scripture*. London: Darton, Longman and Todd, 1990.

Younge, Gary. *The Speech: The Story Behind Dr. Martin Luther King Jr.'s Dream*. Chicago, IL: Haymarket, 2013.

Žižek, Slavoj. *The Parallax View*. Cambridge, MA: MIT, 2006.

———. *Violence: Six Sideways Reflections*. Big Ideas/Small Books. New York: Picador, 2008.

Name Index

Scripture Index